Women's Pictures

Feminism and Cinema

second edition

ANNETTE KUHN

V

VERSO

London · New York

First published by Routledge & Kegan Paul 1982
This edition published by Verso 1994
© Annette Kuhn 1982

Verso
UK: 6 Meard Street, London W1V 3HR
USA: 29 West 35th Street, New York, NY 10001-2291

Verso is the imprint of New Left Books

ISBN 1-85984-910-5
ISBN 1-85984-010-8 (pbk)

British Library Cataloguing in Publication Data
A catalogue record for this book is available from the British Library

Library of Congress Cataloging-in-Publication Data
A catalogue record for this book is available from the Library of Congress

Kuhn, Annette.
    Woman's pictures : feminism and cinema / Annette Kuhn. — Rev. ed.
      p.   cm.
    Includes bibliographical references and index.
    ISBN 1-85984-910-5—ISBN 1-85984-010-8 (pbk.)
    1. Women in motion pictures.   2. Feminism and motion pictures.
  I. Title.
  PN1995.9.W6K8   1994
  a791.43′652042–dc20
                                    94-11624
                                       CIP

Typeset by Servis Filmsetting Ltd, Manchester
Printed and bound in the UK by
Biddles Ltd, Guildford and King's Lynn

For my teachers

Contents

Preface

One sunny Saturday in the spring of 1974, I drove the forty or so miles from Sheffield to Nottingham to attend a screening of 'women's films'. Although I cannot now remember very much about them, they were certainly the first overtly feminist films I had ever seen. What remains in my memory of that occasion, more than the films themselves, was the unpretentious setting in which they were screened – a small room in a community centre or some such place, with a 16 mm projector set up on a table at the back – and the fact that what I saw were films that were not just *about* women, ordinary working women, housewives, mothers, but were also *by* women. Most, perhaps all, of them came from the London Women's Film Group, a pioneering feminist film-making collective that had already, by 1974, been in existence for two years. I came away from the screening with a mimeographed booklet produced by the LWFG explaining how to go about making films in 16 mm – an exercise aimed, clearly, at demystifying an area of work from which women have often felt, and indeed have actually been, excluded. So women were making films, feminists were making films: and they were encouraging other women to do the same.

Coincidentally, or perhaps not so coincidentally, only a few months later, while at a film study summer school, I was struck by the dazzling and somewhat alarming realisation that in all my years of rapt cinema-going, my enjoyment of the movies had depended in large measure on identification with *male* characters. I had, that is, been putting myself in the place of the man, the hero, in order to enjoy – perhaps even to understand – films. This seemed nothing less than a negation of that part of myself that looked at films as a woman. In common, I imagine, with many movie fans who also happen to be feminists and women, I began at this point to indulge in a certain amount of guilt as I continued enjoying Hollywood movies, while at the same time searching with some desperation for positive women characters with whom a feminist could happily and guiltlessly identify. In other words, my feminism began at last to inform the way I looked at films.

It is significant, I think, that the second experience seemed at the time more powerful and more memorable than the first. This, I suspect, may be true of many other film-loving feminists of my generation: one of the things it points to, perhaps, is the gap that existed at the time between feminist film making and feminist approaches to an understanding of what might be called 'mainstream' cinema.

Things are rather different today. Indeed, this book could be written only because conditions now seem to exist for feminist film criticism and feminist film making to share some common concerns and goals: the organisation of my arguments throughout *Women's Pictures* is a reflection of this conviction. My basic objective in dealing here with both feminist film theory and feminist film production is to suggest some ways in which the two are interconnected, either explicitly in their politics, or implicitly in the kinds of thinking that underlie them. What I have attempted to do is trace the development of these two sets of practices and provide an overview of current work centring on the relationship between feminism and cinema. In the process, I have tried to explicate some of the theorising behind such work. Thus Part II is devoted to discussion of work in the general field of film theory which has been taken up, developed, and in the process often transformed, by specifically feminist theoretical approaches to cinema. And while Part III contains an account of feminist film theory as it developed over the first ten years or so of its existence, it includes as well some criticisms and suggestions for future work, and – by way of signalling an important and potentially productive direction for feminist film theory – a case study.

In dealing with these issues I have been faced with some fundamental questions as to the nature of feminism as a method or a perspective as it informs a study of cinema. For if feminism is considered in this way in relation to an existing body of knowledge, the socially constructed nature of that knowledge becomes immediately apparent, as do the political implications of constructing knowledge from a feminist standpoint. It may be argued, therefore, that to do feminist film theory is in itself to engage in a political practice.

Alongside this may be set further questions that are raised more specifically by feminist film production, the topic of Part IV of this book. While in this context, as in any other, theory and practice are not reducible to one another, it nevertheless seems clear that the two areas of work with which I am concerned are increasingly addressing themselves to similar questions. These questions include: relationships between films, film makers and audiences, the kinds of pleasure women may derive from watching films, and the nature and implications of representations of women constructed in different types of cinema.

The three chapters that form Part V are a postscript, written in 1993, to the main body or *Women's Pictures*, which was written in 1980 and 1981 and published in 1982. In the intervening years, feminist critical and theoretical work on cinema has expanded greatly and now enjoys an academic standing that would have seemed inconceivable in the early 1980s. At the same time, the modes of production, the forms and the contents of feminist practices of cinema have themselves undergone considerable transformation, and some have taken off in unexpected directions.

In Part V, I attempt to chart these changes, whilst re-examining the relationship between feminism and cinema in the 1990s and extending, revising or critiquing some of the arguments advanced in the original *Women's Pictures*. An exhaustive report and review, however, would have required not a simple postscript but an entirely new book: and indeed the project of a revised edition turned out considerably bigger and less wieldy than I had anticipated when I took it on. I have not, for example, attempted to deal with feminist experimental video, nor indeed reassessed the status of feminist documentary cinema. My overview of developments in feminist film theory, too, is necessarily not comprehensive, although most of the key areas are, I hope, covered in greater or lesser depth: exceptions include feminist work on stardom and acting as institutional and semiotic features of the cinematic apparatus; on psychoanalytically based metapsychologies of cinema which shift attention from vision towards sound as grounds of subjectivity and meaning; and on masculinity. These exclusions are pragmatic – the outcome of constraints of time and space and limitations on knowledge – rather than strategic.

A number of reviewers suggested that the original *Women's Pictures* made the then new field of feminist film studies seem too tidy: they felt this could close off debate prematurely in what was still very much a messy, unformed body of knowledge. There is some truth in this observation: the book's cut-and-dried quality is perhaps an undesirable consequence of the praiseworthy aim of making difficult ideas accessible. The fact that I would not feel it necessary or desirable today to write such a well-behaved book is possibly reflected in the postscript. Nevertheless, I discover – somewhat to my surprise – that there is little in the substance, as opposed to the style and the emphasis, of the original *Women's Pictures* from which I would seriously depart at this distance of time.

For this revised edition, the glossary has been added to, and the details of films discussed in the book modified to form a new appendix. The bibliography is divided into two sections, the first listing works published before 1982, the second including material that appeared during and after 1982: both sections include only works referenced in the main body of the book. Given the exponential growth of feminist film studies over the past decade, the second section of the bibliography provides a relatively selective coverage of what has become a sizeable literature. All of the material in the updated appendix and bibliography is intended as an aid to further study and viewing, and to the planning of courses, classes and discussion groups.

Acknowledgements

In writing *Women's Pictures*, I have been fortunate in enjoying support
and assistance from a number of institutions and individuals, and I
should like to express my gratitude to all of them. They include the
University of Wisconsin at Madison and Camberwell School of Art,
London, which provided me with employment that made it economically possible for me to spend time researching and writing a book.
Special screenings of some of the films I have discussed were arranged
by Nicky North and Joan Woodhead of the British Film Institute
Education Department. I would like, too, to thank the staff of the BFI
Information Department for the unfailing competence and courtesy
with which they provided their services. Terry Dennett of Photography Workshop assisted with the production of film stills. The late Jo
Spence very kindly gave me permission to borrow the title of a course
which she taught, 'Women's Pictures', and incorporate it in the title of
this book. Sarah Montgomery and Christine Pearce assisted in
preparing parts of the typescript, and I want to thank them for their
enthusiasm and efficiency. James Ferman and Rosemary Stark of the
British Board of Film Censors supplied me with information on the
legal situation regarding obscenity in films for Chapter 6, and James
Ferman responded to a draft of part of that chapter. Audrey
Summerhill and Caroline Spry of the Cinema of Women collective
provided details of the history and activities of COW for Chapter 9.
Rose Cooper staunchly read through the entire typescript of the
original edition in draft and put forward some extremely useful
comments and suggestions for improvements. I want to thank in
particular my friends Philip Corrigan and Ann Ferguson for many

things: for the stimulus and encouragement which have come from our discussions of the central issues of the book, for the time and effort they have spent in reading and responding to drafts of parts of it, and in general for their comradely and affectionate supportiveness during the time it was being written.

The stills reproduced in this book first appeared in films distributed by the following companies, to whom thanks are due: Warner Bros, Twentieth Century-Fox, Paramount, Film Traders, Liberation/ Concord Films and The Other Cinema. The extract from Raymond Bellour's article, 'Psychosis, neurosis, perversion' is reprinted by permission of *Camera Obscura*.

In writing this revised edition, I have found the comments of those who reviewed the original *Women's Pictures* extremely helpful: special thanks are due to Robert Burgoyne, Jacqueline Levitin and Janet Walker. Viewings of some of the films discussed in Chapter 12 were made possible by Helen de Witt of Cinenova, Karen Alexander of the British Film Institute and Julie Rigg of the National Film Archive. Thanks to Gillian Hartnoll, I was allowed access to the stacks of the British Film Institute Library throughout the summer of 1993; and the library's staff met my needs with their customary efficiency and courtesy. Phillippa Brewster, my editor at Routledge and Kegan Paul when *Women's Pictures* was first published, has been instrumental in ensuring that the book has remained in print over the years. I am most indebted to Phillippa, and to Colin Robinson of Verso, for their indispensable encouragement and support, past and present, for this project.

PART I

Introduction

1

Passionate Detachment

This book is about feminism and cinema: it assumes, therefore, a relationship of some kind between two sets of practices, and explores various points of overlap and intersection between them. The linking of feminism with cinema in itself raises a series of questions, some of them analytical or theoretical, others more obviously political. Feminism is a political practice, or set of practices, with its own history and forms of organisation, with its own bodies of theory constructed in and through that history and organisation. And it is not a monolith; it comes in different varieties, offers a range of analyses of the position of women, and different strategies for social change. Because of the forms of organisation it has adopted and developed over the years, and also perhaps because of its current cultural and political marginality, feminism presents itself very clearly as a process, and is therefore hard to pin down. This can be both a strength and a weakness. Cinema, on the other hand, which also has its own history, appears at first sight more concrete. Everyday understandings of it have had more than eighty years to become solidified and institutionalised. But for this very reason, our understandings of what cinema is or ought to be are perhaps all the more impenetrable.

For the purposes of this book, it is easier initially to pose a working definition of what I want to include within the term 'cinema' than of what I understand by 'feminism'. 'Cinema' is understood here in its broadest sense to embrace the various aspects of the institutions historically surrounding the production, distribution and exhibition of films of different types, from the commercial cinema exemplified at its most elaborate by the Hollywood studio system of the 1930s and 1940s, to the varieties of independent and avant-garde cinema which have been developing their own forms and institutions over the years since the 1920s. This definition also takes in the actual products of the institutions – the films themselves – and, very importantly, the conditions and character of the production and reception of films. At this point, I will define 'feminism' very broadly as a set of political practices founded in analyses of the social/historical position of women as subordinated, oppressed or exploited either within dominant modes of production (such as capitalism) and/or by the social relations of patriarchy or male domination. Given that feminism is itself many-sided, the possible dimensions and permutations of interrelations between it and cinema become enormous.

The central question addressed by this book is: what is, can be, or should be, the relationship between feminism and cinema? In even posing such a question I am, of course, assuming that a relationship of some kind is there to be explored, explicated, or constructed. This assumption in turn implies the acceptance of some form of cultural politics; in other words, that the 'cultural' (images, representations, meanings, ideologies) is a legitimate and important area of analysis and intervention for feminists. This argument might be considered in some quarters as contentious, in particular because of its implied assumption that economic factors may not always be paramount in shaping or determining the social and historical position of women. However, it seems to me that one of the major theoretical contributions of the women's movement has been its insistence on the significance of cultural factors, in particular in the form of socially dominant representations of women and the ideological character of such representations, both in constituting the category 'woman' and in delimiting and defining what has been called the 'sex/gender system', 'the set of arrangements by which a society transforms biological sexuality into products of human activity, and in which these transformed sexual needs are satisfied' (Rubin, 1975, p. 159).

To put forward the case for a feminist cultural politics, then, is to hold to a notion that ideology has its own effectivity both in general within social formations, and in particular with regard to sex/gender systems. In other words, everything that might come under the heading of the ideological – a society's representations of itself within and for itself and the ways in which people both live out and produce those representations – may be seen as a vital, pervasive and active element in the constitution of social structures and formations. As regards the sex/gender system as a specific social formation, Rubin's definition may be read as suggesting that it is in some measure an ideological construct. A Marxist-feminist perspective on this issue would focus on the relationship between sex/gender systems and their ideological character in relation to the economic conditions of their existence, perhaps by accepting that the autonomy of the ideological is relative, or operates in interaction with economic conditions. Such a perspective would suggest that cultural factors do not in general act alone or have their effects in isolation from other factors, such as class or the sexual division of labour, in shaping sex/gender systems. It would also suggest that the interaction of the ideological with the economic and other instances of the social formation is historically specific, so that the state of the sex/gender system varies historically.

If it is accepted that 'the cultural' may be subsumed within ideology and thus be considered as having effects in the constitution of the sex/gender system at any moment in history, then it becomes possible to argue that interventions within culture have some independent potential to transform sex/gender systems. In other words, 'cultural struggle' becomes a political possibility. To pose a relationship between feminism and cinema, as this book does, is therefore to suggest two things: one, that there are connections to be made on an analytical or theoretical level between the two sets of practices, and, two, that taken together feminism and cinema might provide a basis for certain types of intervention in culture. Although in specific cultural practices the distinction between analysis and intervention cannot easily be held to, it is in fact useful initially to make the distinction, if only for the sake of clarity of thought and exposition. And indeed although part of the structure of my argument in the main body of the book is founded on this conceptual separation of analysis and intervention, I shall in fact be arguing that they are but two sides of the same coin.

A recognition, implicit or explicit, of the relevance of cultural factors to a consideration of the sex/gender system has informed feminist thought in a variety of ways since the emergence, from the late 1960s on, of the 'second wave' women's movement. Arguments have been put forward regarding, for example, certain kinds of stereotypical images of women marketed via women's magazines, television advertisements, and other media. Here the cultural construction of an ideal female – young, shapely, carefully dressed and made up, fashionable, glamorous – may be considered in itself as 'oppressive' because it proffers an image which many women feel it is important to live up to and yet is at the same time unattainable for most of us. Such images are also criticised by feminists on the grounds that they objectify women – that is to say, legitimate and constitute social support for an ideological construction of women as objects, in particular as objects of evaluation in terms of socially predefined visible criteria of beauty and attractiveness. This analysis of images of women as objects has led also to a consideration of the extent to which women are represented as object-victims, particularly in media addressed specifically to male audiences. The implication is that the distinction between the glamorous female image of 'mainstream' advertisements and the nude pin-ups in male-oriented 'soft-porn' publications such as *Playboy* is only a matter of degree, and that the depiction of women as objects of male sexual violence in certain forms of hard pornography is a final and logical outcome of the cultural dominance of other forms of objectification in representations of women. Further ramifications of this form of cultural analysis may be seen, for example, in critiques of recurrent representations of women within Western fine art traditions – in particular in depictions of the female nude, and the madonna/mother figure (Berger, 1972), and also within literature – where critical arguments tend to centre on the nature of roles played by female protagonists of novelistic narratives (Cornillon, 1972). From such theoretical beginnings, feminist response may begin to extend beyond a critique of mainstream or dominant representations and towards the construction of alternatives: the creation of new feminist fine art forms, for example, or of novels with 'strong' female characters.

Commentaries on and criticisms of films from various feminist standpoints have drawn upon all of these approaches, the initial thrust of which emerges from a combination of a critique of existing, culturally dominant, representations of women with a tendency to emphasise the concepts of image and role. Such analyses, when applied to cinema, are important both in creating awareness of the socially constructed nature of representations of women in films, and also in offering an impetus towards the creation of alternative representations. However, precisely because of its focus on images and roles, there are a number of questions that cannot readily be addressed within the terms of reference of this approach. It tends, for instance, to take readings (particularly readings by professional film critics) very much at face value, and to focus criticism based on such readings upon surface features of story and character, without considering either the operation of elements underlying the surface features of film narratives or, perhaps more importantly, how the 'specifically cinematic' – formal characteristics peculiar to cinema: composition of the cinematic image, lighting, editing, camera movement and so on – operates in films either alone or in conjuction with stories or images and characters. Because of this, such an approach can easily bypass the question of how films make their own kinds of meanings, how they *signify*, in other words. These points are considered more fully in the main body of the book: they are raised here, however, because of the influence that the role/image approach has had, and still has, in feminist film criticism, and also in order to open up the question of what such an approach does not do, the issues to which it does not attend. This in itself raises questions central to my project. With this in mind, I set out with the assumptions not only that there is indeed a relationship fruitfully to be explored between feminism and cinema, but also that one possibly productive avenue of exploration lies in an examination of the operation of specifically cinematic signifiers, and also of elements of plot, characterisation and narrative structure which do not necessarily offer themselves to a 'surface' reading.

The question of feminist alternatives to culturally dominant representations of women is raised – sometimes implicitly, sometimes explicitly – by feminist critiques of such representations. Posing the possibility of alternatives may be allied with a critique of the dominance of males as producers of representations in general, and of representations of women in particular: for example, the advertising and TV industries are dominated by men in positions of authority, art history as an academic discipline has offered us few 'great' women artists, and the film industry has been dominated by male producers, directors and technicians. When the two critiques are put together – the notion of images of women as 'objects' and the observation that males are or have been largely responsible for producing such images – it can readily be concluded that a transformation in the area of representation might in some measure be brought about if there were greater num rs of women artists, advertising executives, film directors, for certain purposes, such an argument can be both use *goes* relation to cinema, for example, there is no d *against* d fewer opportunities than men to invo n, particularly in the commercial film inc ve been employed in the industry, they have b concentrated in jobs which involve relatively little and reward (Association of Cinematograph, Television and Allied Technicians, 1975). It is arguable that the obstacles women face in film production need to be dealt with to provide an opportunity to see what, if any, feminist interventions might be made in cinema. Another important condition for this clearing of the ground may be the rewriting of film history so that some awareness of the past contributions of women film makers, hitherto somewhat effaced, may be brought to light.[1] At the same time, however, it is essential to emphasise that the existence of more women film makers does not in itself guarantee more feminist films.

What then is the relationship between cultural interventions by women and feminist cultural interventions? Put this way, it is easy to see that the two things are not necessarily one and the same. Paintings, novels or films by women may or may not be feminist, and it is possible to argue, though some feminists will disagree, that feminist work may be produced by men. Disagreement on the latter point may in fact be regarded as symptomatic, in that it points up a further issue, one that is implicit in the very way in which the question is posed: the issue of authorship. Is the feminism of a piece of work there because of attributes of its author (cultural interventions by women), because of certain attributes of the work itself (feminist cultural interventions), or because of the way it is 'read'? The questions of authorship and text are central to any debate about the relationship between feminist cinema and women's cinema. The term 'text' refers to the structure and organisation of any one cultural product or set of representations: it may be applied, for instance, to a particular novel, painting, film, poem, advertisement. Its usage implies that works are the object of a certain type of analysis, involving 'an active reading in terms of the contradictions at work in them' (Cook, 1975, p. 9). Any single film may of course claim to be representative of both feminist cinema and women's cinema. What is being argued here, however, is not only that the one cannot unproblematically be reduced to the other, but also that a good deal of productive discussion about the relationship between feminism and cinema emerges through holding to the logical distinction between the two. This is because the very insistence on such a distinction is a necessary precondition of raising questions about the relationship between text and authorship in cinema: it also allows the question of the reception and reading of texts to be opened up. Before this argument is elaborated, however, it is perhaps important to reiterate that I am not suggesting that feminist efforts aimed at increasing the numbers of women 'cultural producers' are unimportant or irrelevant: on the contrary, it can certainly be argued that transformations in dominant modes of representation will not be brought about unless and until this happens. However, such transformations are neither a necessary nor an automatic outcome of such a strategy.

Unpacking the arguments around authorship and gender on the one hand and feminism and textual organisation on the other involves dealing with a number of fundamental issues. These centre around two questions: firstly that of authorship and intentionality, and secondly that of feminism in relation to female subjectivity and the latter in relation to the attributes of texts. The question of authorial intentions has informed debates in theories of art and literature for many years. What has been dubbed in such debates the 'intentionalist fallacy' argues that texts are reducible to the conscious intentions of their producers. That is to say, the meanings obtainable from or readable in texts of various kinds are, or ought to be, no more nor less than the meanings which authors or producers intended to put there. Arguments against authorial intentionality tend to stress either that an author may incorporate elements in texts unconsciously – that she or he may not be wholly aware of the implications of what is being written, or painted, or filmed. Or, as an extension of this argument, it might be suggested that texts can in some sense generate meanings on their own, or at least that meanings which go beyond authors' intentions may be generated in a dynamic moment of reading or reception. Balzac, for example, is often considered to be a novelist who 'knew more than he knew' – whose fictional works can yield textures and levels of meaning which clearly go beyond anything the writer himself could possibly have intended. The literary theorist Lukács, for instance, regarded Balzac's work as embodying the most progressive qualities possible in art produced in a bourgeois society, and this despite the novelist's personal politics, which were conservative in the extreme. To this extent, Balzac's works may be seen as in some way constituting their own meanings above and beyond conscious authorial input, and/or as constructing meanings uncontrolled by the author in the interaction of reader and text at the moment of reception.

Approaches to the question of authorship within film theory have advanced similar positions. 'Auteur theory' puts forward the notion that the primary creative responsibility for a film usually lies with its director (e.g. Sarris, 1968). That is to say, the notion of authorship on the literary model, despite very important differences between film making and literary work in modes and relations of production, is relevant to an understanding of film, and that films by a single director may sometimes be considered and analysed as a body of work, an *oeuvre*. At this point auteur theory may or may not embrace intentionalism. To the extent that it does, it will suggest that films mean only what their directors intended them to mean. Certain forms of the auteur theory have attempted to deal with some of the problems raised by intentionalism by posing a notion of authorship in terms of textual structures. For example, in considering the mythic themes embodied in the films of John Ford, themes which may well have exceeded the conscious intentions of Ford himself (which in any case we are not in a position to know for sure), distinction may be made between John Ford the man and 'John Ford' as a convenient label or signature for a series of themes and structures recurrent in the *oeuvre* of the director (Russell, 1965). If this notion of film authorship is accepted, we cannot necessarily take a film maker's word about her or his films – even if we have it – at face value.

A similar argument may be advanced in relation to the question of feminism and textual organisation. It if is accepted that texts are not necessarily readable purely in terms of the intentions of their authors or producers, then it can be argued on the one hand that a non-feminist is capable of producing a feminist text, and on the other that a feminist is capable of producing a non-feminist text. (This, of course, is to bracket for the moment the question of what is to be understood by the term 'feminist text': it is this which is finally at issue in this whole debate and which – as I shall argue below – cannot be defined either *a priori* or universalistically). Opening up the more general issue of gender in relation to authorship and textual organisation adds a further dimension to the argument. What, if any, relationship can there be between a text produced by a woman and a feminist text? It is evident that not all women are consciously feminists, and not everyone consciously a feminist is a woman, so that even the intentionalist fallacy would reject any attempt to equate women's texts with feminist texts. At this point, a more nuanced and critical approach to intentionalism – one which, in focusing in the first instance on texts as bearers of meaning, begins to transcend the terms of the intentionalism debate – permits the consideration of some important questions centring around notions of, and distinctions between, 'feminine' and 'feminist' texts.

First of all, how might a 'feminine' text be defined, and if 'the feminine' can be considered a principle of textual organisation, an attribute of the text itself, what is the connection between such a principle and 'woman': what possible link can there be between an attribute which informs the structure and organisation of texts, and gender? Even to suggest the possibility of a relationship between feminine-as-text and 'woman' is to pose some kind of connection between 'woman' and representation which, at least initially, side-steps the whole issue of feminism. What is at stake here then is the possibility of a feminine text as opposed to a feminist one: that is, that representations might be considered as either 'feminine' or 'masculine'. This question has been addressed under the rubric of feminine language or feminine writing by a number of theorists. Luce Irigaray, for example, argues on behalf of a feminine language which operates outside the bounds of an 'Aristotelian type of logic' (Irigaray, 1977, p. 64) which she sees as informing masculine language. In constructing this argument, Irigaray sets up a relationship of analogy between gender and language, so that Western discourse is seen as possessing the 'masculine' attributes of visibility, goal orientation, and so on. A feminine language, or a feminine relation to language, would on the other hand challenge and subvert this form of discourse by posing plurality over against unity, multitudes of meanings as against single, fixed meanings, diffuseness as against instrumentality. That is to say, whereas Western discourse – the 'masculine' – tends to limit meaning by operating a linear and instrumental syntax, a feminine language would be more open, would set up multiplicities of meanings.

In considering in this way the relationship between the feminine and signification, it is perhaps useful at this point to focus on signification. If signification and representation are seen as processes of meaning production, and if it is accepted that notions of feminine language and feminine writing may describe a specific relationship to representation, then the feminine can be seen as a subject position, a place which the user – or the subject – of language can occupy in relation to language. This first of all frees the argument from biologism, from any necessary equation of the feminine with woman as defined by bodily attributes, and second allows us to name the defining characteristics of a feminine relation to representation. Irigaray's argument suggests that the feminine describes a relationship to language and not a particular form of language, and also that this relationship is characterised by process and heterogeneity. To telescope a complex argument (Heath, 1978; Kuhn, 1979), 'the feminine' in this view may be regarded as an attribute of textual organisation only in the sense that it poses a challenge to dominant forms of relationship between texts and recipients. This challenging relationship is one in which in the act of reading, meanings are grasped as shifting and constantly in process, and the reader-subject is placed in an active relationship to those meanings. A feminine text would in this way constitute a subversion of and challenge to a 'mainstream' text. By extension, this argument may be viewed as an explanation of and a justification for intervention at the level of signification, for 'radical signifying practice' – modes of representation which challenge dominant modes by placing subjectivity in process, making the moment of reading one in which meanings are set in play rather than consolidated or fixed (Cixous, 1980; Kristeva, 1975).

The notion of a feminine text therefore brings to the very centre of debate the consideration of texts as producers of meanings, as producing meanings in the moment of reading. Thus, meanings are produced for the 'subject' of the text – the reader is inserted into the meanings produced by the text and is thus in a sense produced by them. This dynamic notion of reading as a relationship between reader and text then implies that no texts, 'mainstream' or otherwise, bear specific *a priori* meanings in and for themselves. Although – and this is a different, if related, debate – texts may embody 'preferred' readings, a dynamic notion of texts as processes of signification or meaning production allows for a consideration of the possibility of interventions in cultural practice being generated elsewhere than solely in the consciousness of authors or producers. The theoretical groundings of the notion of a feminine text are complex and open to criticism, centring primarily on the fact that many of the arguments – Kristeva's in particular – seem to be suggesting that all radical signifying practice is, in some way, feminine. In spite of the difficulties, however, I believe it is vital at least to open up the question here, because its implications for feminist interventions in cultural practice are potentially very wide-ranging. What the notion of a feminine text, drawing as it does on theories of feminine language or feminine writing, achieves is to open up for consideration two productive sets of ideas. First of all, in addressing itself to the text, it puts forward arguments concerning the specific character of feminine language or feminine writing, and offers a theoretical justification for such arguments: the feminine text would disrupt, challenge, question and put its reader-subjects into process. In providing a challenge to situations in which the process of signification is not foregrounded, as is the case – it is argued – in dominant texts, in masculine discourse, the feminine would be subversive of such discourse, would constitute a disturbance to dominant modes of representation, and thus to the dominant cultural order.

The argument at this point is still rather abstract, however. What, it might be asked, would a feminine text actually look like? Julia Kristeva, in putting forward her argument for radical signifying practice, introduces the notion of the poetic (Kristeva, 1976). A text may embody or produce the poetic to the degree that it brings to the fore the processes by which it constructs its own meanings. That is to say, a text is constituted as poetic in relation to its reading. Any text may qualify as poetic, as radical signifying practice, or as feminine only in the relations it poses between itself and its readers. Since such relationships are clearly context-bound in that they are likely to vary from place to place, from time to time, and from reader to reader, it is actually impossible to make any universal or absolute prescriptions as to formal characteristics, a point which needs to be borne in mind in considering the question of feminist cinema in relation to that of feminine writing. Kristeva's argument does perhaps constitute some kind of prescription for avant-garde signifying practices. But does this mean that avant-garde and feminine practices are necessarily the same?

A feminine text then has no fixed formal characteristics, precisely because it is a relationship: it becomes a feminine text in the moment of its reading. This conclusion leads to consideration of the second set of ideas generated by the notion of feminine writing: that the moment of reception is crucial. In concrete terms, it might be concluded from this that no intervention in culture can work at the level of the text alone. As far as a feminist intervention is concerned, therefore, it is not really a question of producing a 'feminist *text*'. In any case, if it is accepted that neither authorial intention nor the attributes of the text taken in isolation (if, indeed, that is ever possible) can always guarantee specific readings – even if they may limit the range of readings available – we are led to ask where feminism, as a set of meanings, enters a text. I have already advanced the argument that no set of meanings already inhabits a text, but rather that a text is, in some measure at least, created in its reading or reception. If this is the case, then the whole area of reception becomes a political issue in its own right. Given the distinct nature of the film-viewing situation, this has highly specific implications for cinema.

Nevertheless, to set aside completely both intention and textual organisation is perhaps too extreme a stance to adopt. It might usefully be stressed once more that feminine writing is not necessarily the same thing as feminist writing. For although it may be appropriate in certain circumstances to consider a text which constitutes a disturbance of, or a challenge to, dominant modes of representation as in some sense feminist, it can also be argued that such 'disturbance' is not a sufficient – even if it might be held to be a necessary – attribute of a feminist text. From this it may be concluded that a text is feminist to the extent that something is added to it – precisely some 'feminist' input. Debates on this issue are sometimes conducted in terms of a division of form and content, so that the question becomes: should we seek a specifically feminist form? Or, under what conditions should a feminist intervention in culture operate at the level of content? However, although it provides a useful point of entry to the complexities of the debate, I believe that the form/content distinction does not in the final instance permit a sufficiently nuanced argument: the point that feminine language is not a formal attribute of texts so much as a relationship of reader and text should demonstrate this. Debates which limit themselves to the form/content division end, ironically perhaps, by being overly formalist in that they do not allow consideration of the conditions surrounding the production and reception of texts. It seems important to emphasise that the text is but a single element in a series of social relations of cultural production, all of which need to be taken into account in any work on representation.

What, then, is a feminist text? In the light of this discussion, it would seem more apposite to rephrase the question, and ask: what is a feminist intervention in culture? For to the extent that both authorial intention and formal textual attributes are displaced or relativised as productive of meaning, the question of a feminist text becomes problematic. If a text may or may not be readable in terms of feminist intentions on the part of its author or producer, if it may or may not generate 'unconscious' feminist meanings, it would seem once again that the issue is decided at the moment of reading or reception. If primacy is thus transferred from author and text to reading, then the moment of reception itself becomes a feasible point of political intervention. One possible outcome of the notion of feminism as a property of textual reception is that 'feminist reading' becomes possible. This in fact has been a premiss of certain forms of feminist criticism, which may regard dominant texts as cultural bearers of ideologies which can be mined and exposed – and the texts themselves transformed in retrospect – by readings 'against the grain'. Some feminist readings of classic Hollywood films have in fact been undertaken along these lines, and indeed have been very important in the recent development of film theory.

But this by no means exhausts the debate, which at this point might easily be perceived as advancing a view of the text as nothing more than the site of struggle for the production of meanings. Although it may be true that all texts are indeed open to a range of readings, it is surely not often the case that they are open to any or all readings, depending only on the context and conditions of reception. To some extent, texts do tend to offer 'preferred' readings, so that, for example, a feminist reading of a dominant text might aim to challenge those very preferred readings by uncovering hidden structures and ideological operations, while other texts might not seem to call for such challenge, in that their preferred readings – the readings which they seem immediately to offer – may already appear as 'feminist'.

At this point the somewhat vexed issue of tendentiousness raises itself. 'Tendency' in cultural production was in the forefront of debates about the social and political functions of art in the years immediately following the October Revolution in Russia. Tendentiousness, refer-ring to the artist's desire to take up a political stance, in its original context implied that no specific party loyalty was called for from an artist expressing tendency in her or his work. It did, however, suggest a conscious intent on the part of the artist to incorporate a particular political position or range of positions in that work. We are back, then, with the problem of intentionality, a problem which troubled discussions about the artist's role in the revolution, about the distinction between 'high' art and agitational art, and was an important factor in a series of divisions which increasingly split Soviet artists and writers throughout the 1920s (Vaughan-James, 1973). In spite of the obvious differences in social, political and economic conditions, some of the problems surrounding tendentiousness in contemporary feminist cultural practice do seem somewhat similar. If we are perhaps more aware today that authorial intention does not and cannot necessarily circumscribe the range of meanings available from a work, we are still forced to ask the question: under what conditions are readings in fact determined or determinable by the intended inputs of authors or producers?

The problem with this question is that it cannot be answered in a general way: there is no answer that will fit all possible cases of feminist cultural production. To find the reason for this, I need only reiterate the centrality of the moment of reception in the construction of meanings. Whatever the overt intentions of producers, in many cases readings of their works must often take place outside any control they may wish to exert. In other words, if it is accepted that meaning does not reside purely in the text itself, that it is not something locked within the text waiting for a reader in order to be liberated, but is itself to some degree an independent product or outcome of reading, then it becomes impossible to consider feminism in terms of fixed textual attributes, whether they be of 'form' or of 'content', let alone in terms of whether or not producers intended to put them there. A cultural producer who wishes to take up a feminist stance, therefore, has several options. One might be to continue doing whatever she thinks fit in terms of textual input, and simply hope that the work will be read as it was intended. Another might be to attempt more actively to limit the range of meanings available from the work, which may be accomplished in several ways. This might be by addressing a very specific audience and trying to ensure that the work reaches only that audience, or by dealing with a particular issue on which positions are already to some extent clear, and attempting to determine readings by taking up a very overt stance on that one issue, or by trying to limit readings in other – extra-textual – ways, through interviews, reviews and personal appearances, for example.

A point which should perhaps be emphasised here is that the thrust of tendentiousness is usually in some degree in the direction of closure, of restricting the range of meanings potentially available from a text. For certain purposes and under certain circumstances a cultural practice calling itself feminist may actually be characterised by some degree of closure: it is perhaps even a truism that tendency and closure go together, that a restricted range of possible readings is a defining characteristic of tendentiousness in texts. Posing the issue of feminist cultural practice in this way opens once more the question of a feminine as against a feminist text. One of the arguments on behalf of a feminine language is that it works against that very closure which, it is suggested, is a feature of dominant 'masculine' language, to the extent that such a language embodies a hierarchy of meanings and implies a subjection to, a completion and closure of, meaning.

It has been argued, too, that closure is a feature of certain types of textual organisation, such as that of 'classic' narratives. The structure of classic narratives works in such a way that stories are opened by a disruption of some equilibrium (say a murder or a disappearance) and work towards a resolution of the initial disruption, so that the resolution coincides with the end of the story. Roland Barthes makes a distinction between the pleasure to be obtained from the closure or resolution of this classic form of narrative, and the 'bliss' (*jouissance*) of the text which challenges such closure. Both are clearly relationships of reading: the pleasure of the first is the satisfaction of completion, of having all the ends tied up, whereas the bliss of the second is the unsettling, the movement of the subject produced by the reading, which goes beyond, or is outside, the pleasure of the fixation of the subject-reader of the classic narrative (Barthes, 1975).

It is clear that openness as a defining characteristic of the feminine is something very different from the closure, fixation or limitation of meaning implied by the tendentious text. In this difference two distinct forms of cultural practice may in fact be at stake. And indeed it does actually underlie a series of strategic dissensions and contradictions within contemporary feminist cultural politics. Such dissensions may be summed up briefly by distinguishing between two extremes of oppositional cultural practice, one which tends to take processes of signification for granted and one which argues that the meaning production process is itself the site of struggle. The first would draw on dominant forms, such that the oppositional character of the representations produced is guaranteed by mobilising the signification process as a vehicle of already constituted meanings and by taking readers as also already formed (in this instance, in relation to certain political positions) prior to the moment of reception: thus meanings are seen, as it were, as being handed unchanged from source to recipient. Here it is meanings, rather than the process of their generation, which are constituted as in some sense oppositional. Such forms of cultural practice would therefore tend to operate within culturally dominant modes of representation, but would use those modes as a means to convey a 'message' constituted as culturally or politically oppositional.

The second form of oppositional cultural practice would take as its object the signification process itself, giving it a central place in the organisation of the work. Thus in this case meaning production would not be taken for granted, exactly because the ideological character of the signification process is regarded as itself something to be challenged. The argument here is that dominant modes of representation constitute forms of subjectivity – the subject fixed by closure, for example – characteristic of a masculinist or patriarchal culture, and that to write 'in the feminine' is in itself to challenge the ideological constitution of dominant modes of representation. It is in this respect that such a cultural practice may be considered as feminist. The question of feminist interventions in culture, therefore, goes beyond – though of course it must include – considerations of tendentiousness, and involves a number of fundamental questions about the ways in which texts create meanings and define and constitute their reader-subjects.

Feminism, considered in relation to cultural practice, is perhaps even more complex and many-sided than might at first be imagined. My purpose in this book is to explore as many of the dimensions of the relationship between feminism and cinema as I can, and in as open a way as possible. At various points in this chapter, I have indicated that feminist cultural practice may take up various moments in the production of representations as legitimate points of intervention, if only because there are so many more dimensions to the situation than simply the text. If this argument is accepted, the relationship between feminism and cinema may usefully be explored in a variety of ways. It may be appropriate, for example, to include in the terms of the relationship not only forms of textual practice, and the production, distribution and exhibition practices surrounding texts, but also interventions at the level of reading, so that under the umbrella of feminist film practice may be sheltered not only feminist film production, work with audiences, conditions of reception, and textual organisation, but also feminist film analysis itself.

PART II

Dominant Cinema

The second section of this book is an examination of the characteristics of dominant cinema, which will lead, via a consideration of representation of women in dominant cinema, to the discussion which follows in Part III of the various ways in which dominant cinema may be taken up in feminist film criticism and analysis. It is important, however, to understand what dominant cinema is: how it works, and how it has developed its peculiar forms and institutions over the hundred years since its beginnings. Because it must be a prior condition both of criticism and of analysis, as well as of the creation of alternatives to dominant cinematic forms and institutions, such an understanding is essential to any feminist approach to film – particularly when it involves feminist cultural politics.

2

The Pleasure Machine

In this chapter, I will examine dominant cinema from two points of view: first in terms of its nature as an economic and social institution, and then in relation to its textual features. Dominant cinema may be defined both as the institutional frameworks surrounding the production, distribution and exhibition of films for world-wide mass markets, and also as the distinctive characteristics of the films themselves – what they look like and the kinds of readings they construct. Hollywood is usually considered to be the limit case, the ideal-type, of dominant cinema, although of course the institutions and forms characteristic of dominant cinema are by no means confined to the Hollywood film industry. Indeed one of the principal features of dominant cinema is its pervasiveness as a model for modes of production and modes of representation in film industries all over the world. This has important consequences for the presuppositions audiences bring to their film viewing. Most of the millions of people throughout the world who have had contact with cinema would share certain assumptions about it: for example, that 'cinema' is constituted of films of a certain length (between one and two hours, say), which tell stories with beginnings, middles and ends, stories which usually involve fictional characters as pivots of narrative action. It would perhaps also be assumed that films are normally viewed in a special place set aside for the purpose, darkened, with seats facing a screen onto which a large image is projected. Film viewing, in this model, is a collective and semi-public undertaking: it is also an activity which is, as a rule, paid for by spectators. An exchange takes place – of money in return for representations. Spectators, as part of their socialisation as cinema-goers, build up an understanding of how to read films, so that the act of reading may eventually become automatic or taken for granted.

Although this common experience of dominant cinema may seem quite obvious today, there is in fact no historical inevitability about it. Dominant cinema could well have taken directions other than the ones it has, developed a variety of forms and institutions. The fact that dominant cinema has taken the contingent forms it has is no coincidence, but the outcome of the interaction, at different points in time, of certain economic and ideological factors. Although it is not my purpose here to detail these interactions, it is important to clarify the general terms of discussion. Economic conditions, then, include the institutions of film production, distribution and exhibition, and the ways in which they are financed, organised and administered. The ideological is formed by a variety of factors, including the history, prevalence and formal strategies of popular non-cinematic fictional representations, the ways in which cinema speaks to or addresses audiences, and the ways in which certain visual representations carry over into cinema from non-cinematic media. It is in the historically specific relationship between the economic and the ideological – in the 'cinematic apparatus' – that dominant cinema takes its concrete forms.

If dominant cinema is shaped by historically variable conditions of existence, it is clearly not a fixed entity. Its forms change along with variations in the character and interaction of its economic and ideological contexts. The definition of dominant cinema I am advancing here, turning as it does on the conjunction of certain modes of cinematic representation with certain cinematic institutions, is offered simply as a model. There will be variations on the model at different times and places. It might therefore be more to the point to talk about dominant cinemas, or varieties of dominant cinema. Dominant cinema can be a comprehensive category: nevertheless, even the broadest definition of it is highly exclusive, in that an enormous range of possible practices will be excluded. Some of these – like political cinema and avant-garde cinema – have developed their own histories alongside that of dominant cinema.

Although the apparatus of dominant cinema acquires its historically specific character from the relationships between its economic and ideological conditions of existence, I will examine these two categories separately, as 'institutions' and 'texts' respectively. It cannot be emphasised too strongly, however, that in concrete situations institutions and texts do not operate in isolation from one another, but are interrelated in any and every specific form taken by dominant cinema. Nevertheless, the conceptual distinction is quite useful for the purpose of dealing with the relationship of feminism and cinema, because it permits a consideration of feminist film practices which focus, implicitly or explicitly, on the one rather than the other, as well as of practices aimed at transcending any distinction between them.

Institutions

As dominant cinema is not a fixed, historically invariable formation, it is impossible to make general statements about its institutional side at any other than an abstract level. Although general statements may be useful in marking out the terrain of debate – by showing what the institutions are not, as much as what they actually are, for instance – any detailed consideration of particular moments in the institutional formation of dominant cinema calls for a more finely drawn set of parameters. This, of course, is an argument on behalf of a study of cinematic institutions in their historical specificity.

However, the institutions of dominant cinema do assume certain general characteristics of their own as against those of other types of cinema. In dominant cinema, for example, every film typically becomes a commodity possessing two aspects: first of all, a film is a commodity in its physical existence – actual reels of celluloid are at various points products and objects of exchange. But film is more than this, in that representations may also constitute objects of exchange within institutions of dominant cinema. The cinemagoer's purchase of a ticket at the box office buys the right not to take home reels of celluloid, but only to look at a series of images projected onto a screen. This exchange is, moreover, only the last in a series of transactions which turn not on concrete commodities but on commoditised meanings. Film is therefore a commodity in at least two senses: both as reels of celluloid and as bearers of meanings. In dominant cinema, the product film takes on a certain character, defined by its distinct modes of production. The institutions of dominant cinema characteristically embody industrial production relations, in the sense that the film-making process usually involves the labour of large numbers of people with different skills – a division of labour, in other words. In many forms of dominant cinema, there is also a high level of demarcation and hierarchisation of skills and labour in film production, institutionalised in the practices of both managements and unions. The centrality of trade unions in the film industry, taken together with the commodity status of the films themselves, serves to underline the fact that most or all of those involved in film production in dominant cinema are employees. The commodity film is consequently not the property of the majority of those involved in its production. The right to the use of the film as an object of exchange belongs with its owners, and ownership is typically vested in production companies.

A further series of exchanges centring on the commodity film takes place at the point of distribution, when a production company will sell either the celluloid itself, or more often certain rights in the celluloid, to a distribution company. Distribution companies in turn rent films to exhibitors, who then screen them for audiences. The exhibitor again acquires not the actual film, but only the right to exhibit it. Films are screened, as a rule, in theatres, and audiences pay for the right to look at a film at a particular place and time. In dominant cinema, then, film constitutes a set of relations of production and exchange centring on a commodity whose exchange value has a range of aspects. Film production is usually, in the final instance, financed by revenues from distributors, exhibitors and audiences. In capitalist or mixed economies, such revenues may also constitute the major source of return for investors in the industry.

Beyond this point, it is impossible to generalise: it becomes necessary to consider variations in cinematic institutions in greater historical detail. The ideal-type of dominant cinema is commonly regarded as the Hollywood studio systems of the 1930s and 1940s: the foregoing description of the institution might in fact be of exactly this conjuncture. But even Hollywood in its 'classic' years has its own characteristic departures from and elaborations on the model. These might include the star system in relation to the industry, the industry's self-censorship institutionalised in the early 1930s with the studios' agreement of the Production Code, and the tendency, until the late 1940s, to monopoly among certain major Hollywood production companies who also owned or controlled distribution companies and chains of film theatres (French, 1971). It is significant that much feminist work aimed at exposing the ideological operation of dominant cinema through practices of reading and analysis of texts (see Chapter 5) is directed exactly at the products of the Hollywood studio system of the 1930s and 1940s.

However, I wish now to focus discussion on the implications of variations in the institutional model of dominant cinema outlined here. There have, for example, been a number of changes within Hollywood since the 1950s – the decade in which, it is commonly agreed, the studio system began to break down. In recent times, films addressed to mass audiences have increasingly been made by independent producers as well as, or sometimes rather than, directly by the corporations owning what were once the film studios. As a result, much labour in the film industry has become casualised – many actors, technicians and 'creative' workers are no longer on company payrolls, but work freelance. The studios themselves have diversified, and much of their routine work consists of television productions. While on the one hand large corporations – such as Warner Bros, which began in the 1920s as a family business devoted solely to film production – have extended their activities into a wide range of non-cinematic media, relatively few cinema films are now being made, and most entrants to the film industry tend either to operate on its fringes as independents, or to serve their apprenticeships by working on television productions.

Other changes within the institutions of dominant cinema may constitute a challenge to the very boundaries of the category itself. Developments in technologies of representation have the potential of transforming the social relations and modes of address characteristic of ideal-type dominant cinema. Audiences can now, for example, buy films as physical commodities, in the form not usually of celluloid, but as video-cassettes and video-discs, which can be viewed, given the machinery, in the home. And many of the media corporations, with their activities already highly diversified, are promoting the technologies and relations of production and reception associated with these shifts in the commodity status of film. The potential implications of such developments are wide-ranging: they may transform the actual institutions of dominant cinema, the social relationships underpinning the exchange value of representations, and the institutional characteristics of the conditions of reception and reading of films.

This is certainly true as regards the relationship between cinema and feminism. It seems clear, first of all, that film – considered as a complex commodity having certain relationships with structures of production, distribution and exhibition – has become, as a vehicle of representations, relatively marginalised. Film theatres must compete for audiences with functional equivalents of this form of cinema – network television producing TV movies, home video and subscriber cable television broadcasting films round the clock. This particular formation of the institutions of dominant cinema, which is frequently regarded as symptomatic of a state of crisis in the film industry, has a number of implications with regard to feminism. Firstly, the rise of small film production companies on the fringes of institutions of dominant cinema has opened up a space within the purview of dominant cinema for films which may be read as 'feminist': such a space did not exist during the period of ascendancy of the studio system. These films operate broadly within the institutional and textual parameters of dominant cinema, while at the same time appearing to offer alternative representations of women. The situation also has implications for the position of women and feminists working within the industry and for the degree of control which they are able to exert over their own work.

Claudia Weill's film *Girlfriends* (1977) – which is discussed in Chapter 7 – is a significant case in point, in that it highlights some of the contradictions within dominant cinema. The film began as a low-budget ($10,000) independent short, financed by a series of grants, loans and private donations. It then grew, over a production period of several years, into a full-length narrative feature. When it attracted attention at a number of film festivals, Warner Bros acquired world-wide distribution rights to the film, and it was widely exhibited and favourably received. Weill, whose directorial experience had come from work on documentaries for American public television, was then contracted by Warners to make three more feature films. *Girlfriends* is interesting because, although it was widely read as a feminist film, it constructs a kind of feminism which is in some degree assimilable by the structures of dominant cinema. First, it can be situated within the recently revived genre of 'women's pictures', and, second, the fact that it is a feature narrative permits it to be slotted relatively easily into existing structures of distribution and exhibition, while its approach to cinematic narrative is compatible with the textual characteristics of dominant cinema. At the same time, however, the film's conditions of production marginalise it in relation to dominant structures. The history of *Girlfriends* may be understood as marking a crisis over representation, of women and of feminism in particular, within the film industry.

A further set of potential consequences in relation to feminism of changes in the institutional structures of dominant cinema revolves around transformations in the conditions of reception of films. The fact that films can now be viewed not only in the public or semi-public setting of the film theatre, but also in the privacy of the spectator's home, has a variety of consequences. One is that, to the extent that film viewing takes place in private, it is no longer susceptible to the forms of censorship to which public representations may be subject. This immediately raises the question of texts as they intersect with institutions: various institutions for the control and censorship of cinematic representations have, precisely because their domain is 'the public', sought to circumscribe what is representable in cinema. To the extent that institutions of film censorship concern themselves with the nature and the audience of films considered to be 'pornographic', for example, cinematic representations of women are at stake (see Chapter 6). A change in relations of exchange and reception of films whereby they are increasingly consumed in private may thus open up a space for transformations in certain representations of women. This in turn may operate retroactively on the textual characteristics of certain types of films to generate, for example, changes in the nature of pornographic representations.

Finally, the increasingly privatised conditions of film reception, taken together with changes in relations of production, distribution and exhibition in dominant cinema, suggest that the social characteristics of cinema audiences are themselves likely to be transformed. While, with relatively few exceptions, films in the 1970s and 1980s were decreasingly being produced for mass general audiences, low-budget independent films began to address themselves to small audiences with specialised or sectional interests. This has implications for the reading and reception of film texts. The point to be emphasised here is that among these fragmented or specialised cinema audiences are audiences for films of feminist interest. Indeed, certain recent examples of Hollywood (or, like *Girlfriends*, quasi-Hollywood) films may be read as addressing themselves exactly to such audiences. All this may take place largely within dominant cinema, but might none the less be considered in some respects as a challenge to its institutional boundaries.

Texts

If it is possible to advance general statements about the institutional structures of dominant cinema only in the form of a model, and if in consequence concrete instances of dominant cinema vary in some degree within the parameters of the model, much the same can be said of the textual characteristics of dominant cinema. Nevertheless, there are some core constituents of the dominant cinematic text which pervade all forms of dominant cinema, and indeed – such is their power as ideological constructs – also spill over into a variety of institutionally 'non-dominant' film practices. The textual model for dominant cinema is the 'classic realist text', in relation to film sometimes called the classic Hollywood text, classic cinema, or classic Hollywood cinema. I take all these terms to refer to a type of film text organised around both a certain kind of narrative structure, and a specific discourse or set of signifiers, which become the vehicle of the narrative, the means by which the story is told. It should be emphasised that this set of textual operations is not confined to films made in Hollywood. However, Hollywood films, and in particular the products of the studio system of the 1930s and 1940s, may again be regarded as ideal-typical. I shall examine in turn narrative structure and narrative discourse, at this stage simply signalling a number of points which are of relevance to the question of cinema and feminism. Most of the points made here are taken up again in subsequent chapters.

Narrative structure is considered here within the terms adopted by literary critics working in the Formalist tradition. In analysing narratives, Formalists distinguish between, on the one hand, story – the events of the narrative given chronologically – and, on the other, plot – the order in which narrative events appear in the actual telling of the story. Work on narrative structures is directed at narrative events and their ordering within the plot, and is based on the assumption that any one narrative will share common structures with innumerable others. In other words, the presupposition of Formalist approaches to narrative analysis is that individual narratives are simply expressions of underlying structures, or ground rules, common to whole groups of narratives (Barthes, 1977). Such an approach also assumes that the basic structures of narratives are limited in number, but can at the same time account for all individual cases. Plot may be understood as the trajectory of the narrative, the process of movement between its beginning and its end, and the beginning and the end of a narrative seen as constituting two states of equilibrium. The movement of the plot, according to this model, is from an initial state of equilibrium – which is ruptured by an event or 'enigma' that sets the narrative in action – towards a new equilibrium which constitutes a resolution of the initial enigma and a closure of the narrative.

Within this model, different plot orders may structure the movement between beginning equilibrium and end equilibrium: there are a variety of ways of getting from the one to the other, of devices to delay narrative closure (Todorov, 1977b). Elements of story and plot are traced along the path from one equilibrium to the other, while the plot itself may be considered as simply, in the Formalist term, a 'retardation device' – the pleasure of the narrative being derived in some measure from the recipient's anticipation of the held-off narrative closure. The Formalist critic Propp, for example, in examining the fairy tale as a particular narrative form, concludes that its typical motivator is a 'villainy' or a 'lack' which disrupts a *status quo* – a child is spirited away, say, or a king wants a husband for his daughter. The task of the tale is to restore order to the world of the narrative by vanquishing the villain or liquidating the lack. In the fairy tale, resolution is brought about in a limited number of ways: by a battle in which the hero conquers the villain, perhaps, or by the marriage of the hero and the princess (Propp, 1968).

Structural analysis can be applied to various forms of narrative expression, and the method provides a useful point of entry to the narratives of individual films. For example, a breakdown of the plot of *Mildred Pierce* (Curtiz, Warner Bros, 1945) can be instrumental in untangling the somewhat complex interrelationship between story and plot in this film. The film's story follows, more or less, the story in the novel by James Cain on which the film is based. It concerns the rise to wealth of an 'independent' woman who parts from her husband, opens up a successful restaurant business, and has an affair with a millionaire playboy. The woman, Mildred Pierce, has two daughters, with one of whom she has an almost incestuously close relationship that ends in the downfall of both of them. The film's plot reverses the story order by setting up as its narrative disruption the central element in the heroine's downfall – the murder of her lover. The task of the plot of the film, as against that of the novel, is to solve the murder. The story is told in three flashbacks which relate events leading up to the murder: it is this which makes for the complexity of the film's plot-story relationship. A breakdown or segmentation of the plot of *Mildred Pierce* based on the film's articulation of narrative time is given in Figure 2.1. The first segment sets up the villainy – a murder – which it is one of the tasks of the narrative to explain and solve. The plot may be regarded as a series of retardation devices which function to delay the solution until the penultimate segment, when the 'truth' is revealed by the detective and the murder solved. The second segment constructs a further enigma, this time in the form of a lack centring on Mildred's relationship with her husband: the lack is liquidated in the final segment, when the two are reunited. These resolutions constitute a final equilibrium and permit narrative closure at the levels of both plot and story. The complex relationship of plot and story in this film turns on its peculiar manipulation of temporal order, such that the end of the story becomes the beginning of the plot, which then moves in and out of various levels of narrative time. This is effected by the film's juxtaposition of flashbacks from different narrative viewpoints (Mildred's and the detective's) with sequences in the film's narrative present. A breakdown of narrative structure along these lines may clear the way for further textual analysis, as is demonstrated by feminist readings of *Mildred Pierce* itself (Cook, 1978a; Nelson, 1977).

Another procedure for a structural analysis of narratives involves isolating the basic units, or moves, of the story – the 'functions' of the narrative. In the relatively simple case of the fairy tale, Propp deals with only one type of function, which he defines largely in terms of narrative action. Since narrative function is regarded as 'an act of a character defined from the point of view of its significance for the course of the action' (Propp, 1968, p. 21), characters in fairy tales are seen simply as vehicles for narrative action, or agents. Analyses of narrative forms have elaborated on Propp's model by putting forward

1	2	3	4	5	6	7
narrative present	flashback 1: indefinite narrative past (Mildred)	narrative present	flashback 2: indefinite narrative past (Mildred)	narrative present	flashback 3: narrative past (Detective)	narrative present

1 The murder. Mildred is found on the beach and taken to police station.
2 Mildred tells detective events in her past.
3 Detective interrupts.
4 Mildred proceeds with her story.
5 Mildred's daughter is brought into police station.
6 The 'truth' is revealed by the detective and the murder solved.
7 Mildred leaves police station with her former husband.

Figure 2.1 Mildred Pierce: a segmentation of the plot

other kinds of function. Barthes, for example, has added three groups of functions to Propp's in order to account for data relating, for example, to the spatial location of the narrative and to characters in the story (Barthes, 1977).

The notion of character is in fact crucial to any consideration of the classic realist text, cinematic or otherwise. While the classic realist text may mobilise elements of story and plot and produce enigmas and resolutions in the ways I have described, it derives its specificity from its articulation of character as a narrative function. In the classic realist text, action typically pivots on central characters who are rendered in psychological depth and tend to become objects of identification for readers. These characters are fictional persons whose fate is tied up with the progress of the narrative, indeed on whom may be centred the very disruption that sets the narrative in motion. For example, the second sequence of *Mildred Pierce* shows the heroine in a series of close-ups (see Still 2.1) and medium close-ups: this immediately signals the centrality of the Mildred character to the film's narrative. Because a sequence showing a murder has immediately preceded these shots of Mildred, the villainy becomes linked with the figure of the heroine, and her fate becomes tied up with the solution of the crime. In classic Hollywood cinema, character and action are typically intertwined in this way. To the extent that, as in *Mildred Pierce*, the central character is female, we may consider how 'woman' as a structure or narrative function operates within the textual organisation of certain types of film. Is it possible, for example, to isolate recurrent or typical narrative functions or interactions of character and narrative action in dominant cinema, and if so, how do these relate specifically to 'woman'?

There are a number of possible approaches to this question. The one which perhaps presents itself most immediately, and which was in fact adopted early on in feminist critical work on dominant cinema, actually departs from the premisses of structural analysis in being inductive rather than deductive (in induction, general conclusions are drawn from particular cases). An inductive approach ideally demands a thoroughgoing empirical critical method, which is exemplified to some extent by Molly Haskell's historical/critical survey *From Reverence to Rape* (Haskell, 1975). Haskell deals largely with changes over time in the images and roles of female figures in Hollywood films, from the vamp of the 1920s to the victim of male violence of the 1960s and 1970s. She then relates these stereotypes to female 'star' images in each of the periods in question. Her method is basically a descriptive survey of a large number of films, with some general inductive conclusions. In Haskell's analysis, cinematic representations of women tend to be perceived in terms of roles, stereotypes or images, a perspective which is often accompanied by the assumption that there is some direct or reflective relationship between these representations and the social formation of which they are part (see Chapter 4). A structural approach to narrative, on the other hand, starts out with a rather hermetic view of the film text, focusing in the first instance on its internal structures. It is deductive in the sense that it advances a general model of underlying narrative structures and suggests ways in which particular narratives may be read as expressing or articulating their ground rules. These rules are both logically prior to the innumerable narratives existing in the world and also not open to immediate observation. It is clear, then, that a structural approach to the study of narratives does not necessarily demand an empirical methodology, at least in a positivist sense. It may be considered sufficient, for example, to examine a single narrative in terms of its expression of underlying structures, for the structures themselves are seen as manifest only in their operation in actual narratives.

The point at issue here is that any structural approach to the analysis of 'woman' in narratives is faced with a model of woman that departs from the one characteristic of inductive approaches to film narratives. No longer is 'woman' regarded as a concrete gendered human being who happens to exist on the cinema screen rather than in 'real' life: 'she' becomes, on the contrary, a structure governing the organisation of story and plot in a narrative or group of narratives. The ways in which a 'woman-structure' activates narratives must clearly be related in some way to the wider question of the position of women in the society which produces the narrative, but in a structural model a simple relationship of reflection cannot be assumed. The question of how the woman-structure informs cinematic narratives may be rephrased, then, within the terms of structural analysis, by asking whether there are any recurrent structures of enigma resolution, of movement of plot from disrupted beginning equilibrium to resolution, associated with woman as a narrative function. Such a question calls for inductive and empirical study of films as well as for analysis of individual narratives on the deductive model.

A project which opens up this area of study has been undertaken by Mary Beth Haralovich, who has analysed ten randomly sampled Warner Bros films of the 1930s and 1940s. Within the terms of an

2.1 A central character in close-up: Mildred Pierce (Joan Crawford)

explanatory model which takes in the narrative structures of the films, the roles of their women characters, and the place of the films within their immediate institutional and broader historical contexts, Haralovich has concluded that narrative closure is always dependent on the resolution of enigmas centring on heterosexual courtship:

> If a woman is in a non-normative role in economic control and production, she will cede that control to a man by the end of the film. Romantic love seems to be the normative role which most strongly influences her decision (Haralovich, 1979, p. 13).

Not only, then, is woman recuperated into the male/female bond by the closures of these films (Dalton, 1972), but the courtship process itself constitutes a structuring element of their entire narratives.

There seems, therefore, to be a tendency on the part of the classic Hollywood narrative to recuperate woman. Moreover, it is often woman – as structure, character, or both – who constitutes the motivator of the narrative, the 'trouble' that sets the plot in motion. In *Mildred Pierce*, for example, the narrative's reconstruction of Mildred's life is a prior condition of the detective's access to the truth of the matter, and thus to the solution of the murder. In this way, the film's resolution depends on the resolution of the particular 'woman-question' set up by its narrative: woman may thus have to be returned to her place so that order is restored to the world. In classic Hollywood cinema, this recuperation manifests itself thematically in a limited number of ways: a woman character may be restored to the family by falling in love, by 'getting her man', by getting married, or otherwise accepting a 'normative' female role. If not, she may be directly punished for her narrative and social transgression by exclusion, outlawing or even death. In *Mildred Pierce*, both forms of resolution of the woman-question are at work. Mildred is restored to the family in the film's final sequence by being reunited with her former husband. Her daughter, on the other hand, is punished for transgressing the law: not only by having committed the crime of murder, but also through the unbridled and quasi-incestuous sexuality (she sleeps with her mother's lover) which is the unspoken narrative motivation for the actual act of murder.

Fortunately for feminists, things are not always so clear cut in dominant cinema. Perhaps the only thing that can be concluded with any degree of certainty is that, structurally and thematically, the classic Hollywood narrative attempts to recuperate woman to a 'proper place'. This attempt may not always be completely successful, though, particularly in cases where the narrative sets up questions that cannot be contained by any form of closure. Such excess of narrative disruption over resolution has been seen as signalling Hollywood's intermittent failure to contain woman within the confines of the classic narrative structure. An interesting case of persistent narrative excess in Hollywood cinema is exemplified by the film noir genre of the 1940s. In films noirs, whose narratives are typically structured around crime and its investigation by a detective figure, it is very common for a woman character to be set up as an additional mystery demanding solution, a mystery independent of the crime enigma (Kaplan, 1978). In many films noirs, in fact, the focus of the story may shift between the solution of crimes and the solution of the woman-question. However, if only because of the way in which enigmas are constituted in films noirs, there is a tendency to narrative excess inbuilt in the genre. This excess often centres precisely on the inability of the narrative to cope fully with the woman-question. As a genre, film noir is, historically speaking, very much a part of dominant cinema and yet at the same time it contains the potential, within its own characteristic narrative structure, to subvert the textual organisation of dominant cinema. This internal contradiction is a point at which are directed a number of feminist readings of films. These readings are aimed exactly at exposing some of the ideological operations and contradictions embedded in the textual practices of dominant cinema (see Chapter 5).

So far, I have been considering the textual characteristics of dominant cinema in relation exclusively to narrative structures. Much of what I have said could therefore be applied not only to cinema but to all narrative forms of expression. My discussion has not yet touched on cinematic discourse – the ways in which stories are told through film as opposed, say, to the novel. Is it possible to identify modes of discourse intrinsic to dominant cinema? It is commonly accepted that across all its forms of expression, the classic realist text is marked by a denial of its own operation in the signification process, in that the discourse seems to be nothing more than the vehicle of telling the story (MacCabe, 1974). The point here is that all narrative discourse does produce meaning in and by itself, and does therefore constitute a form of address to its recipients, but one of the defining features of the classic realist text is that its recipients are not normally aware that this is taking place.

In any consideration of the textual characteristics of dominant cinema, then, an important question must be: how do signifiers in cinema produce meanings, and how does this work specifically in relation to narrative meanings? To answer these questions, it is necessary to penetrate the surface transparency of classic narrative discourse. Signifiers in film texts may or may not be specific to cinema: cinema mobilises some vehicles of meaning production, or codes – written and spoken language, for instance – which also operate in other narrative forms of expression, as well as some – such as editing – that operate exclusively, or virtually so, in cinema. All films create meanings through the articulation of their signifiers, and each narrative film creates its own meanings through a particular configuration of signifiers, some of which are cinematically specific (Heath, 1973: Metz, 1974). According to this argument, classic Hollywood cinema produces narrative as it produces meanings – that is, it produces narrative meanings. Not only, then, is meaning conterminous with narrative meaning in this form of cinema, meaning also presents itself as transparent, as 'already there' in the story, rather than as the outcome of active processes of signification. In dominant cinema, it might be said, signifiers work unobtrusively in the service of the narrative. How does this operate in actual films? In dealing with this question, I will consider four sets of codes: the photographic image, *mise en scène*, mobile framing, and editing. I will argue firstly that the operations of these codes in dominant cinema are historically specific and contingent, and secondly that they construct modes of address which draw spectators into film narratives by making the reading of film texts seem effortless.

Cinema uses the technologies of cinematography as a basis for its own practices of meaning production. As such, while it draws on some of the codes of still photography, the cinematographic image also possesses codes of its own. Moreover, further codes are associated with narrative discourse in cinema. Among the signifying features of the cinematographic image is framing: long shots, medium shots and close-ups, for example, generate their own meanings. A cut-in close-up, for instance, can emphasise detail which may be read as having some significance within the narrative (see Still 2.7). Close-ups very commonly also operate in relation to characterisation: close-ups of players' faces became increasingly common in Hollywood films of the 1920s and after as a means of conveying the emotions of characters (see Still 2.1). To the extent that close-ups are most commonly of central characters in film narratives, they may function to constitute that psychological realism of character which is a mark of the classic narrative.

Mise en scène is a term employed in theatre to designate the contents of the stage and their arrangement. In cinema, however, the reference is rather to the contents of the film frame, including the arrangement of the profilmic event, of everything, that is, which is in front of the camera – settings, costumes and props. *Mise en scène* also refers more broadly to what the spectator actually sees on the screen – the composition of the image and the nature of movement within the frame. As an element of *mise en scène*, composition of the cinematic image, for example, may produce narrative meanings relating to the spatial location of the story. Movement within the frame, particularly the movements of players, can also have narrative functions in relation to characterisation. In any one film, *mise en scène* will work in conjunction with other codes to produce narrative meanings. In a scene from Howard Hawks's film noir, *The Big Sleep* (Warner Bros, 1946), for example, the signifying effects of within-frame movements of the hero, Philip Marlowe, around the house of the film's first murder victim, Arthur Geiger, in the course of the detective's search for clues (see Stills 2.2–2.7) combine with the effects of camera movement and editing to establish the series of disruptions and enigmas which structure the narrative of the first part of the film (Kuhn, 1981). Mobile framing – the effect of zooming and of camera movements of different kinds (Bordwell and Thompson, 1979, p. 121) – can also produce narrative meaning in a variety of ways. For instance, a zoom-in, like a cut-in close-up, can emphasise detail which may then be read in context as bearing particular significance within the narrative. Camera movement may operate simply to move the plot along, as in the case of the series of pans and tracking shots which orchestrate Marlowe's movements around Geiger's house in his search for clues to Geiger's murder.

Finally, the question of the forms of editing developed and privileged in classic Hollywood cinema is of the utmost importance to any consideration of the textual operations of dominant cinema and their construction of narrative meaning. The term 'editing' refers basically to the practice of splicing together pieces of film. Nevertheless, editing may be performed according to various principles. Dominant cinema, however, has institutionalised a highly specific set of rules for film editing, and the mobilisation of these rules has important consequences for cinematic signification. Continuity editing, as this set of conventions is called, was not firmly established in Hollywood itself until the early 1920s, but it is the culmination of a series of experiments with the cinematic rendering of narratives which began in the earliest years of

2.2 The Big Sleep: Marlowe enters Geiger's house, to discover . . .

2.3 . . . a corpse . . .

2.4 ... a flashbulb ...

2.5 ... a concealed camera ...

2.6 ... a drugged woman ...

2.7 ... a coded 'sucker list' of blackmail victims

cinema. The rules of continuity editing are written up in manuals of film technique and are invariably represented to learning film makers as the only possible approach to editing. The explicit objective of the continuity system is to construct – by ensuring that cuts are as unobtrusive to the spectator as possible – the appearance of a seamless and coherent narrative space and time. The effect of this is to make cinematic discourse – the process of meaning production – invisible. Each of the rules of continuity editing functions to this end (Bordwell and Thompson, 1979, p. 163; Reisz and Millar, 1973). In narrative cinema, an apparently coherent fictional world is produced which carries with it the 'impression of reality'. Spectators are thus drawn effortlessly into a narrative which seems to unfold before them as a series of already constituted meanings. At the same time, the invisible ellipses of space and time brought about by continuity editing move the story along, keeping the plot on track towards its resolution.

The question of the woman-structure in the textual organisation of classic narrative cinema may now be raised in relation to the specific question of cinematic signification. What, then, is the relationship between 'woman' and narrative discourse in dominant cinema? This begs two further questions: in what sense may 'woman' be regarded as a signifier in cinema? And what kind of relationship of reading might a notion of 'woman' as signifier suggest? Much of the discussion in the present chapter concerning the textual characteristics of dominant cinema may, because of its emphasis on the internal features of film texts, seem overly formalistic. However, it is perhaps worth repeating a point which was made earlier in this chapter: despite the fact that analytical work on film texts may be justified to the degree that it sheds light on the ideological operation of dominant cinema, it is important to remember that texts do not function independently of their institutional conditions of existence. Texts are part of the cinematic apparatus, and the cinematic apparatus is also constituted by the contexts within which film texts are received. What a discussion of cinematic codes and narrative structures in dominant cinema suggests is that the point at which cinematic discourse departs from non-cinematic discourse rests precisely in its address, in the ways it speaks to and is received by spectators. Cinematic address operates visually and through time: the pictures we see are moving pictures. The implications of this fundamental fact for the question of 'woman' as signifier in dominant cinema are examined in the next chapter.

3

Textual Gratification

In the previous chapter, I opened up discussion of dominant cinema by making a conceptual distinction between its institutional and its textual aspects, but also stressed that the two cannot in practice be held to operate independently of one another. I also looked at various formal attributes of film texts in dominant cinema, some of them specific to cinema and others not. What may be concluded from such a discussion is that these textual attributes can never be considered as operating independently of their reception, because they constitute forms of rhetoric, or ways of addressing spectators. Therefore the spectator and the moment and conditions of reception are each crucial and integral components of film texts. At this point the very notion of a film text is itself opened to challenge, for we are faced not with a concrete and self-contained textual body but with a series of dynamic textual operations and relations which become fixed only in the moment of reading. And since the question of reception and reading of film texts has to be considered in its historical specificity as part of the institutional apparatus of cinema, the argument comes full circle and we return once again to a consideration of cinematic institutions. Therefore to raise the question of address and the relationship between spectator and film is to return, in a certain sense, to a totalising model of dominant cinema and its institutional apparatus.

In the moment of reception, cinematic signifiers become at one level objects of exchange and at another elements in a process of meaning construction. Meaning production in cinema in turn involves certain kinds of spectator–text relationships which are peculiar to cinema. In looking at the place of 'woman' in all this, it is necessary first of all to consider in what specific ways dominant cinema works in its address to spectators: how, that is, it positions spectators in and through the signification process. How then is 'woman' to be conceptualised within this process, as representation, sign or signifier? In answering this question, I need to raise some of the issues addressed in the last chapter, but I will be approaching them here from a rather different angle.

There is a body of work which concerns itself exactly with the question of spectator–text relations in dominant cinema: this is a psychoanalytic approach to cinema which is informed by semiotics. Semiotics is the study of the operation of signs in society, of the cultural constitution of processes of meaning production. Until fairly recently, the fields in which semiotic work took place were largely those of written and spoken language, although other sign systems which do not immediately or exclusively mobilise linguistic signifiers can also qualify: film is such a one. Arguments concerning the ways in which film produces meaning through its articulation of signifiers draw heavily upon semiotics. A psychoanalytic approach to the question, however, goes further than this, by considering the question of how cinematic meanings are constituted for viewing subjects: how, that is, in the moment of reading, spectators are caught up in, formed by, and at the same time construct, meanings. What makes this approach psychoanalytic as opposed to semiotic is that it rests on a theory of unconscious processes at work in the constitution of the subject of cinema. The specific argument is that the subject of cinema is actually formed within the processes of language and representation.

The work I refer to is complex and notorious for its inaccessibility, but it is important in my view that some attempt be made here to render it more approachable. This is because although work on cinema and psychoanalysis was first developed, and is in fact being broached here, in relation to the operation of dominant cinema as signifying practice, it actually has repercussions for many aspects of the relationship between cinema and feminism. However, in the present context, although such work does open up a number of potentially productive areas of investigation, it is also, from a feminist standpoint, susceptible to some criticism, and suffers from a number of gaps to which feminist work on cinema can usefully attend. What I am suggesting here is not only that psychoanalysis of cinema be productively drawn upon in dealing with the question about spectator–text relations in dominant cinema which opened this chapter, but also that in spite of its drawbacks – some of which I shall discuss – it can still offer a productive frame of reference within which to consider various aspects of the question of cinema and feminism.

In examining the question of cinematic address in terms of the positioning of the viewing subject in the meaning-production process, I shall discuss five interrelated issues raised by work on signification and subjectivity in cinema. I will first advance a general outline of the concept of 'the subject' and of the unconscious relations within which the formation of the subject is said to take place. Second, I will look at certain features of cinematic address, some of the ways in which viewing subjects are positioned by the rhetoric of cinema. Third, I will look more closely at an aspect of cinematic address which is important as a specifically cinematic mechanism of subject positioning: suture. The fourth area of discussion is concerned with the notion of a cinematic apparatus considered in terms of unconscious processes. Finally, I will consider the ways in which cinema may be regarded as evoking psychic structures of 'scopophilia' – the drive to pleasurable looking – in viewing subjects. Although my exposition as a whole is somewhat schematic and perhaps even oversimplified, I hope that it will provide a broad frame of reference within which to place, understand, and develop work which seeks to consider the question of spectator–text relations in cinema from a feminist standpoint. The chapter concludes with an examination of some psychoanalytic work in the area of women and representation, of the potential of such work, and of the range of questions relevant to the topic of this book which are raised by it.

The Subject

In considering the relationship between text and spectator in cinema, psychoanalytic work has drawn upon a particular model of the human subject (in this instance the viewing subject, the subject of cinema) as constituted by unconscious processes: that of the post-Freudian analyst Jacques Lacan. According to this model, the human subject is formed in relations with the world outside, in relations which are constructed developmentally in the process of language acquisition. The Unconscious is a by-product of these processes. Subjectivity thus entails on the one hand a positioning in relation to the Symbolic or language and on the other unconscious formations. Work on psychoanalysis and cinema draws on a model of the 'field of the subject' as constituted by three distinct areas: the Unconscious, language, and specularity (relations of looking and seeing). The field of the subject may thus be represented as in Figure 3.1. Although I shall consider each of these three terms separately, it is important to bear in mind that in their actual constitution of the subject, as the figure suggests, they operate in interrelation with one another.

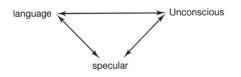

Figure 3.1

In Lacanian psychoanalysis a central polemic, indeed its very foundation, is the claim that the Unconscious is structured like a language. This means that the Unconscious is produced in the same process in which the subject is produced – that of language acquisition: in other words the human subject is a speaking subject. Lacan advances an account of the developmental processes in which this takes place, and argues that human subjectivity is also continually structured by these processes. At various privileged moments (the mirror phase and the Oedipus complex in particular) the subject undergoes formative stages in the course of which a series of repressions which become the content of the Unconscious is produced. The arguments are complex, and it is in any case not necessary to my project to reiterate them at length here (see Coward, 1976; Coward and Ellis, 1977). I simply wish to signal the argument linking together human subjectivity, the Unconscious and language.

In the Lacanian model, the speaking subject is a subject in language: this means, among other things, that subjectivity is constituted in and through speech acts. A useful way of illustrating this point is to look at how the pronoun 'I' works. In order to be able to use 'I', the speaker has to have a conceptualisation of her or his own subjectivity as separate from the outside world, while at the same time in saying 'I', the speaker also produces that subjectivity. Thus the process of signification is the process of the subject. The notion of process in this context is important, for two reasons. First, the formation of human subjectivity is not solely developmental: the subject is not 'made' once and for all when language has been acquired – it is in constant flux, being formed in and through every speech act. Second, the notion of the subject in process consequently suggests that subjectivity is not always nor necessarily cohesive, unitary or final. There is in fact an argument that ideology is definable as exactly the process whereby human subjectivity takes on the outward appearance of wholeness and unity, and furthermore that – in relation specifically to cinema – one of the central ideological operations of dominant cinema is precisely the positioning of the viewing subject as apparently unitary. This point has a number of consequences, some of them considered elsewhere in this book (see Chapter 8) for forms of cinema which aim to subvert the ideological operations of dominant cinema. If signification is considered as ceaseless productivity, and if it is accepted that the process of meaning production is the process of the subject, then the operation whereby meanings are produced in cinema must be considered as a dynamic one which not only draws in and forms the viewing subject, but is also a product of this positioning of the subject.

If specularity refers to relations of looking and seeing, it is easy to see its relevance to a consideration of the subject of cinema. One of the arguments put forward by Lacan suggests that a crucial moment in the process of subject formation is established by relations of looking. In looking at an object in the world outside its own body, the subject begins to establish that body as separate from and autonomous of the world outside. The mirror phase is a privileged moment of specularity: the infant's reflection in the mirror establishes the contours of its own body as separate from, say, that of its mother. This separation is a prior condition for entry into language, because the use of language is premised on a distinction between subject and object (Coward and Ellis, 1977, p. 110). Another important point about the mirror phase, in the Lacanian model, is that it is governed by Imaginary relations. The Imaginary is the order which governs the subject's experience (or 'misrecognition') of itself as whole. Thus, to take up an argument mentioned above, the Imaginary is the site of ideological operations. Therefore if the mirror phase is governed by specular relations and is instrumental in the construction, in ideology, of the unified subject, then relations of looking may be regarded as ideologically implicated.

The mirror phase corresponds more or less with that aspect of scopophilia defined by Freud as autoerotic: narcissism, when the object of the look is one's own body – or, presumably, its reflection. Freud also outlines other types of scopophilia which, he implies, are somewhat more developed than narcissism. These are voyeurism, the desire to look at an object outside the subject, and exhibitionism, the introduction of a new subject as the source of a look back at the exhibitionist/subject (Freud, 1915). The implications of narcissistic identification, voyeurism and exhibitionism for spectator–text relations in cinema are dealt with later in this chapter: at this point my concern is to indicate the centrality of specular relations in the overall constitution of subjectivity, in that specularity is held to govern both the subject–object split built into language, and also the Imaginary relations whereby subjectivity is misrecognised as unitary.

The question of Imaginary relations is also crucial as regards the third term in the field of the subject. Notions of subjectivity in relation to language and specularity do not, taken together, exhaust the issue of human subjectivity, either in general or in relation specifically to cinema. What is missing is that which makes psychoanalysis a distinct body of knowledge: the Unconscious. In Lacanian psychoanalysis, the Unconscious is said to be formed in the same process in which the subject is produced: that is, in the acquisition of language. In the course of this process, a series of repressions takes place, and these repressions form the Unconscious. The Unconscious, then, may be regarded as the price paid for language and human culture. The fact that the Unconscious is produced in and through signification is what makes the speaking subject, despite the misrecognition effected by ideology, not in fact unitary. For the Unconscious is the site of those splits, tensions and contradictions which are the hidden underside of the apparently whole human subject.

Although by its nature the Unconscious does not make itself available to direct observation, its operations are in fact indirectly discernible in what analysands say – particularly in their 'Freudian slips', jokes and accounts of fantasies and dreams. This, taken together with the notion that the Unconscious is formed by repressions produced in and through the subject's relation to language, underpins the claim that the Unconscious is structured like a language. Unconscious processes which inform dream thought or dream language may be seen to have certain elements in common with waking language, for example (Freud, 1900; Lacan, 1970). The points about the Unconscious which I want to focus upon, and to which I shall return in the course of more detailed discussion of the forms of subjectivity constituted in cinematic address, are twofold. One, that the Unconscious is held to be the condition of language and therefore of subjectivity, and, two, that unconscious language operates its own forms of rhetoric.

Cinematic Address

In considering cinematic address, it is necessary to return to the question of the place of language in the process of the subject. I have already referred to the way in which use of the pronoun 'I' can constitute the subjectivity of the speaker in relation to some 'other'. This 'other' may be not only the outside world in general, but also more specifically the person(s) implicitly or explicitly addressed in the speech act ('you'). The use of a form of language in which 'I' and 'you' are uttered or implied in speech acts, however, is only one form of subjectivity available in language use. Speech acts may operate in two registers: on the level of the enounced, or the purport of what is said, and on the level of enunciation, the ways in which the recipient of a speech act is addressed and situated by it. In considering the question of address, therefore, our concern for the moment is exclusively with enunciation. Enunciation in its turn may operate in two registers: *discours* and *histoire*[1] (see Figure 3.2). These registers are extremely important in relation to cinematic address. In written and spoken language, *histoire* is that mode of address characteristic of narrations of past events, in which the narrator is not foregrounded as a 'person': 'I' is not enunciated, and events are typically told in an indefinite past tense. In *discours*, on the other hand, every utterance inscribes both a speaker ('I') and a hearer ('you'), so that 'person' is present throughout. The typical tenses of *discours* are the present and the perfect (Benveniste, 1971). A statement such as: 'Once upon a time, there were three bears ...' would therefore be exemplary of *histoire*, whereas: 'Mum, I've just seen three bears at the bottom of our garden' is a typically discursive enunciation. What emerges from this is basically that *discours* foregrounds subjectivity in its address, while in *histoire* address is impersonal. How does this relate to cinematic address, to the ways in which cinema, as a specific mode of expression distinct from written and spoken language, addresses spectators?

The film theorist Christian Metz argues that cinematic address – by which he means its specifically cinematic aspects – operates largely within the register of *histoire*, in that films appear to 'speak to' spectators impersonally (Metz, 1976). Cinematic enunciation does not, says Metz, normally identify itself as proceeding from anywhere in particular: a film seems simply to be 'there' as it unfolds before our eyes. To the extent that it has no identifiable source of address, cinema hides the marks of its enunciation. Culturally speaking, of course, all

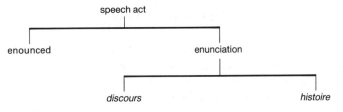

Figure 3.2 Language and address

enunciations originate from somewhere: the point is that *histoire* operates to give the impression that they do not, or at least that the enunciator is not a subject but an omniscient impersonal narrating instance, the mouthpiece of some overarching 'truth'. Metz's argument may be held to suggest that cinematic enunciation can never be discursive, which is in fact not the case. Even classic Hollywood has certain devices through which subjectivity can be incorporated in a film's address: shots which suggest the optical point-of-view of a character, for example. Another classic device which is in some measure discursive is the subjectively marked flashback. Each of the heroine's flashbacks in *Mildred Pierce* is marked by a close-up of Mildred talking in the first person about her own past, which then dissolves into flashback – a cinematic rendering of the events being narrated by the character, but not from the character's optical point-of-view (see Still 3.1). It may be argued, however, that in cases such as this, in which subjective material in film lasts longer than one or two shots, the discursive mode of address tends to merge back into *histoire* because without optical point-of-view cinematic enunciation has difficulty in retaining a sense of subjectivity.

If all this suggests that cinema – or dominant cinema, at least – does indeed privilege *histoire* as a mode of address, it is important to point out that *histoire* in itself may incorporate variations in address. I am referring here to variations in narrative point-of-view, or narrative voice. In the case of the novel, it can readily be seen that even an impersonal narration can incorporate different points-of-view. Todorov distinguishes three narrative viewpoints within *histoire*: the 'view from behind' when the narrator (and the reader) knows more than the characters, the 'view with' when narrator–reader knows no more and no less than the characters, and the 'view from outside' when narrator–reader knows less than characters (Todorov, 1977a). Most classic films operate the view from behind, in that the spectator is placed in a privileged position of knowledge in comparison with the

3.1 Discursive enunciation in classic cinema: the dissolve into flashback 2 in *Mildred Pierce*

characters in the film about what is going on in the story. Some films, however, speak 'with' their characters – this is a defining feature, for instance, of the film noir. In *The Big Sleep*, for example, although Marlowe has no first-person voice-over, the spectator is never in a position of knowing more about what is going on than the detective himself, who is therefore the 'enunciator'. Other films may be less straightforward about narrative point-of-view. In *Mildred Pierce*, for example, the fact that Mildred 'narrates' her two flashbacks might suggest that the film's narrative voice is hers. It is not until the final reel that we see that the 'truth' about what has happened can be told not by Mildred but by the detective who is questioning her. It is 'his' flashback that finally resolves the enigma set up by the narrative (Cook, 1978a). Narrative point-of-view in classic cinema is an element of cinematic address which is worth examining for what it reveals about the place of woman as enunciator, her place in relation to narrative 'truth' and knowledge.

To permit investigation of different forms of cinematic address, some kind of structural method may be called for. In all forms of *histoire*, the narrating instance presents itself as somehow 'already there', omniscient and above subjectivity. In the last chapter I argued that one of the marks of classic Hollywood cinema is the invisibility of its devices of meaning construction: the audience is on the whole not aware of processes of signification. It can now be seen how certain forms of cinematic address work to produce this effect of transparency. Because in dominant cinema meaning presents itself as 'already there' in the film text, the viewing subject is positioned as recipient of apparently preconstructed meanings. This is the ground of the argument that it is the work of ideology to produce an appearance of wholeness and 'already-thereness' on behalf of the subject. Therefore, to the extent that *histoire* is instrumental in producing this appearance, it is an ideological operation. I would argue that *histoire* is not necessarily, as Metz sometimes seems to suggest, a mode of address common to all forms of cinema, but rather that it is a defining feature of dominant cinema. If this is indeed the case, then it is perhaps possible to envisage modes of cinematic address which, in mobilising the discursive, constitute viewing subjects rather differently – a point which is of relevance in any consideration of alternatives to dominant modes of cinematic representation (see Chapter 8).

Suture

Meanwhile, however, I want to look at an argument which outlines some specific ways in which the viewing subject is positioned in relation to signification in dominant cinema. This argument is centred on the concept of suture, which has been defined as 'the relation of the individual-as-subject to the chain of its discourse where it figures missing in the guise of a stand-in' (Heath, 1976, p. 261). This definition refers back to the point that in *histoire*, the source of cinematic enunciation is typically absent from, or invisible in, the text. Suture is the process whereby the gap produced by that absence is filled by the spectator, who thus becomes the 'stand-in', the subject-in-the-text (Oudart, 1977–8). The process of subjectivity in cinema is seen as both ongoing and dynamic in that the subject is constantly being 'sewn-in' to, or caught up in, the film's enunciation. The notion of suture has been concretised in an argument advanced by Daniel Dayan, who suggests that in cinema the subject is produced in place of an absence in the text by means of a mechanism of optical point-of-view. A characteristic device of classic Hollywood cinema is the shot/reverse shot structure, which establishes the optical point-of-view of characters within the fictional space of the film at moments (during conversational exchanges, for example) when they are looking at one another. A typical shot/reverse shot sequence is detailed in Stills 3.2–3.4. There are a number of variations on this classic point-of-view structure (Branigan, 1975), but the basic issue here is that in all its forms it establishes point-of-view by means of devices of continuity editing. In Still 3.3, for example, the look of the spectator seems to come from a place identical to the source of the look of character A: this appearance is brought about by constructing, through editing, an 'eyeline match'. The spectator therefore stands in for A, who is of course absent from this shot. When this is followed by Still 3.4, in which A is once again present in the image, the shot/reverse shot figure is closed and the gap in the spectator's relation with the film is for the moment 'sewn up', sutured. Such moments of absence, presence and suture are repeated throughout the film, thus ensuring an ongoing process of subject positioning in cinematic enunciation.

The Cinematic Apparatus

It should be clear by now that the model of the subject of cinema under consideration here poses the spectator as central in the process of

3.2 Shot 1: close-up of character A

3.3 Shot 2: close-up of character B, from A's angle of vision

3.4 Shot 3: close-up of A, from B's angle of vision

cinematic signification. Not only can spectator and text not be considered in separation, the one simply receiving preconstructed meanings from the other: it is clear also that the process of meaning construction itself involves an interaction of the two. In cinema this interaction takes place under specific conditions. The entire context, structure and system of meaning production in cinema has been termed the 'cinematic apparatus', a concept which has generated its own body of work on cinematic signification. It has been argued, for instance, that the ways in which the apparatus constructs the spectator's subjectivity are identical to the operations through which the subject is produced, that they are in fact 'a simulation of the condition of the subject' (Baudry, 1976, p. 123). There is a tendency in arguments of this kind to emphasise one aspect in particular of subject formation – unconscious relations. To the suggestion that the process of cinematic signification is the same as the process of the subject, the theory of the cinematic apparatus adds the twofold argument that cinematic rhetoric is analogous to the rhetoric of unconscious language, and that the 'filmic state' or the 'cinematic condition' (Augst, 1979; Barthes, 1979) is similar to the dream-state, or is in some sense an evocation of the Imaginary. To make an analogy between the filmic state, dreaming, and unconscious language is, of course, to invoke a very old metaphor: film as celluloid dream. Used more precisely in psychoanalytic terms, however, the analogy sets up a comparison between dream-thought and cinematic address, so that for instance the distant and timeless character of dream-thought is regarded as analogous to *histoire* in cinematic enunciation. In this sense, work on the cinematic apparatus is an extension of work on cinematic enunciation.

However, to suggest that the form of subjectivity set in play within the cinematic apparatus 'mimes a form of archaic satisfaction experienced by the subject by reproducing the scene of it' (Baudry, 1976, p. 118) is to engage a rather different argument. What is being suggested here is that the filmic state reproduces the scene of the Imaginary and re-evokes the relations of the mirror phase. Does this mean that the filmic state is in some sense pre-linguistic? Some of the writings on the cinematic apparatus would seem to suggest as much: Baudry, for example, constructs a model of the apparatus and the place of the subject within it in terms of a fusion of exterior and interior, so that the subject of cinema appears to be regressed within an apparatus which reproduces the scene of a pre-Oedipal, pre-linguistic satisfaction. Metz, on the other hand, offers a more cautious argument in suggesting that cinema does operate on the side of the Symbolic relations of language and culture, but through the play of the Imaginary (Metz, 1975). I do not intend to go into further detail here about theoretical work on the cinematic apparatus, partly because much of it is tangential to the immediate concerns of this book, and partly because – in putting forward a monolithic model of the apparatus – I feel it closes off the possibility of making distinctions between different types of cinema. Nevertheless this work is important in advancing the argument that the moment of reception is integral to the operation of cinema. It also opens up the question of the look as a component of the relationship of spectator and text in cinema.

The Look

In outlining the three terms of the field of the subject, I made reference to relations of specularity and to the various forms of scopophilia outlined by Freud in his work on the drives. Looking – or rather certain types of looking – is clearly an activity that distinguishes cinema from many other forms of expression. The most obvious instance of the look in cinema is the one that originates with the spectator, whose gaze is directed at moving images on the screen. But looking in cinema is more complex than this. Cinematic address may also, for example, construct looks *at* the spectator. This is particularly clear in the shot/reverse shot structure (see Stills 3.2–3.4): the viewing subject, in standing in for the look of a protagonist in the film, becomes the object of the fictional gaze of the other protagonist. In addition to this relay of looks between spectator and screen/image, the exchange of looks between characters within the space of the film itself may also be taken into account. At moments, of course – and this perhaps constitutes an instance of *discours* in classic cinema – the fictional look of a character may effectively coincide with the look of the spectator. This is what occurs in the (optical) point-of-view shot, which marks a further instance of looking in cinema – the look of the camera.

Taking up the Lacanian model, Metz argues that although cinema evokes the Imaginary relations of mirror-identification, the subject of cinema – like the speaking subject – cuts across the linguistic and the specular, the Symbolic and the Imaginary (Metz, 1975). In other words, the subject of cinema is not the regressed pre-Oedipal subject suggested by certain work on the cinematic apparatus. In his argument, Metz links psychoanalytic work on the look with his own earlier work on cinematic specificity by outlining some ways in which cinema mobilises more of the axes of perception than any other matter of expression: herein lies a justification for examining the concept of scopophilia in relation to the cinematic apparatus. The drive to looking is, according to Freud, one of the sexual or libido drives: a drive, that is, which operates through the play of pleasure and unpleasure. Active scopophilia demands, in its pleasurable aspects, a distance between subject and object, in that it is in the play of absence and distance that desire is activated. Given that in cinema the object of the spectator's look is indeed both distant and absent – a 'primordial elsewhere', as Metz says – the filmic state must be particularly prone to evoking the pleasurable aspects of looking. Pleasurable looking here takes the form of voyeurism, in which the object of the look is outside of, and distanced from, the subject, and there is apparently no comeback for the spectator in the form either of a returned look or other response, or of punishment for looking. Cinema, according to this argument, involves a kind of 'lawless seeing', and this is one of the major sources of its pleasure.

The look in the cinematic apparatus is therefore a relationship between the spectator and what is going on on the screen. Looking involves a condition in which the spectator identifies with, or is positioned in relation to, the apparatus. Identification, according to Metz, is potentially twofold. It may be narcissistic, in that in looking at representations of the human body, or parts of it, the spectator identifies with himself (the degree to which the spectator identifies with *herself* is another question). Here the connection between narcissistic identification and the identifications of the mirror phase is evident. The process of identification may also be more actively voyeuristic, as is the case when the spectator's identification is with the camera: in this case the viewing subject in effect stands in for the camera. In a voyeuristic relation, when the spectator occupies the place of the camera as source of the look, the subject in the cinematic apparatus is set up as the centre and origin of meaning, because the image and the points-of-view of spectator, camera – and indeed projector – coincide. The instance of looking in the cinematic apparatus may therefore constitute the viewing subject as whole and unitary, by inaugurating 'a total vision which corresponds to the idealist concept of the fullness and homogeneity of "being"' (Baudry, 1974–5, p. 42).

*

This brief exposition of the psychoanalytic model of the subject is intended to broaden the discussion of cinematic specificity begun in the last chapter. Given this model, it is possible to advance a relatively nuanced perspective on the operations of dominant cinema, on the place of the spectator as viewing subject within these operations, and on the ways in which the subject is positioned and constructed by the rhetoric of classic cinema. Such an understanding is a useful, even an essential, precondition of an engagement with two areas of work that are crucial to the question of the relationship of cinema and feminism. It is necessary both to consider the place of woman – as representation and as viewing subject – within the apparatus of dominant cinema, and also (and consequently) to move towards an understanding of how modes of subjectivity other than those privileged by dominant cinema might be set into play. The remainder of the present chapter is devoted to a consideration of the first of these two areas, with the aim of setting out some terms for discussions around feminism in relation to dominant and non-dominant forms of cinema which are taken up in later chapters.

Although I believe that psychoanalytic film theory offers a productive frame of reference for a consideration of issues of relevance to a feminist analysis of dominant cinema, much of the work in the field is conspicuous for its failure to raise explicitly any such issues. Since within this model, what actually takes place on screen tends to be bracketed in favour of considering either on the one hand a relationship – that of screen image and viewing subject – or on the other constitution of the viewing subject, questions directly concerning representation are not usually dealt with (though Dayan's work on suture is an exception). Moreover, the viewing subject at the centre of debate appears to be either androgynous, or neuter, or male: subject positioning is in any case generally taken to be undifferentiated as to gender. No attention is given, therefore, either to cinema as it constructs meanings around 'woman', or to how dominant cinema addresses spectators as gendered subjects. Both questions are of vital concern for feminism: on the one hand for understanding the mechanisms of dominant cinema and on the other for effecting transformations in those mechanisms. The question of gendered subjectivity in relation to cinematic representation must be central to a feminist critical and theoretical exploration and interrogation of cinema. It is the task of feminist film practice, too, to continue opening up and mapping this terrain. Because these issues are raised repeatedly throughout this book, I shall simply outline them here by concentrating firstly on the question of the relationship between the look in cinema and woman as representation, and secondly on the notion of the viewing subject as feminine or masculine.

Laura Mulvey has addressed the question of voyeurism as a feature both of the relationship of spectator and text and of representations of woman in classic Hollywood cinema in an article in which she looks at the question of visual pleasure and cinematic narrative. In arguing that cinema is 'a hermetically sealed world which unwinds magically, indifferent to the presence of the audience, producing for them a sense of separation and playing on their voyeuristic phantasy' (Mulvey, 1975, p. 9), Mulvey implicitly invokes the notion of *histoire* as a feature of cinematic address, linking it with pleasurable looking. Like Metz, Mulvey argues that in this spectator–text relationship, structures of identification may be both narcissistic, in that the spectator's identification is with his own likeness, and also more specifically voyeuristic to the extent that the spectator's look stands in for the look of the camera. Mulvey also suggests – like Metz, Oudart and Dayan – that this relation of looking/identification describes the way in which a spectator becomes caught up in a film narrative. Where Mulvey departs from the others, however, is in her argument that, as far as the look is concerned, the element of spectacle in dominant cinema may at times work against the flow of the narrative by halting it in favour of moments of erotic contemplation of the image: and that, as representation, woman may often operate on the side of spectacle and therefore constitute a potential disturbance to the spectator's voyeuristic/narcissistic identification. The assumption here is either that the spectator is male or – a more complex position – that cinematic address works to constitute the spectator as such.

What Mulvey suggests is that, as spectacle, cinema constitutes woman as the object of looking (not only on the part of spectators but also on the part of protagonists within the fictional space of the film), but that as such woman evokes not only the pleasurable, but also the threatening, aspects of looking. This point is premised on a psychoanalytic argument linking castration anxiety with the infant's awareness, gained from looking at its mother's body, that the mother lacks a penis. In the social-historical context of the patriarchal family, it is argued, this apparent lack constitutes a threat because of its association with certain power relations: in the Oedipus complex, the intervention of the father shows the infant that the mother is not, after all, as omnipotent as she once seemed. It is in this process, Freud suggests, that the body of the mother begins to signify the threat of castration and powerlessness, and the relations of looking associated with the Oedipal process carry over into representations of women in general. Therefore representations of women may in certain respects constitute a threat to the observer: 'Thus the woman as icon, displayed for the gaze and enjoyment of men, the active controllers of the look, always threatens to evoke the anxiety it originally signified' (Mulvey, 1975, p. 13). This anxiety may be dealt with by turning woman, or the figure of woman, into a fetish: that is, by disavowing and defusing the castratory aspects of the image by making them their opposite through idealising the image (Freud, 1927). In classic cinema, the woman-image is typically fetishised both by means of lingering close-ups which, through interrupting the flow of the narrative, constitute woman as spectacle; and also by means of the glamorous costumes, make-up, settings and lighting surrounding female stars. Mulvey is able, therefore, to explain the excessive idealisation of the female star-image in dominant cinema in terms of fetishisation.

A good deal of the work discussed in this chapter, despite its attention to the specifics of the question of cinematic address and spectator–text relations, tends to homogenise the cinematic apparatus by representing it as an undifferentiated monolith in which all forms of representation and relations of looking are reduced to a single model. Mulvey's argument, on the other hand, stretches the psychoanalytic perspective by forcing a consideration first of all of possible alternatives to dominant cinema, and secondly of the specificity of the positioning of the gendered spectator in dominant cinema.

In examining psychoanalytic arguments concerning the constitution of subjectivity, I have made no specific reference to its potential as either masculine or feminine. Lacan does, however, offer a theory of the formation of the gendered subject in language. Briefly, the argument suggests that the privileged moment, developmentally speaking, in the construction of the gendered subject is the Oedipus complex, which structures awareness of sexual difference. Lacan argues that the moment when the look of the infant establishes the mother as without a penis forms the model for the inauguration of language as a play of presence and absence, and as difference. Lacan further argues that the phallus – which is the symbolic representation of the penis – takes on the characteristics of a signifier, a bearer of meaning in language. The full entry of the infant into the Symbolic order of language turns, according to this view, on Difference and Lack. Difference, because sexual difference in relation to signification (having or not-having the phallus) is mapped onto the operation of language as difference – the linguistic premiss being that meaning emerges through differences between signifiers, in their articulation with each other, rather than from signifiers in themselves. Lack, because the girl-child and the boy-child occupy different positions in relation to having and not-having the phallus: thus Lacan can argue that the relation of woman to the Symbolic order of language is structured by Lack (Coward *et al.*, 1976). The female child therefore does go through the Oedipus complex to enter the Symbolic – she is not, as is sometimes suggested, locked in the 'half-light of the Imaginary', forever outside language. But unlike the male child, in doing so she has to make sense of Lack, which means she occupies a gender-specific relation to language. It may be argued that this is one of the central operations of patriarchy, in that patriarchal social–familial relations inform the historically specific character taken by the Oedipus complex, so that the developmental acquisition of language takes place according to the same process as the structural organisation of sexuality in patriarchy (Kuhn, 1978b).[2]

The point of discussing the Lacanian account of the formation of the gendered subject is that it immediately raises the question of the relationship of the female subject, or the feminine, to signification. Consequently, it also poses the issue of the spectator as a gendered subject. The answers to the numerous questions raised by this issue might well in effect force a transformation of the very perspective in which the questions are posed. My discussion of these questions is focused around two interrelated issues: that of address in dominant cinema in relation to gender and the viewing subject on the one hand, and that of a specifically feminine relation to language and significa-tion and what this might mean for cinema on the other. As is so often the case with issues raised within a feminist perspective, these two questions together immediately begin to transcend the terms in which they are raised, spilling over from the confines of an examination of the operations of dominant cinema and into all the areas of concern of this book.

Mulvey's analysis of the operations of voyeurism and fetishistic scopophilia in narrative cinema and the constitution of woman as spectacle suggests that the spectator is male: or perhaps, and this is not quite the same thing, that such a cinema addresses itself to male spectators. The notion of representations of woman evoking castration anxiety, for example, is predicated on a psychoanalytic argument which centres specifically on the male child's relation to the Oedipus complex. Scopophilia might take different forms were the meaning of the mother's lack of a penis – or indeed, for that matter, her possession of a vagina – not in fact sexual difference. The question then is, are there specifically feminine relations of looking, and if so, what are they? If Mulvey's argument is correct, and in a sense also if the arguments of Metz and the others are correct, dominant cinema is actually distinguished by an address which, at least through its evocation of certain kinds of looking, advances masculine subjectivity as the only subjectivity available. What exactly does this mean for women as spectators in cinema, given that women do go to the cinema, and indeed that for certain types of films they have constituted a large part of the audience?[3] It may mean several things: for example, that the female social audience can be caught up by the rhetoric of dominant cinema because on some level they identify with 'masculine' modes of address. This is perhaps another way of saying that the viewing subject is, at this moment in history at least, not constituted as gendered by cinematic address: or perhaps that socio-biological gender and gendered subjectivity are not necessarily coterminous, so that the specificity of the 'masculine' becomes in some way culturally universalised. If this is indeed the case, it certainly speaks to the hegemony of the masculine in culture that dominant cinema offers an address that, as a condition of being meaningful, must in effect de-feminise the female spectator. Women, on the other hand, may in these circumstances be regarded as peculiarly able to stand at a distance from the ideological operations of dominant cinema, in that the marginal place they occupy in relation to its address may be conducive to the formation of a critical perspective. It this is so, then the readings of classic Hollywood texts undertaken within feminist film theory (see Chapter 5) acquire that much more incisiveness.

The question of whether there are specifically feminine relations of looking also raises the issue of feminine language as against masculine or dominant language and what this might mean for cinema. This question may be approached in different ways. Lacan, for example, in suggesting that the specificity of woman's relation to the Oedipus complex means that her entry into language is structured by Lack, is saying in effect that woman's relationship to language does indeed have its own specificity. But in constituting woman as 'other', the argument stops here without taking the question of woman and language very much further. Other views have accepted the notion of woman as 'other' and taken it to mean that women exist outside of language, that they are consigned to the pre-Symbolic order of the Imaginary, that in effect they have no language. Although this may be true to the extent that, as many feminists have argued, language does not belong to women, or that it is inadequate for our needs (Spender, 1980), nevertheless taken literally it does negate the arguments concerning women's specific relation to the Oedipus complex as structuring the entry into language and culture. What could be argued here is that woman may retain a privileged place in relation to the Imaginary, or may be particularly close to the Imaginary. This is by no means the same as saying that women are outside language. Arguments concerning the foregrounding of voice, sound, rhythm and the 'poetic' in feminine writing tend to draw on this latter position (see Chapter 1).

These arguments about woman, the feminine and language are all in one way or another founded on the Lacanian view that the phallus is the privileged signifier structuring Symbolic relations, in that woman is regarded in various ways as 'other' in relation to language. Other arguments, however, may offer a view of woman and language based on alternative versions of the Oedipus complex. Luce Irigaray's conceptualisation of the specificity of woman's relation to language (see Chapter 1) takes up exactly this point: the significance and signification of the 'two lips' of the vagina suggests a non-fixity of meaning and subjectivity as against the coherence and apparent wholeness of subjectivity implied when the monolithic phallus is erected as primary signifier (Irigaray, 1977). What this means is that a feminine relation to language would constitute a challenge to the ideological wholeness of subjectivity constructed, according to the Lacanian model, in and through signification. In consequence, a feminine relation to language could effect a subversion of the Symbolic order.

What does this mean for alternative film practices, given the centrality of the look in the cinematic apparatus? This, I feel, remains very much an open question. Mulvey's view is that any alternative to dominant cinema should challenge the relations of looking characteristic of this form of cinema. To do this, it would have to 'free the look of the camera into its materiality in time and space and the look of the audience into dialectics, passionate detachment' (Mulvey, 1975, p.

18). She does not, however, explicitly link this with any notion of a 'feminine' cinematic language (Heath, 1978). It could be argued, however, that a cinema which evokes pleasures of looking outside the masculine structures of voyeurism might well set up a 'feminine' approach to cinematic signification.

PART III

Rereading Dominant Cinema:
Feminism and Film Theory

The focus of the third part of this book is the question of feminism in relation to film criticism and film theory. Feminist film theory constitutes one area of work within the wider sphere delineated by the relationship between feminism and cinema. Feminist interventions in film theory have been developed alongside – sometimes independently of, increasingly hand in hand with – feminist film making, which now has an extensive body of theory on which it may draw. In examining the question of feminism and film analysis, I begin in Chapter 4 by looking at some theoretical and methodological issues surrounding the notion of a specifically feminist analysis of film, or a feminist approach to film theory. The subsequent two chapters are devoted to discussions concerning the application and potential of the first phase of work in feminist film theory dealing with texts and images, particularly those of dominant cinema.

3

Making Visible the Invisible

I shall open the debate around feminist film theory by raising and examining some questions which are immediately posed by the conjunction of two substantive areas of thought and practice, each one independently pre-existing the other, within a single critical endeavour. How may the body of work called feminist film theory be defined? And, more important perhaps, what are its objectives, and what perspectives or methodologies has it adopted, or might it adopt? In relation to its objectives, how productive have been the perspectives and methods drawn on up till now? Are there any gaps or absences in feminist film analysis which might usefully be attended to? Are there any dead ends, or conversely, any areas that call for further development? In dealing with these questions, I shall return to some issues which have already been raised in previous chapters. However, at this point discussion will be focused distinctively on feminism as a standpoint which may shape, inform, or even transform certain types of film analysis. The main concern here, in other words, is with the specificity of a feminist approach to film theory.

An immediate question, and extremely important in this context, is one that is less simple than it might at first appear: if some notion of feminist film theory is to be advanced, what exactly is to be inferred from the use of the term 'feminist'? What is it that feminism does to film theory that turns it into something special, something different from the general run of film criticism that makes no claim to be 'feminist'? In this context, a useful distinction may be advanced between feminism as a perspective and feminism as a methodology. That is to say, feminism might be regarded on the one hand as a way of seeing the world, a frame of reference or a standpoint from which to examine whatever it is one wishes to examine. Or alternatively it might be seen as constituting a set of conceptual tools, a method or a series of methods, even an analytical model, by means of which to examine its object: in this case, film. Put in this way, it is obvious that perspective and methodology can never in actual operation be held to be independent of one another, but none the less the conceptual distinction is fundamental and important. Feminism, I would argue, offers not so much a methodology as a perspective – a pair of spectacles, as it were – through which we can look at films (Kaplan, 1976; *New German Critique*, 1978). What we see through our feminist spectacles will of course inform what we choose to analyse, and perhaps also to some extent how we choose to analyse it. Feminist theory involves taking up a distinct stance or position in relation to its object, therefore, and thus in this sense cannot be regarded as politically neutral. To do feminist theory is, consciously or otherwise, to engage in an intervention within theory or culture. But to state this merely opens up a further series of questions, questions which resolve themselves into two sets of interrelated issues. The first centres on methodology: if feminism does not of itself embody or advance any particular methodology for, say, analysing films, what tools are in fact available to a feminist analysis? The second set of issues concerns the degree to which feminism may itself be regarded as a unitary perspective, and the implications for film theory of the multifaceted character of feminism. Here I am faced with a difficulty, in that the directions taken up to now by feminist film theory and the directions potentially available to it are two rather different matters. In my discussion, therefore, I shall try to keep this distinction as clear as possible.

On the question first of all of methodology, it seems to me that there are two options. The first would be founded on the premiss that a methodology may, or should, emerge from the feminist perspective itself: to this extent, then, it would be held either that an autonomously and characteristically feminist methodology may be adopted or developed, or perhaps that feminism in itself already embodies an adequate methodology. The second option would be founded on a complete separation, at least initially, of perspective and methodology, so that tools for, say, analysing films from a feminist perspective would be drawn from methods of cultural analysis already available to, and in operation outside the sphere of, feminism in itself. This latter option calls for the appropriation of existing methodologies for a newly constituted project. It can further be suggested that an appropriation for feminist analysis of methodologies originating elsewhere might effectively transform the body of thought from which the methods were taken in the first place – a claim in fact frequently made on behalf of all types of feminist theoretical work.

Feminist film theory has on the whole tended to take the second methodological option rather than the first – that is, it has tended to adopt or appropriate methodologies developed outside the sphere of feminism itself. These methods have largely been drawn from the sociological analysis of cultural production, from cultural studies, and from the more limited field of film theory. Sociologically based methods would locate images, roles and representations of women in cinema as phenomena reflecting, or perhaps determined by, the position of women in the 'real' world or the wider society. Feminist film theory which draws more specifically on film theory for its methods has tended, on the other hand, to premiss itself largely on a notion of representation as mediated, as a social and ideological construct, an autonomous or relatively autonomous process of meaning production which does not necessarily relate immediately to or reflect unproblematically a 'real' social world. Here therefore the main focus of interest has been the ways in which woman has been constituted as a set of meanings through processes of cinematic signification. In that its topic is the processes whereby meanings are produced in cinema, the body of work drawn upon by this form of theory has been semiotics, together with the related fields of structuralism and psychoanalysis (Kaplan, 1977). In fact much of the work in the present book is very evidently informed by semiotic forms of theorising, if only because I would regard semiotics and its allied methodologies as having been instrumental in generating a considerable and useful body of work in film theory in general and in feminist film theory in particular. This is not to suggest, though, that a feminist theory of cinema based in semiotics is entirely without its drawbacks. For one thing, other approaches in film theory have often tended to be pushed aside in favour of this form of analysis, which has sometimes meant that certain issues crucial for a feminist film theory are not easily dealt with (Gledhill, 1978): I shall be considering this point more fully below. Moreover – though this is perhaps not in the final instance so much problem as a benefit – the appropriation for feminist film theory of the methods of cinesemiotics has generated a critique of that very body of work, and has thus actually inaugurated a retroactive transformation of cinesemiotics itself. In other words, a feminist approach constitutes a questioning of the very methods it has adopted for itself. This is one reason why feminists engaging in this kind of film theory have felt able to defend their appropriation of what have sometimes been considered 'patriarchal' methodologies and theories (Johnston, 1973a; Mulvey, 1975; *New German Critique*, 1978).

Developments in feminist film theory have been very much informed, then, by developments in other fields and vice versa. There is, however, nothing either necessary or inevitable about this process: it has happened for a variety of reasons, not all of them having to do with the character of feminism itself. Setting aside for the moment the actual developments which have taken place up to now in the field of feminist film theory, it is evident that the theoretical and methodological options potentially available to feminist film theory must in some measure be delimited by the range of perspectives and practices constituted by feminism itself. That is to say, it seems plausible to suggest *a priori* that different feminist perspectives will tend to privilege different methodological approaches. However, it seems to me that this relationship is likely to be mediated in practice by the different political questions addressed by various forms of feminism.

Methodological differences, however, do not necessarily follow immediately from political differences. And in fact for feminist film theory as it actually developed over its first ten years or so, things are neither as simple nor as cut and dried as a categorisation of different types of feminism might suggest. First of all, differences between political practices of feminism are in themselves not that easy to pin down; and, second, feminist film theory has not on the whole developed out of any overriding concern with purity or consistency in relation to any particular feminist position or positions. Despite the quite large degree to which feminist film theory has been self-conscious about its own development, it has in general not overtly espoused any particular brand(s) of feminism: such differences in feminist perspective as do exist tend to be implicit and discernible only after the fact. Most kinds of feminist film theory actually share a broadly based concern to look at the cultural products and institutions of a patriarchal society from a feminist standpoint. This concern has tended to be focused on the silences of film *texts* in relation to women, to 'the exclusion of the woman's voice and her position within the text as object' (Martin, 1976, p. 12). This is a focus which, theoretically speaking, has the potential of cutting across various feminist discourses. The concern then is one which can be held in common by different feminist practices: that of becoming sensitive to what often goes unnoticed, becomes naturalised, or is taken for granted within a sexist society. The common object of such attention was initially, and largely continues to be, dominant cinema – and particularly its apotheosis in the products of the Hollywood studio system of the 1930s and 1940s. Feminist film theory thus starts out with a common objective of looking at existing films, especially Hollywood films, and drawing attention to certain matters which often go unnoticed in these films. These matters are centred not only around presences – the explicit ways in which women are represented, the kinds of images, roles constructed by films – but also around absences – the ways in which women do not appear at all or are in certain ways not represented in films. Given the argument that in a sexist society both presences and absences may not be immediately discernible to the ordinary spectator, if only because certain representations appear to be quite ordinary and obvious, then the fundamental project of feminist film analysis can be said to centre on making visible the invisible.

Making visible the invisible is an analytical activity that can work at a number of levels. The most obvious object of this kind of activity is perhaps the film text itself: a feminist analysis may offer a reading of a film which starts out by exposing the absences of the text, or by pointing to the ways in which it constructs women through its images or its narrative structure. But the activity of making the invisible visible can also work at the level of film production itself, through an examination of the place of films within the contexts in which they are produced, by looking at the question of how films are put together in the ways they are, the kinds of social relations involved in that process, and the relationships between modes of production and the formation of textual structures and operations foregrounded by a feminist perspective. Feminist film theory may therefore operate at the levels of both text and context, and would ideally aim to delineate the relationship between the two. Such a model for feminist film theory probably constitutes a prescription or an objective, rather than a description of the state of the art. According to one view, for example, feminist film theory should

> develop and use an analysis of our culture that includes a political perspective, knowledge of economic conditions, and the role of ideology. Second, feminist [theory] must be both able and willing to analyse films themselves. . . . The entire dynamic of a narrative structure must be

considered, and the tools for most thoroughly comprehending films must be utilized by the feminist critic. Lastly [the critic] must have an analysis of the possible relationships between art and ideology in all their complexities (Place and Burton, 1976, p. 56).

Another writer suggests that

A good theory includes an explanation of the mechanisms operating *within* the film (form, content, etc.) and the mechanisms that go beyond the product that is the film (such as the film industry, distribution, audience expectation, etc.) (Lesage, 1974, p. 13).

What is being demanded of feminist film theory here is that it focus both on film texts and also on their social and historical contexts, although there is perhaps a difference between these writers as to the precise ways in which the notion of context is conceptualised. The point about both models, though, is first of all that they are exactly that – models, something to be aimed for by feminist film theory; and, second, they are both with different degrees of explicitness suggesting that feminist film theory should, while taking into account the specific operations of film texts, not at the same time seize those texts from their broader contexts as cultural productions. Despite these counsels of perfection, feminist film theory has, in its actual development, taken rather different paths, although it might well be that the objectives are in fact being moved towards, if somewhat circuitously. An account of the history and development of feminist film theory may cast some light on this process: it can also serve to place the discussions which follow in the next two chapters. In any brief overview, positions are bound to be oversimplified and accounts selective: in this instance, though, I hope not to the point of inaccuracy. Also discussion is limited for the most part to developments in the English-speaking world, particularly Britain and the USA.

Self-consciously feminist approaches to film began to be developed on both sides of the Atlantic more or less simultaneously, and in large measure independently of one another, during the early 1970s: 1972 in fact seems to be the watershed year for feminist film theory. In North America, a number of women's film festivals – the first New York International Festival of Women's Films (1972) and the Toronto Women and Film Festival (1973) – coincided with the publication of three books of feminist film criticism: Molly Haskell's *From Reverence to Rape* (1975), Marjorie Rosen's *Popcorn Venus* (1973) and Joan Mellen's *Women and Their Sexuality in the New Film* (1974). Although there are important differences of approach between the books (Johnston, 1975c; Place and Burton, 1976), all three are devoted to examining the place of women in dominant cinema: Haskell's and Rosen's concern is largely with Hollywood, Mellen's with the European 'art' cinema. At around the same time, 1972, the journal *Women and Film* began publication, and in that year another American journal, *Velvet Light Trap*, devoted an entire issue to articles on women and Hollywood. This writing was in part descriptive or journalistic, and where theoretical approaches were taken up, their methodologies tended to be sociological or quasi-sociological. Female characters in films might be considered in terms of roles and stereotypes, for example, and stereotyped women's roles – the vamp, the girl next door, the mother, and so on – assessed according to the degree of their 'truthfulness', the extent to which they either reflected, or constituted a smoothing over of, contradictions and conflicts in the 'real' lives of women. Or changes over time in the ways in which women have been portrayed in films might be viewed as in one way or another reflective of changes in the wider society. The title of Molly Haskell's book in fact sums up an argument concerning the relationship, sometimes regarded by her as direct, sometimes as inverse, between images of women in cinema and the contemporary social status of women. The frame of reference for all this work is defined by a shared and usually implicit assumption concerning the relationship between cinematic representation and the 'real world': that a film, in recording or reflecting the world in a direct or mediated fashion, is in some sense a vehicle for transmitting meanings which originate outside of itself – within the intentions of film makers, perhaps, or within social structures. Since wherever their source is located, meanings are regarded as pre-existing their transmission via film, cinema tends to be viewed entirely as a neutral means of communicating already constituted significations.

At around the same time, a rather different approach to feminist film theory was beginning to develop in Britain, inaugurated by the first women's film event at the Edinburgh Film Festival in 1972 and the publication in 1973 of *Notes on Women's Cinema*, a pamphlet edited by Claire Johnston. Variations in approach at this period between feminist film theory in the USA and Britain have subsequently been characterised and explained in terms of differing attitudes towards theoretical activity. Whereas, it has been suggested, feminist film theory in Britain 'wanted first to develop a viable theoretical position based on a thorough investigation of the nature of cinema' (Kaplan,

1977, p. 394), the American approach was seen as more descriptive and less analytical. American criticism was however, as I have already indicated, also based on a set of theoretical and methodological presuppositions: it is simply that these theoretical groundings were not made explicit in the work itself, and were certainly not in themselves a topic of debate, as they were in Britain. Another distinction between the two approaches was that, whereas the American was based loosely on various forms of social–cultural and journalistic criticism, the British version drew consciously on theories and methods which were being developed within the narrower field of film studies, and combined them with a feminist perspective to produce a variant of feminist film theory which was self-conscious and aimed at being theoretically rigorous.

The areas of film theory drawn upon at this point were structuralism, semiotics and, to a certain extent, psychoanalysis. Each of these is premised on an assumption that meanings, far from being seized out of the 'real world' and simply transmitted through the medium of film, are actually produced in and through the operations of film texts themselves. It is perhaps this, more than their relative degrees of theoretical rigour, which in the early 1970s distinguished British from American feminist film analysis. The adoption of semiotics-based methodologies had two initial and interrelated consequences. First, the primary object of analysis became in the first instance the film text itself, so that questions of context tended to be bracketed or ignored. Second, however, this did have the important and positive consequence of permitting, even of necessitating, an examination of the independent operation of ideology within film texts. This is because text-based criticism founded in a structuralist method posits the notion that meanings are constituted at least partially in and by texts themselves and that there is not necessarily any direct or unmediated relationship of determination between context and text.

Such an approach also assumes that the actual operation of the meaning-production process is not always immediately discernible, that texts will on the contrary often actually present themselves exactly in the way in which they are often read: as neutral vehicles of pre-existing meanings-in-the-world. The operation of the meaning-construction process has, as it were, to be unearthed, for it is precisely the work of ideology to conceal its own operations: 'The reluctance to declare its codes characterises bourgeois society and the culture issuing from it: both demand signs which do not look like signs' (Barthes, 1977,

p. 116). A textual analysis whose objective is to uncover this process of signification will, according to this argument, also – as an intended or unintended consequence – uncover the textual operation of ideology. That is to say, such an approach can constitute what has been termed an ideological analysis. Structuralist and semiotic approaches to textual analysis which take up this notion of ideology are founded, therefore, on the twofold assumption that part of the work of ideology is to conceal its own operation, and that this operation can have its own independent effects within cultural productions. Thus a necessary prior step in any textual analysis informed by structuralist methodology is to break down the text, to deconstruct it (Barthes, 1972): an ideological reading of a text is then a reconstruction of it in which what was previously hidden is now brought to light.

Bearing in mind the frequently taken for granted character of assumptions about women and images of women in society, the relevance of ideological readings of texts to any feminist approach to cultural analysis is immediate and clear. Such readings can at least chart and begin to analyse some of the ideological operations of patriarchy: this is what is implied in feminist film theory by the use of the term 'patriarchal ideology'.[1] If it is the case that one of the effects of ideology is to make what is cultural and therefore historically variable appear natural and therefore immutable (Barthes, 1973), then a film may be seen to embody a series of ideological operations through which woman is constructed as eternal, mythical and unchanging, an essence or a set of fixed images and meanings, 'a sign within a patriarchal order' (Kaplan, 1977, p. 404). In this way a structuralist/semiotic method appropriated for feminist film theory would aim to expose the processes whereby woman is constructed as myth, as a fixed signifier, within textual practices of meaning construction. These were the grounds on which, during the early and middle 1970s, feminist film theorists in Britain appropriated certain existing methods from film theory for their purposes. The need, it was felt, was for a sound theoretical position based on the investigation of the nature of cinema in general, a position which would be secured by the use and extension of existing methods of film analysis. In addition to semiotics and structuralism, psychoanalytic approaches were at this point also called upon, usually as a means of opening up further possibilities for textual analysis. Psychoanalytic readings are premised on a view of film texts as analogous to the discourses of persons undergoing psychoanalysis, so that textual analysis may be based on certain kinds of analytic methods, such as those developed by Freud for interpreting dreams. This of course is also a method aimed at uncovering meanings which are at first sight hidden, in this particular case hidden because they are embedded in unconscious processes. Psychoanalytic approaches to textual analysis seize the operations of ideology as in some sense the 'Unconscious of the text'.

By the middle 1970s, the distinctive British and American approaches to feminist film analysis began to seem rather less clear-cut than had previously been the case. In 1976, the first issue of a 'journal of feminism and film theory', *Camera Obscura*, was published from Berkeley, California by a collective of women who had previously worked on *Women and Film*. *Women and Film* had ceased publication in 1975 and its later issues had increasingly manifested internal differences in theoretical approach. The new journal immediately took up, from a feminist standpoint, some of the concerns of structuralism and semiotics: in the first issue, the editorial collective stated that its perspective was based on a recognition that 'women are oppressed not only economically and politically, but also in the very forms of reasoning, signifying and symbolical exchange of our culture' (*Camera Obscura*, 1976a, p. 3). The methodologies proposed for describing and analysing this form of oppression were on the one hand textual analysis, which 'considers the film as a dynamic process of the production of meanings' (ibid., p. 5), and on the other psychoanalysis, which may be called upon to analyse how 'the dominant patriarchal view conditions us at the level of psychic structures' (ibid., p. 6).

Psychoanalysis is being called upon in this instance not to provide a model for the analysis of texts, but as a metapsychology, a means of explaining the construction of certain relationships between spectator and text in the film-viewing situation. This particular appropriation of psychoanalysis reflects the impact on film studies of certain critiques of structuralism and semiotics: these critiques were answered within the field itself by what has come to be known as 'post-structuralism'. Textual analysis in itself is always susceptible to criticism on grounds of formalism: that is, that on focusing on the text, such analysis can readily emphasise textual operations to the exclusion of all else, and thereby imply that an account of the processes of the text offers an exhaustive explanation of the work of signification. Post-structuralist analysis attempts to answer this by broadening the field of signification to take in, as well as its internal operations, the moment of reading or reception of the text, and to posit a model of the signification process as involving the interaction of text and recipient. This in turn calls for ways of conceptualising both recipient and moment of reception, and a means of doing this is offered by structuralist variants of psychoanalysis, which advance theories of human subjectivity based on a notion of the subject as producer of, and produced by, meaning (see Chapter 3). It is this version of psychoanalysis which was advanced by *Camera Obscura*.

An article by Jean-Louis Baudry on the 'cinematic apparatus' included in the first issue of the journal deals with the question of 'psychic structures' evoked in the film-viewing situation, but does not explicitly address the question of specific types of meanings – around representations of women, for instance – constructed in and by the apparatus, nor of the potential implications for spectator–text relations of the gender of viewing subjects. The latter point is also largely true of Laura Mulvey's article on visual pleasure and narrative cinema, which appeared in *Screen* in late 1975.[2] Mulvey did, however, extend within a psychoanalytic perspective the terms of the debate on the cinematic apparatus: this extension was effected by the insertion of the earlier preoccupation of feminist film theory with the question of woman as signifier in a patriarchal order within a discussion of the psychic structures evoked by the cinematic apparatus. Mulvey was thus able to address the question of the ways in which spectators of narrative films are positioned by representations of women, in terms of how spectator–text relations are mobilised in a series of looks which evoke early, even infantile, forms of pleasure and unpleasure. The feminist perspective is manifest here in the concern with woman as the object of looking, but it is not yet extended into a consideration of the question of whether or in what specific ways the gendered subjectivity of spectators may inform these relations of looking.

By the late 1970s then, feminist film theory on both sides of the Atlantic was taking up a number of issues raised by semiotics, structuralism and psychoanalysis. At the same time, approaches of a more journalistic and sociological kind continued to have wide currency. However, in the USA, where in comparison with Britain both film studies and women's studies are relatively firmly institutionalised within higher education, semiotics-based approaches in film theory in general began to be set alongside other types of criticism and in some degree institutionalised and recuperated as academic discourses, and their broader cultural impact consequently weakened to some extent. In Britain, on the other hand, semiotics-based approaches became – paradoxically perhaps – relatively influential whilst at the same time remaining institutionally marginal: they have never become part of the discourse of academic institutions to the extent that they have in the USA. At the same time, though, they seem to have acquired a greater cultural and political currency. These national differences are worth signalling to the extent that they shed light on differences in the ways in which feminist film theory has been taken up and developed on either side of the Atlantic.

Textual analysis is considered at some length here not only because of the central place it has occupied up to now in feminist film theory, but also because it has actually been quite productive in itself. Nevertheless, although I would argue that textual analysis is a crucial area of work for feminist film theory, I would also suggest that a purely text-based criticism does have a number of limitations that should be signalled. The rest of the present chapter is devoted to a discussion first of all of the place and importance of textual analysis in feminist film theory, and then to a consideration of what a text-based criticism can easily exclude, of how it may be extended, and of the kinds of questions which feminist film theory might usefully address for its future work.

In the late 1970s, while feminist textual analysis continued to be developed and refined, other demands on feminist film theory became increasingly pressing. The significance of such pressures lies, I believe, in the fact that the question of what feminist film theory is, or ought to be, is in the final instance a political one. It is necessary constantly to ask: what is feminist film theory for? and who is it for? These questions are clearly about the relationship of theory and practice, and in addressing them it is useful to be aware that the impact of feminist film theory can sometimes be defused by its becoming one more subject on the curricula of educational institutions. This is not to deny the political significance of changes in institutional knowledge so much as to point out that feminist film theory can also have other equally important relationships to practice. It can be instrumental, for instance, in the promotion of a general understanding of the ideological operations of patriarchy at work in various kinds of representations: and such an understanding may in turn inform attempts to effect transformations at the level of representation itself.

The productivity of textual analysis arises from the fact that it is premised on a notion of film as a dynamic process of meaning construction. From this it follows that social meanings centring in one way or another on women can be constituted as the focus of textual analysis, whose objective then becomes to expose the processes by which such meanings are constructed. In this sense, simply by laying bare the process by which it operates in actual films, a feminist textual analysis may inaugurate a deconstruction of patriarchal ideology. A feminist perspective provides ways into a text, poses the kinds of questions asked of a textual analysis. These may include: what functions does a woman character perform within the film's narrative? How are women represented visually? Are certain fixed images of women being appealed to, and if so how are they constructed through the film's image and/or narrative? How do women not function, how are they not represented in the film? And perhaps, at a deeper level, a textual analysis might attend to disjunctions, ruptures or inconsistencies in the text, at the level of narrative or image, or both, and ask whether and in what ways woman as signifier or structure informs or relates' to those absences.

The objects of feminist textual analysis have often, in fact almost invariably, been the products of the Hollywood film industry. It is sometimes argued, however, that an analysis of Hollywood cinema along these lines constitutes an unwarranted forcing of texts which in no way present themselves as open to this kind of reading. While accepting the argument that Hollywood films do not always readily offer themselves up to feminist readings, there are perhaps two grounds on which such readings may none the less be justified. The first is that this is just the point – that it is exactly the work of ideology to naturalise and therefore to efface the 'patriarchal' character of film texts, and that it is in turn the work of textual analysis to demystify this process by uncovering the work of ideology: precisely, that is, to render the invisible visible. The second point is that a feminist perspective can offer a privileged point of entry into the workings of ideology, because under patriarchy for a woman, film viewing can often be a dialectical experience in a way it cannot be for a man: that woman – socially constructed as 'other' or 'outsider' in sexist society – is, like the exile, in an excellent position to stand apart and analyse its workings (*New German Critique*, 1978; Rich, 1978). A feminist textual analysis, in uncovering the processes whereby certain sets of meanings surrounding 'woman' are constituted in a film, opens it up to readings 'against the grain' and thus also in some sense finally transforms the film itself.

An analysis which begins and ends with a text is open, however, to the criticism that it brackets or ignores the conditions and contexts of the production and reception of that text. At the time when feminist film theory was, in its semiotic variant at least, focusing largely on the internal operations of texts, some feminists were, as I have already indicated, demanding that it do more than this, that it attend in fact to a film's various contexts (Kuhn, 1975; Lesage, 1974; Place and Burton, 1976). The demand that analysis go beyond the text can in some measure be met within the terms of a semiotic approach, by extending the area of analysis to take in the relationship between film and spectator, thereby deepening the understanding of the ways in which both text and spectator operate as sites of signification. This approach, drawing as it does on certain psychoanalytic theories, has led to the development of a model of the institution of cinema as an entire apparatus – embracing the technology of the medium, the movie theatre, the spectator, the film itself, and the whole range of processes of human subjectivity. This psychoanalytic model has been useful to feminist film theory because it opens up – though in its original form it does not actually address – the extremely important question of the gender of the spectator, of gendered subjectivity in cinematic representation. One question, for instance, which is posed with some urgency for feminist film theory is exactly that of the place of the female or feminine spectator in the relay of looks set up within the cinematic apparatus.

However, although this psychoanalytic approach does indeed address some of the limitations of a purely text-based analysis, it does have the drawback of posing as an alternative a totalising model of the cinematic apparatus which appears to be somewhat impervious to analysis centred on the historical location of texts, spectator–text relations and contexts – of the concrete conditions of production and reception of film texts, in other words. Reviewing feminist film analysis, Christine Gledhill argues that

> there is a danger that, once the object of Feminist criticism is defined solely
> in terms of the cinematic production of meaning, we lose the ability to deal
> with its relationship to women as defined in society (Gledhill, 1978, p. 460).

This is perhaps another way of saying that questions of context can easily become evacuated in favour of the formalism that is readily privileged in semiotic and psychoanalytic approaches to cinema. Whether such approaches are inherently impervious to contextual analysis, or whether the focus on meaning foregrounded by the semiotic model can be brought to bear on an analysis of the historical and social conditions and contexts of individual films, is very much an open question. Approaches which in some way bring the two together are often regarded as desirable, even essential, ways forward for cultural analysis (Barrett *et al.*, 1979). The point about this issue, however, is that it can only be resolved by actual historical/analytical work: we will not know whether a semiotics-based contextual analysis of the institution of cinema from a feminist standpoint is possible until it has been seriously attempted. In the next two chapters, I shall attempt first of all to provide a picture of the development of feminist textual analysis, by discussing some specific examples. This is followed by a consideration of some ways in which attention to the internal operations of film texts may inform analyses of their institutional, social and historical contexts.

5

Trouble in the Text

I have defined textual analysis as a form of reading which starts out with the aim of uncovering processes and structures at work in a text that may not be immediately discernible. Analysis may lay bare the ways in which a text works within, or is an expression of, ideology. It is a premiss of textual analysis that the apparently natural qualities of ideology can be brought into question through 'de-naturalisation' – rendering ideology visible and thus open to critical examination. It is also a contention of textual analysis that structuralist (or post-structuralist) approaches of one kind or another offer a useful set of methods for doing this. Textual analysis, therefore, is founded on an understanding of texts as constructs, as structured by the work of ideology, while at the same time naturalising that work – embodying, in other words, a denial or effacement of the operation of ideology.

Cinema is peculiarly open to the appearance of 'naturalness' because of its specific signifying qualities, notably the fact that the film image, because it draws on the recording potential of photography, in conjunction with the projection of an apparently moving image, presents all the appearances of being a 'message without a code', an unmediated duplication of the 'real world'. Film's potential for re-presenting the appearances of the filmed world is what lies behind frequently impenetrable presuppositions as to the inherent 'truthfulness' of certain types of film, documentary in particular: but it informs the ways in which fiction films, too, are commonly regarded as 'uncoded'. In the case of the classic film narrative, for example, the seemingly analogical character of the film image in relation to the profilmic event is overdetermined by various elements of identification on the part of the spectator – notably identification with the central characters of the narrative, and with the process of unfolding of the narrative itself. The operations of ideology, according to this argument, insert themselves within these cinematic structures of identification, thus taking on the appearance of being natural, obvious, and 'already there' in the world. The recovery and examination of the hidden work of ideology within film texts is the project of ideological analysis. Because it has been so important in certain feminist approaches to film, a brief account of the premisses, methods and applications of ideological analysis is in order here.

Probably the earliest example of an ideological analysis of a film text to appear in English was the collective reading by the editors of *Cahiers du Cinéma* of *Young Mr Lincoln*, a film directed by John Ford and released in 1939. Originally published in *Cahiers du Cinéma* in 1970, the analysis appeared in translation in *Screen* two years later, and was seen by its authors as part of a larger project of reading classic films in order to pinpoint

> the relation of these films to the codes (social, cultural . . .) for which they are a site of intersection . . . therefore the relation of these films to the ideology which they convey, a particular 'phase' which they represent, and to the events . . . which they aimed to represent (*Cahiers du Cinéma*, 1972, p. 6).

The objective at this point was clearly in part to situate the operations of the classic film text within their historical context. Further on in the introduction to their project, the authors also state that they are interested as much in what is not in a film as in what is actually in it – that in other words they regard silences, absences and 'repressions' as crucial in structuring the ideological operation of texts, and that readings of films should 'make them say what they have to say *within* what they leave unsaid' (ibid., p. 8). In its twofold aim to attend to the ideological character of the 'structuring absences' of film texts and to situate textual operations historically, the *Cahiers du Cinéma* analysis looks beyond the initial limits of ideological analysis as I am defining it here. However, the actual reading of *Young Mr Lincoln* seems to be founded on a more concretely text-centred approach to analysis than might be suggested by the introductory claims for historicity made on its behalf. This, I believe, is because of the author's indebtedness to certain arguments about the relationships between cinema, ideology and criticism which had been put forward in an earlier issue of *Cahiers du Cinéma* (Comolli and Narboni, 1971).

These arguments are based on the notion that every film, as well as being part of an economic system, is also part of an ideological system, but that ideology does not necessarily operate similarly in all films. On the contrary, it is suggested: even in dominant cinema, films may construct a variety of ideological relations, and these ideological relations may be categorised. Thus, it is suggested, although in dominant cinema 'the largest category comprises those films which are imbued through and through with the dominant ideology in pure and unadulterated form' (ibid., p. 31), there are various exceptions to this general rule. Textual analyses founded on Comolli and Narboni's arguments took up one category of exception in particular. This is the group of films which appear at first sight to operate fully within the dominant ideology, but which on closer inspection turn out to be rather more complex. In such films

> An internal criticism is taking place which cracks the film apart at the seams. If one reads the film obliquely, looking for symptoms, if one looks beyond its apparent formal coherence, one can see that it is riddled with cracks: it is splitting under an internal tension (ibid., p. 33).

What is being suggested here is that certain classic films lend themselves particularly readily to ideological analysis because there are already disjunctures of some kind in their relation to ideology, and that such disjunctures are discernible within the text in the form of 'symptoms' – cracks, ruptures, on so on. These symptoms provide us with clues as to what, ideologically speaking, is going on. Since, in dominant cinema, cracks in the smooth operation of ideology are by definition not there intentionally or consciously, the disjunctures of the text may be regarded as analogous to the symptomatic manifestation of unconscious repressions in the discourses or on the bodies of the human subjects of psychoanalysis. In other words, ideological operations in films are seen here as in some sense unconscious, or repressed, within texts. But, like unconscious processes in general, they can sometimes put in an unexpected appearance in disguised or displaced form. For the *Cahiers du Cinéma* writers at this time, the hidden (unconscious) work of ideology in classic cinema could sometimes show itself in the form of a radically ruptured text, as a series of structuring absences in the text.

For example, in the analysis of *Young Mr Lincoln*, the *Cahiers du Cinéma* editors point out that history and politics are important structuring absences of the text, in that certain obviously crucial (but politically divisive) aspects of Abraham Lincoln's life, such as his position in relation to the abolition of slavery, are simply not explicitly dealt with in the film. It is further suggested that this omission has political significance in itself: its effect in the context of the film is to imbue the figure of Lincoln with qualities of universalism – precisely to represent the man as outside history, and thus to elevate him to the ahistorical status of myth. It is also argued that the political divisiveness which is not mentioned in the film is none the less present 'unconsciously' in displaced form, as for example in the repetition on the soundtrack of a musical theme based on the Southern patriotic song 'Dixie'. Structuring absences can therefore operate as gaps or fissures in a film's discourse: but they may also work in conjunction with displaced or disguised representations of whatever it is that is not explicitly spoken in the text. In either case, a symptomatic reading – a reading of the 'symptoms' of the text – would, in attending to these things, open it up for analysis in terms of its ideological operations.

Methods employed in ideological readings of film texts call for some initial breakdown of the film under analysis into its constituent parts – that is to say, for a deconstruction. The methods employed in the reading of *Young Mr Lincoln* are in this respect fairly typical, in that the analysis proceeds from a division of the film into a number of narrative segments or sequences, with a detailed examination of each one. In this case, the text in its entirety is constituted as the object of analysis, and the reading is a kind of 'slowing-down': a commentary on each segment in turn, an analysis of its underlying operations and a signalling of the processes at work in individual segments and across the text as a whole. However, textual analysis need not necessarily take as its object an entire film, but may instead either concentrate on specific moments of the film which are seen as in some sense condensing its ideological processes, or may foreground particular sequences which are regarded as 'key' and then subject these sequences to analysis in depth. The earliest feminist textual analysis tended in fact to focus on 'pregnant moments' in films, on specific examples of textual rupture.

Early examples of feminist textual analysis inserted a feminist perspective into procedures of ideological reading by raising as their central concern the question of the specifically patriarchal character of the ideological operations of the classic Hollywood film. Although the notion of patriarchal ideology was not explicitly defined or argued through in feminist film theory, the implication was clear enough: that in dominant cinema the voice of woman, the woman's discourse, is systematically absent or repressed, and that the controlling discourse is almost invariably male. In other words, in dominant cinema, women do not tell their own stories or control their own images, but are ideologically positioned in patriarchal terms (Johnston, 1973a). At this point, basically two strategies were adopted in feminist textual analysis. The first takes up the Comolli and Narboni argument concerning films of rupture in dominant cinema and uses it in an examination of the operations of patriarchal ideology. The second is focused on films which appear, in the Comolli and Narboni definition, to be completely under the sway of patriarchal ideology, and attempts to unpack their ideological operations. Thus while in the second case the assumption is that it is the task of textual analysis to lay bare the operations of patriarchal ideology, the first strategy assumes the existence of a body of Hollywood films which already contain an internal criticism of that ideology. Such films, it is argued, are cracked open internally by the contradictory operations of ideology. This internal tension facilitates the de-naturalisation of ideology because it opens films up for 'oppositional' interpretations, or readings that go against the grain of dominant cinema (Johnston, 1975a). According to this view, one of the tasks of feminist film theory is to seek out such films and, in producing readings of them, reappropriate them for feminism. In this instance, part of the feminist project is seen to be the rewriting of film history, and at the same time the transformation of that history by means of a theoretical approach which it has hitherto lacked, an approach informed by a feminist perspective.

This is the context in which, during the mid-1970s, two feminist film theorists, Claire Johnston and Pam Cook, took up and re-examined the work of Dorothy Arzner. Arzner was one of the very few women to have worked as a film director during Hollywood's classic years – the 1920s, the 1930s and the early 1940s – and to have produced a substantial body of work (Johnston, 1975b). Although part of Johnston's and Cook's project – in effect if not in intent – must have been to reinsert a forgotten woman director into the mainstream of film history, their main stated aim was to focus on film texts rather than on directors' biographies: on the ways in which the 'discourse of the woman' foregrounds itself in Arzner's films as working in contradiction with the 'patriarchal discourse' prevailing in Hollywood films. An argument that the internal criticism of patriarchal ideology seen to be at work in Arzner's films is in some sense informed by the director's gender is implicit in the actual choice of objects for analysis – films directed by a woman – although at the same time such a simplistic version of the auteur theory is overtly rejected. Johnston's and Cook's analytical strategies are neverthelsss informed, at least initially, by auteurism, simply because their work is founded on general statements applicable to a number of films by a single director. Textual readings focus on specific features of individual films only to the extent that these features structure other films by the same director.

For Claire Johnston, the overall defining characteristic of Arzner's films is that 'the woman ... determines her own identity through transgression and desire in a search for an independent existence beyond and outside the discourse of the male' (Johnston, 1975a, p. 4). Johnston then looks at individual films directed by Arzner for evidence in support of this statement. The statement contains a presupposition about the place of woman in film narratives: that 'woman' operates as a narrative function – an element, that is, of narrative structure – while at the same time in her fictional character/role she represents a person embodying human traits with which the spectator may (or may not) identify (see Chapter 2). Johnston's argument about the women in Arzner's films is that because, as characters in stories, their desires are transgressive of the patriarchal order, they function as disruptions to the linear flow of the classic narrative, thus posing a 'trouble' in relation to narrative closure. On *Christopher Strong* (RKO, 1933), for example, Johnston suggests that the central female character, Cynthia Darrington (Katharine Hepburn), a world champion aviator, transgresses male discourse through the element of sex-role reversal inherent in her characterisation. Johnston also argues that, to the extent that the discourse of the woman is foregrounded in Arzner's films, the male universe is rendered 'other', made strange, and therefore de-naturalised. The ending of *Christopher Strong* – in which Cynthia, pregnant by her married lover, commits suicide on a solo flight which turns out to be record-breaking – is seen as expressing the contradictions at work in the narrative. These contradictions are embodied in the central female character as the conflict between career and sexuality. The conflict is encapsulated in an ending to the story which is not actually a full resolution of all the questions set up by the narrative. This narrative excess, Johnston suggests, is in fact the 'continued existence of the woman's discourse' (Johnston 1975a, p. 7). The discourse of the woman exceeds the bounds of the film narrative.

Pam Cook too justifies her reading of Dorothy Arzner's work in terms of developing strategies for bringing to light the operations of patriarchal ideology (Cook, 1975). Unlike Johnston, however, she suggests that because – *pace* Comolli and Narboni – the operations of ideology lay themselves bare within ruptures, fissures or disjunctures in the text, textual analysis can examine such moments of rupture in order to see what clues they may offer about the operation of ideology. These moments, according to Cook, function in Arzner's films much like the 'pregnant moments' of Brecht's plays: to distance the spectator, to break down identification, to render her or him potentially critical of what is going on on screen. Cook advances a fairly detailed analysis of two of Arzner's films – *Merrily We Go To Hell* (Paramount, 1932) and *Dance, Girl, Dance* (RKO, 1940) – in terms of their narrative interruptions, reversals and repetitions, and their ironic play with fixed images and stereotypes of woman. In these processes, she argues, the unity of the classic Hollywood narrative is challenged, its working-over of patriarchal ideology is exposed, and the spectator is positioned at a distance from the work of ideology by means of a breakdown of classic structures of identification.

As against these ideological readings which claim that the films of one woman director constitute a challenge to patriarchal ideology, some earlier work by Cook and Johnston takes a rather different approach to Hollywood cinema in suggesting that a feminist perspective may productively also inform the analysis of films which are not films of rupture, but which appear on the contrary to function like that majority of Hollywood films which, according to Comolli and Narboni, are completely under the sway of dominant ideology. In an analysis of the place of women in the films of Raoul Walsh, and in a reading of one film in particular, *The Revolt of Mamie Stover* (Twentieth Century-Fox, 1956), Cook and Johnston argue that in their representation in dominant cinema women 'function as a signifier in a circuit of exchange where the values exchanged have been fixed by/in a patriarchal culture' (Cook and Johnston, 1974, p. 94).

Mamie, a beautiful but misunderstood trouble-maker from the wrong side of town, falls foul of the San Francisco police and embarks for Honolulu. On board ship, she meets Jim Blair, a rich novelist, who lives in Honolulu, and he tries to dissuade Mamie from working for the notorious dance hall there. But Mamie, on learning that he is to meet his girl friend Annalee, determines grimly to concentrate on making money. Jim, however, has found Mamie's allure potent, and when Pearl Harbour is bombed, his first thought is for her. He joins the army, and Mamie buys up real estate at bargain prices. Jim proposes marriage and Mamie accepts, but Bertha, owner of the dance hall, offers Mamie a bigger cut in the takings and she succumbs to the temptation. Mamie graduates to the exclusive golf-club set. Jim returns but is unimpressed by Mamie's loot. She finally understands his scruples and makes her way back to her humble home town (*Monthly Film Bulletin*, vol. 23, 1956).

The approach of Cook and Johnston permits them to examine not only the narrative function of the central character of the film, Mamie (Jane Russell), but also leads them into a consideration of her representation as image. In an analysis of the relationship between the central character's function in the film image and her function in the narrative, it is suggested that her characterisation as an economically independent businesswoman is undercut not only by the fact that the resolution of the narrative constitutes a recuperation of the threat posed by the independent woman (by the end of the film, Mamie has lost both lover and fortune), but also by the very manner in which she is represented in the cinematic image. Cook and Johnston argue that Mamie/Jane Russell is constituted as a fetish, an object of erotic looking, on the part of (male) spectators. But this is not the only sense in which Mamie's image becomes an object of exchange: her role as a 'hostess' in a club/brothel, too, renders this quite literal within the film's narrative. It is, significantly, a pin-up photograph of 'Flaming Mamie' – a representation that is also an object of economic exchange – that turns out to be the heroine's undoing (see Still 5.1). The foregrounding – through cinematic codes of costume, gesture, framing and composition – of the body of Mamie/Jane Russell underscores this argument: in *The Revolt of Mamie Stover*, the star's body becomes a fetish (Mulvey, 1975). In this way, the threat posed by Mamie as subject of desire – an economically independent woman – at the level of the narrative is recuperated at the level of the image. In this analysis, Cook and Johnston indicate some ways in which the various codes of image and narrative in a film text may sometimes work in opposition to one another. These contradictions open up the text for ideological reading, not because it makes itself already available for reading as a film of rupture, but because the film is ruptured, pulled apart as it were, in the process of textual analysis itself.

The distinction between Johnston's and Cook's approaches to the films of Dorothy Arzner on the one hand and to *The Revolt of Mamie Stover* on the other raises important questions about the status of reading and the objectives and consequences of feminist textual analysis. In the work on Arzner, the writers' readings or interpretations tend to be taken as given (Bergstrom, 1979b) in the assumption that the films under consideration are in some sense 'already' ruptured and that it is the task of analysis simply to chart and describe the function of these pre-existing ruptures. The act of reading itself is regarded as neutral: it is implied that anyone would produce similar readings of Arzner's films. The feminist character of the work is seen as residing in the films themselves as much as emerging from readings of the films. The obverse seems to be the case with the analysis of *The Revolt of Mamie Stover*, in which no claims are made that it is a film of rupture. What analysis does in this latter case is to offer a reading of a film which pinpoints some of the ways in which a classic narrative text functions as ideology, a reading situated by the perspective which informs it. If the reading is informed by a feminist perspective, 'feminist' questions are asked in relation to the film text, and a feminist analysis of it is produced. That is to say, the reading both comes out of and also constitutes a political position.

Once a notion of reading as an active and situated practice is adopted, the distinction between films which embody an internal self-criticism and films which are completely ideologically complicit becomes redundant. This is because at this point the focus of analytical activity becomes the process of reading as much as the text itself: if reading is seen as dynamic and situated, then it is possible to argue that film texts are in some measure constituted or re-constituted in and through the act of reading. This is not to suggest that all texts are open to all possible readings, but rather that meanings are not fixed and limited for all time within a text – locked inside it, so to speak, and only waiting to be released through reading. The suggestion is rather that films may proffer a range of possible meanings, and that it is likely that they will be read in different ways at different times and places. If this is the case, it becomes difficult to argue that some films are inherently 'ruptured' while others are not. Who in any case is to judge which films are which? It is perhaps more to the point to argue that the ideological operation of most or all dominant films can be pulled apart, if necessary, by means of textual analysis. There is then no need to argue, for instance, that Dorothy Arzner's films contain, and perhaps always have contained, a critique of patriarchal ideology. It is sufficient to suggest that certain meanings – centred on the notion of a female discourse as against a male discourse, say – can be got from the films by a situated reading made at a particular historical moment. The apparently inevitable, but ultimately unanswerable, question of

5.1 *The Revolt of Mamie Stover*: the woman's body as object of the male gaze

whether or not the original audiences for the films read them as critiques of patriarchal ideology then becomes irrelevant.

In relation to the question of a feminist approach to Dorothy Arzner's films, this argument is supported by a reading of *Christopher Strong* which departs in its approach from those advanced in the work of Cook and Johnston, and arrives at some rather different conclusions about the film (Suter, 1979). The object of Suter's analysis is a single film in its entirety, and not the body of work of a director, which means that she is able to emphasise how the film operates as an 'expression within a patriarchal order' (ibid., p. 148) rather than as exemplary of common structures discernible across the work of one auteur. Although Suter suggests that the central female character of the film does constitute a 'disturbance', in that it is her transgression of the codes of heterosexual monogamy that sets the narrative in motion, she argues that in committing suicide Cynthia also functions to bring about a resolution in which these codes are in fact re-established as the desired ethic. The film as a whole, argues Suter, does (as Johnston and Cook also suggest) raise the issue of the discourse of the woman, but Suter's conclusion is that this discourse is in the end recuperated by a dominant male discourse: '*Christopher Strong* would seem to be structured around the containment of feminine discourse and all that this implies regarding the repression of feminine desire' (ibid., p. 145). This argument, in focusing on the ways in which the film constitutes, rather than transgresses, patriarchal ideology, suggests that while *Christopher Strong* is perhaps not, after all, a film of rupture, it is none the less of interest to feminists for the ways in which it does begin to articulate, even if it finally represses, the 'feminine voice'. It also suggests how textual analysis centred on quite 'ordinary' products of dominant cinema can be of interest and significance to a feminist film criticism.

Feminist (re)readings of classic Hollywood films may be seen as having political impact in at least two areas. First, they can be instrumental in building up an understanding of the specific ways in which sexism operates as ideology. Second, feminist textual analysis, by removing its objects from their original contexts within dominant cinema, may be said actually to transform films by advancing ways of looking at and understanding them that 'go against the grain' of their 'preferred' readings. Feminist textual analysis then, by examining ways in which films embody and construct patriarchal ideology, by undercutting these ideological operations and by offering alternative ways of looking at films, may be regarded as an intervention within ideology.

Without the notion of inherent rupture, the question of the degree to which a text is internally self-critical is perhaps less important than the actual process of reading which ruptures that text by deconstructing it. Textual analysis may proceed on the premiss that all analysis at least starts with deconstruction. There is a distinction to be made between two rather different types of textual analysis, a distinction which turns basically on the difference between structuralist and post-structuralist analysis. In the former, analysis would tend to be text-based and Formalist, while in the latter there would also, or instead, be a concern to deal with meaning production as a process of the reading subject:

> The insistence in this second phase on *structuring* (the *production* of meaning) rather than on virtual *structures* or patterns in a text is seen . . . as a shift in emphasis rather than . . . a rejection of what structuralism had brought to critical theory (Bergstrom, 1979a, p. 33).

A model for this second variant of textual analysis is provided by *S/Z*, an analysis by Roland Barthes of a short story by Balzac in which the entire story is subjected to a kind of deceleration and a highly detailed reading (Barthes, 1974). The objective of this reading is to elucidate the functioning of abstract systems, a set of codes, in the text by means of exploring concrete details. Cinema presents a somewhat more complex object for textual analysis than does literature, however, largely because of the diversity of codes, both cinematic and non-cinematic, at work in any film, and also because of the specificity of the relationship between spectator and film text, a relationship involving forms of subjectivity which evoke a series of psychic structures turning on relations of looking (Chapter 3). This has meant that detailed analyses of films, or even of sequences from films, according to this post-structuralist model are few in number and tend to be lengthy and toilsome. Moreover, they are for the most part not available in full in English (Bellour, 1972; Hanet, 1976), although Stephen Heath's analysis of *Touch of Evil* is an exception here (Heath, 1975a; Heath, 1975b). For these reasons it is difficult to discuss this form of textual analysis both adequately and succinctly. However, I shall none the less attempt to deal with this question by looking at one example of such analysis. The example I have chosen is taken from work by Raymond Bellour on the films of Alfred Hitchcock.

Bellour argues that the films he examines both voice and also function in terms of the abstract psychic systems of psychosis, neurosis and perversion (Bellour, 1979). The extract from Bellour's article reprinted here refers to a sequence in *Psycho* (Shamley, 1960) which precedes the murder of the film's central female character, Marion, and suggests that the murder, as well as other elements in the film, is prefigured in this particular sequence by a series of operations in which the images of birds, Marion, Norman and Norman's mother are linked together as associations across a complex and interrelated set of cinematic and narrative codes. These associations centre on the notions stuffed/mummified/dead, threat/penis/knife, and looking/ object of look/voyeurism. Bellour describes how this process works on the level of cinematic signification in the specific instance of a particular shot/reverse-shot figure in which Marion is positioned as being 'seen by the birds as much as she sees them' (see Stills 5.2–5.5), and suggests that this figure rhymes with a short sequence a little later in the film in which Norman spies on Marion through a hole cut through a picture on the wall adjoining the motel office and Marion's room (see Stills 5.6–5.10) – a sequence which, as Bellour points out, 'mimics the cinematographic apparatus itself'.

> The long segment during which Marion and Norman are face to face in the small reception room of the motel thus places face to face, fictitiously, two psychic structures: man and woman, the latter destined to become the prey of the former. The mirror arrangement that organizes their dialogue in a regulated alternation of shot-reverse shots ensures, between the two characters, the interchangeability necessary to their future substitution. It is here that Norman's family romance is presented, in the deceptive form in which it has been restructured by his desire, by the truth of his delirium, thus echoing the more disparate elements of Sam's and Marion's family romances, scattered throughout their dialogue in the hotel room. Thus, the two mental forms are brought together by similarity and exclusion: Marion grows aware of her own derangement because of the much more absolute derangement she senses in Norman. Their differential assimilation is concentrated in a metaphor with endless ramifications. '*Norman:* You – you eat like a bird.' The metaphor is no sooner spoken than it is denied. 'Anyway, I hear the expression "eats like a bird" – . . . it – it's really a fals-fals-fals-falsity. Because birds really eat a tremendous lot.' Marion has to be a bird, in order to be constituted as a body potentially similar to that of Norman's mother, object of his desire, stuffed just like the birds who survey their exchange. But Marion cannot really be a bird, because the bird's 'psychotic' appetite has been reserved for Norman, as the body transformed into the mother's body (even if, by a remarkable reversal, Norman eats nothing during the entire scene: 'It's all for you. I'm not hungry.').

5.2 *Psycho*: Marion in the motel office 'seen by the birds as much as she sees them'

5.3

5.4

5.5

5.6 *Psycho*: Marion as object of Norman's voyeuristic look

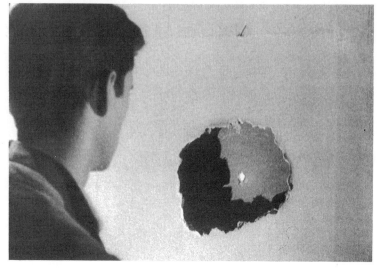

5.7

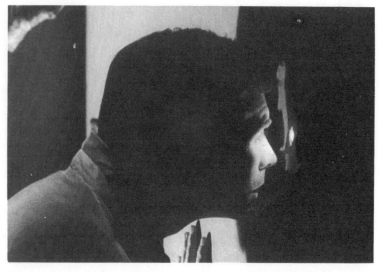

5.8

5.9

The reception room scene is meticulously organized to lead up to the murder scene. After an opening shot during which Norman appears amidst the stuffed birds disposed about the room, there are four shots showing Marion, standing, in alternation with the birds: the order of these shots (bird *a* – Marion – bird *b* – Marion) denotes her feeling that she is seen by the birds as much as she sees them, and that this disturbs her. After a repetition of shot 1 (Norman standing), there is a shot showing Norman and Marion together, seated on either side of a tray of food prepared by Norman. Then a classical alternation is established, dividing the shot between the two characters to distribute their dialogue. At the same time, a formal opposition emphasizes the fact that Norman, in this second alternation, has come to occupy, with respect to Marion, the place of the birds. In the various ways in which Norman is framed, he is associated with the outstretched beaks and widespread wings of one or several of the stuffed birds. Conversely, Marion is defined successively in two framings: she is beneath an oval painting whose theme was clearly visible during the second bird shot of the preceding alternation. The painting distinctly shows a band of angels, or, more precisely, a group of three women in which the central figure seems to be rising up to heaven, wings outspread. Next to the painting, in the same shot, the menacing shadow of a crow is projected onto the wall, penetrating the picture like a knifeblade or a penis. It is this complex whole that rivets Marion's attention, then splits apart when she takes her seat beneath the painting and becomes – through a double, metaphorical–metonymical inflection – defined by it, just as Norman is later emblematically defined by the birds. Thus the differential assimilation is continued: Marion, angel–woman–bird; Norman, bird–fetish–murderer. And thus is prefigured, in the intertwined motifs of alternation, the aggression of which she is soon to be the object (announced, when she rises, half concealing the painting, by the black beak of the crow that reappears inside the frame).

A few shots later, the alternation between Norman and Marion recommences, this time through an apparatus that mimics the cinematographic apparatus itself. Norman is concealed, significantly, by a painting which prefigures the effect he is to produce: *Suzanne and the Elders*, virtually at the moment of the rape. Beneath the painting is a large hole that reveals, in the wall itself, the tiny luminous hole to which Norman puts his eyes, creating – just like the projector's beam – an image which is for us virtual and for him almost real: Marion undressing, once again in the proximity of two birds, the portraits hanging on the wall of her bedroom near the bathroom door. The alternation then continues, obsessively marking the insert of the bulging eyeball, and shifting from the relationship between shots to the relationship between segments (or subsegments).

The next double series of shots, postponing voyeurism, intensifies it to the extreme:

a) Norman, under the influence of what he has seen, goes back to shut himself up in the house in order to imagine what will happen next – or better yet, what will happen metaphorically for him, given the premisses that catalyse his desire.

b) Marion, in her room, soon gets into the shower: the spectator, by this advance intrusion, is witness to the scene for which Norman's obsession has prepared the way.

The moment of the murder marks the invasion by the subject (hero and spectator together) of the constituted image of his phantasy. Here, alternation must be abandoned; it is ruptured by the brutal inscription on the image of the living body–knife–bird of Norman-the-mother, the reiterated fragmentation of Marion's body, the insert of her mouth agape in a horrendous scream and that of the dead eye that answers – at the opposite extreme of this very long fragment – the bulging eye of Norman given over to the inordinate desire of the scopic drive (Bellour, 1979, p. 114–16).

Bellour's analysis, even of this small part of a film, possesses all the detail and density of a dream analysis – which is exactly what makes it impossible to summarise. The comparison is in fact quite apt, because it is basically a psychoanalytic method that is being used here. The film, or the sequence, is being treated as analogous to a dream, and analysed by unpacking the condensations and displacements at work in the text. Thus the stuffed birds in the motel office are analysed as a condensed representation of a series of associations and issues governing the trajectory of the film – death, mummification and voyeurism, to name but a few. And the obsessive repetitiousness with which voyeurism is represented throughout the narrative content of *Psycho* may be regarded as constituting a series of displacements of both the central voyeuristic act of the film's narrative – Norman's aggressive, and finally murderous, gaze at Marion – and also, of course, of the voyeurism built into the cinematic apparatus itself. This kind of textual analysis therefore treats the text as a kind of discourse whose underlying system – its Unconscious, so to speak – must be unravelled, laid out and laid bare by the examination of concrete details. Such an examination would ideally attend to the whole range of cinematic and non-cinematic codes at work in a film, and provide as exhaustive an analysis as possible (although, of course, no analysis is ever complete). In this respect at least it differs from ideological analysis in degree rather than in kind. In ideological analysis, the objective is to expose the underlying operations of a text by means of a symptomatic reading, an attention to its silences, gaps and absences.

Textual (psycho)analysis simply extends the process by applying it to a wider range of textual operations and taking analysis a good deal further. If there is any qualitative distinction between ideological analysis and textual (psycho)analysis, it resides in the fact that the latter aims to organise analysis around attention to the dimension of cinematic address, of spectator–text relations as structuring the reception of a film, while the former would tend to focus more exclusively on the internal operations of the text.

But what does a psychoanalytic approach to textual analysis have to offer feminist film analysis? What space does it open up for feminist questions? The matter becomes rather more complex at this point than a notion of simply 'asking feminist questions' would indicate, for it begins to turn on the issue of the unconscious operations of the text. What actually emerges from a number of textual analyses is that the unspoken, or the unspeakable, in a text – its repressions, in other words – often pivot on what may be termed, in general, 'the feminine'. The repressed feminine may include, for example, certain aspects of sexuality which are not openly 'spoken' in a film's image or narrative but which in some measure nevertheless structure the text and make symptomatic appearances in it in various disguised or displaced forms. Or it may be a question of the repression of the discourse of the woman, of woman's narrative voice, by means of a cutting-off (as, for instance, in *Mildred Pierce* – see Chapter 2) of female control over the film's enunciation. Female sexuality and the discourse of the woman may in concrete instances operate in conjunction with each other through textual repressions. This is implied in the notion of 'woman's desire' as informing a film text. If female sexuality and female discourse are regarded as together posing the threat of disruption to the linear process of the classic narrative, then that threat must be recuperated or repressed if the story is to have any kind of 'satisfactory' resolution – a closure, that is, in which most or all the ends of the narrative are tied up.

Raymond Bellour's analyses of the films of Alfred Hitchcock – and indeed of the sequence from *Psycho* discussed above – do raise these very issues, if only tangentially. It has been said about Hitchcock's films that

> The woman is central ... insofar as the woman's desire is the central *problem* or challenge for the male protagonist ... Her desire, as evidenced by her look, narrativises the possibility and therefore the problem of sexual difference. The narrative then moves to reduce the image of the woman's

sexuality as a threat, thus the work of fetishisation: the pleasure of seeing the woman's body in pieces, a guarantee of the safety (coherence, totality) of the man's (Bergstrom, 1979a, p. 53).

What Bergstrom is suggesting here is first of all that the annulment of the threat posed by the feminine tends to be brought about in Hitchcock's films by a specific form of fetishisation in which the woman's body is cut up: not only at the level of cinematic representation, by a practice of editing which fragments the body of the woman in the film image, but also at the level of the narrative itself, in that the woman may be murdered, or at least subjected to or threatened with physical violence (see Stills 5.11–5.13). It is also implied that this fetishisation is an unconscious operation of the text, and that it is the work of textual analysis to uncover it.

The famous shower-bath murder sequence in *Psycho* is obviously a prime example of this operation. Bellour argues that the early part of the shower sequence sets up the possibility of the woman's autonomous pleasure, by making great – and in terms of the requirements of the narrative, even excessive – visual play with Marion's enjoyment of the shower: we see, for example, close-ups of parts of her naked body intercut with shots of gushing water, close-ups of her face showing pleasure, and so on (see Still 5.11). Furthermore, up to this point in the film, the story has been told largely through Marion's eyes: narrative point-of-view has been constructed as Marion's by means of a large number of shots from her optical point-of-view, so that the spectator has been quite literally put in the place of the central female character by a discursive enunciation. Before the murder, this identification opened up the possibilities of both female sexuality and female discourse. However, both are cut off with extreme violence at the moment of the murder, after which point the enunciation immediately assumes a much greater degree of distance and impersonality. It is as if at the same time as the woman (Marion) must be punished for her crime (stealing money), so the feminine must be repressed because of the threat it poses to a patriarchal order. Bellour concludes:

> The masculine subject can accept the image of woman's pleasure only on condition that, having constructed it, he may inscribe himself within it, and thus reappropriate it even at the cost of its (or her) destruction (Bellour, 1979, p. 121).

It is clear that this reappropriation by the 'masculine subject' refers not simply to the masculine as it informs culture, nor even only to the male

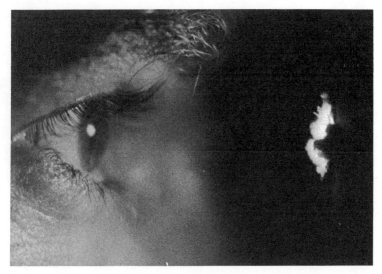

5.10

5.11 *Psycho*: the woman's autonomous pleasure . . .

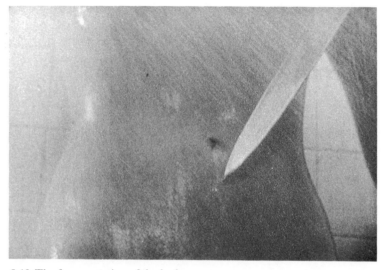

5.12 The fragmentation of the body ...

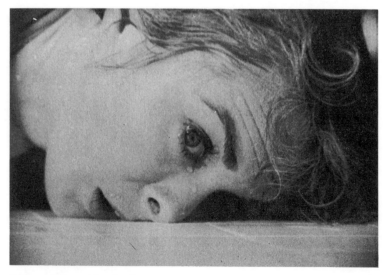

5.13 ... followed by death

protagonists of the film narrative, but also to the male spectators of the film. In seeking thus to account in detail for repressions in a film text and how these may be related to or written into its address, textual (psycho)analysis can begin to consider the question of the repression of the feminine in a patriarchy, and to chart some of the processes by which such repression operates at an unconscious level within cultural productions.

6

The Body in the Machine

While feminist perspectives in film theory and criticism have generated a substantial body of work on film texts, other potentially productive areas remain virtually unexplored. Textual analysis, in focusing on the internal operations of films as texts, tends to bracket questions concerning the institutional, social and historical contexts of their production, distribution and exhibition. An important step forward for feminist film theory would be work that attempts to bring together the focus on meaning production foregrounded in textual analysis with studies of the social and historical contexts in which films are made. Such work does actually raise methodological problems, not least because the epistemological groundings of most existing historical and institutional studies of cinema are often at some variance with those of structural, semiotic and psychoanalytic approaches to cinema. Moreover, the question of the significance of a specifically feminist perspective probably poses itself in rather different ways in relation to contextual analysis, in that a feminist perspective may inform the choice of what conjunctures – what instances and moments in the history of the institution, that is – to study, as well as the perspectives on, the character of, and the questions asked in, analysis. Nevertheless, no one will know whether a semiotically informed conjunctural analysis of the institution of cinema from a feminist perspective is possible unless it is seriously attempted. I intend in the present chapter to attempt to make some inroads in this area. Both the structure and the substance of my arguments here are therefore conditioned by the fact that this is a mapping of the field, an outline of potential areas of work, of questions that might be raised, approaches which might be taken.

There are a variety of areas in which feminist work on text and context could usefully proceed. Feminist analyses of individual film texts or groups of texts might be extended to take in their institutional, social and historical conditions of production: to permit, for example, study of the relationships between 'woman' as signifier in cinema and the position of women in society (Haralovich, 1979). Or an institutional structure within dominant cinema – the star system, say (Dyer, 1979) – might be examined for its embodiment of relationships between individual female stars, their films, the images constructed by fan magazines, publicity, and so on, and other components of the cinematic institution such as the social characteristics of audiences. Or a study of representations of women in films could inform a broader cultural analysis of representations of women across a variety of media in terms of the social and historical conditions of existence of such representations (Turim, 1979). Relationships between the operations of film texts and the institutional structures and processes at work in their moment of production can be properly uncovered, however, only by means of detailed studies of particular instances. I will therefore deal with feminist contextual analysis by demonstrating its procedures in one specific instance, that of a study of pornography. Pornography links a particular group of film texts with other media and with various institutional apparatuses. An important reason for my choice of this topic for investigation is its currency and urgency within feminist politics. Other significant but less immediate reasons should emerge in the course of discussion.

Before embarking on a discussion of pornography, some attempt at a definition is obviously in order. But even this first step is not a simple one. As a number of writers on the subject have pointed out, pornography is by no means a static and unchanging entity. On the contrary, it is a social construct, and thus subject to historical variation: no absolute or universal definition is possible. What is regarded as pornographic at one time or place, or within one cultural context, may not be regarded as such in other situations. None the less, I shall begin here by advancing a basic definition and considering the implications of such a definition for a feminist approach to pornography. I will then proceed by examining first of all some of the conditions surrounding historical variations in definitions of pornography, and then the nature and conditions of what I shall call, by analogy with my usage of the term 'cinematic apparatus', the pornographic apparatus. By this I mean the products, textual and institutional, of the historically specific interactions of economic, ideological and other conditions of existence of pornography. I shall follow the discussion of conditions of existence by a consideration of the pornographic apparatus as it relates specifically to cinematic institutions and film texts in Britain today.

First of all, how may pornography be defined? An examination of the word's origins in itself demonstrates the historical specificity of the concept: this nineteenth-century coinage originally – and perhaps from today's perspective, rather quaintly – referred to writings about prostitutes and their activities. Present-day pornography, at least in advanced capitalist societies, does not for the most part involve either writing (given the predominance of visual media) or exclusively prostitutes (pornographic representations now cover a much wider range of subjects and models). A definition with some degree of general cultural and historical applicability would need to cover all the various media – photography, film, video, literature – in which pornography appears, as well as the varied 'contents' of pornography. At the same time, since any such definition would, in order to cover all possible instances, have to be extremely general, it can really serve only as a beginning point for any more detailed consideration of the issue.

An important point to stress at the outset is that all pornography is representation. The implications of this obviously depend on whatever position is taken with regard to the nature of representation. I have argued throughout this book that representation is never a direct rendering or duplication of 'real world' events or actions, but is in varying degrees and in different ways coded. I have also argued that, as representations, films may nevertheless present themselves as uncoded: analysis of texts will then involve penetrating this uncoded appearance and tracing the operations of meaning construction. This applies equally to media other than cinema, thus to all media in which pornography appears, and hence to the textual characteristics of pornography itself. What, then, are the textual characteristics of pornography?

The Williams Report, the work of a committee appointed in the mid 1970s to report to the Home Office on the state of legislation on obscenity in England and Wales and to make recommendations for reforms, offers this definition:

> [A] pornographic representation is one that combines two features: it has a certain function or intention, to arouse its audience sexually, and also a certain content, explicit representations of sexual materials (organs,

postures, activity, etc.). A work has to have both this function and this content to be a piece of pornography (Home Office, 1979, p. 103).

The definition of the 'content' of pornography, in limiting itself to sexual material, probably restates a widespread understanding of what pornography is 'about', although what precisely constitutes the sexual is neither specified here, nor is it a matter of general consensus. However, the inclusion of a notion of 'function' in the definition is interesting in that, despite its conflation of intention and effect, the term does open up the question of a particular rhetoric, or mode of address, for pornography. In representing sexual material of various kinds, pornography sets up a position of a particular sort for a specific spectator or reader. In calling forth sexual arousal, it addresses the reader in certain ways as a sexed and sexual subject. Clearly, pornography may not have this effect all the time for all possible readers: what I want to suggest is that the rhetoric of pornography privileges a reader–text relationship of this kind.

The definition of pornography as involving both representations of sexual material and also a certain (function) – or, as I have specified it, a certain reader–text relation – is one which is probably general enough to cover all the forms, media, and social–historical contexts of pornography. However, the question of what 'sexual material' means, of what is representable in what degree and in what context, is historically variable, as is the nature of material which will tend to evoke sexual arousal. The differences between nineteenth-century Japanese and contemporary Western pornography illustrate this point quite clearly (Bos and Pack, 1980). In their own cultural contexts, both types would fall within the terms of the Williams Committee's definition, and yet they are completely different from one another in a number of ways. If discussions of pornography are to proceed beyond a very general level, therefore, our definition clearly needs some refinement. But since any refined definition immediately loses some of the range of its applicability, certain types and manifestations of pornography in different contexts will automatically be excluded by it. Given then that pornography is contextually specific, it would perhaps be more to the point here to abandon any further search for a definition covering all cases and concentrate instead on attempting to delineate the terms of its specificity. In other words, a discussion of pornography at any but the most general level calls for a model which will define and describe the conditions of its social and historical variability.

Among feminists, pornography is a much-discussed and often highly charged issue, and it has also inspired a good deal of political activity. In this context, two questions call for consideration. First, why is pornography of interest to feminists? And second – and related – is a feminist analysis of pornography possible? I will address the first question by taking up the general definition of pornography discussed above. Full consideration of the second, however, demands – and must also inform – a theory or model of the pornographic apparatus in its historical specificity. Any attempt to address the question of why pornography is of interest to feminists demands in itself some measure of specification of the general definition. To the extent that pornographic representations involve 'sexual material', pornography will frequently, though not necessarily always, also involve representations of women. To take the matter any further than this, however, it is already necessary to introduce a measure of contextual specificity into the debate, bearing in mind that the current feminist interest in pornography is confined for the most part to its contemporary Western visual variants. In these, women are frequently portrayed in particular ways: either unclothed or, if not, strategically clad in garments or accessories which represent anything from slight states of undress to various fetishes and sexual perversions – unbuttoned blouses, high-heeled shoes, suspender belts, black stockings, through to leather and rubber gear, whips, chains and so on. But it is perhaps the rhetoric of these representations as much as, or more than, their immediate connotations which has seized the attention of feminists. In an address to male spectators,[1] the body of woman is constructed as a spectacle and the *mise en scène* of representations of women's bodies coded in various ways as both to be looked at by the spectator and, in the same process, to evoke sexual arousal in him. These codes include the way in which the body is posed and lit, the overall composition of the image – including props, gesture, clothes and accessories – and the nature and direction of the gaze of the model. This is what is implied by the notion of 'objectification' in certain representations of the female body.

Feminists may argue that many of the codes at work in pornographic representations operate similarly in less esoteric and more 'everyday' representations of women – in advertisements, fashion magazines and elsewhere – and that the connotations surrounding such representations and their typical modes of address cut across various matters of expression and constitute (and are constituted by) socially prevailing forms of sexism (Coward, 1981). Pornography is therefore of interest to feminists to the extent that, in constructing certain representations of women, it codes *woman* in a general way as sign, as an object, that is, of (implicitly male) looking. At the same time, it may have this property in common with other more readily available and culturally prevalent representations of women.

Pornographic representations of women may therefore be of interest to feminists to the extent that they trade on a series of relations of reading whereby the signifier 'woman' is coded as object. This works not only in relation to various psychic structures of looking but also, because pornography is business, in an economic exchange:

> The female body is not only a sex-object, but also an object of exchange; its value can be sold (prostitution) or it can be incorporated into another commodity which can be sold ([e.g.] ... film) (Turim, 1979, p. 56).

But there is another sense in which pornography may be of interest to feminists, and this relates to the fact that, in some of its variants, pornography depicts sexual acts involving women. These are not necessarily the same as the representations discussed above, in that representations of women's bodies may not, and indeed frequently do not, also involve representations of sexual activity. The distinction I am making corresponds in part with current understandings of the distinction between 'soft-core' and 'hard-core' pornography. The stock in trade of soft-core is mainly representations of women, nude or strategically accessorised, usually involving most or all of the body, and coded in such a way as to constitute an address directed immediately outward to the spectator – a 'come-on' – or to suggest a private masturbatory fantasy in relation to which the spectator is situated as voyeur (Bos and Pack, 1980). Only in the latter is sexual activity represented: and in this case, it is autoerotic. Hard-core pornography, on the other hand, represents other-directed sexual activities of various kinds, and in so doing constitutes a spectator–text relation of a rather different character from that typical of soft-core. The mode of address of hard-core is distinguishable primarily by the fact that it is sexual activity, rather than the bodies of participants, which is constituted as the object of the spectator's look. In this sense, hard-core representations of sexual activities involving women may pose the question of women's sexual pleasure in a way that soft-core does not. The questions of representation on the one hand and of women's sexual pleasure on the other may thus also be instrumental in defining the terms of a feminist interest in pornography.

At the same time, however, while most non-feminist discourses around pornography – legal discourses in particular – tend to be directed at what I have defined here as hard-core, feminist analysis and activity tends rather to be concentrated on soft-core: on pornography, that is, whose address is constituted predominantly by certain coded representations of the female body. There are good reasons for this, reasons that may be sought in differences between the premises of feminism as against those of other discourses. The law in particular tends to constitute pornography as socially pathological, or at least as exceptional, and therefore as containable by legal sanction: to regard it, in other words, as qualitatively different from other culturally available representations. Feminist discourses, on the other hand, are more likely to regard pornography as merely occupying one point on a continuum of representations of women, a continuum along which are also situated such commonly available and highly socially visible representations as advertisements. The latter may generate as much protest from feminists as the former, moreover, on the grounds that 'For the statement "pornography is part of everyday sexism" it is the everyday which is perhaps more galling than the exotic' (Brown, 1981, p. 6).

This suggests that a feminist approach to pornography immediately challenges other definitions of, and discourses around, pornography current in society. With this in mind, I want to outline a model for analysing the pornographic apparatus in its different forms at particular moments in history. In attempting to specify the various conditions bearing on what is constituted as pornography in different social and historical contexts, such analysis necessarily moves beyond a general definition of its object. At this point, however, I shall still consider pornography across the various media – photographs, magazines, films, and so on – in which it appears, despite the fact that differences between media may have important consequences for the operation of the pornographic apparatus. The nature of the representations of the female body and female sexuality that are part of the province of pornographic texts in various media is historically specific. That is to say, the ways in which women are depicted in pornography are not static and unchanging but vary according to time and place. Any feminist analysis of pornography needs not only to take this into account, but also can usefully aim to specify the conditions or determinants of the state of the pornographic apparatus at any particular conjuncture. What, in general terms, are these conditions, and in what ways do they shape the pornographic apparatus? The model I am advancing here is based on the premiss that the pornographic apparatus is a social structure which takes its specific form from the state and conjunction of a set of other structures or social formations. These structures may sometimes operate in concert with one another – they may, that is, be overdetermined – in defining the state of the pornographic apparatus. On the other hand, structures may sometimes work autonomously, or even in contradictory ways.

I have defined the pornographic apparatus, or its state at any moment, as the textual and institutional product of the historically specific interactions of its economic, ideological and other conditions of existence. However, in order to consider how the pornographic apparatus is actually shaped in any one context, analysis needs to descend from this level of abstraction and examine the actual state of its 'conditioning' structures. I shall look briefly at three such structures, which I term, rather loosely, the economic, the legal and the patriarchal. In my discussion I shall attempt to specify their operation in as concrete a manner as possible while holding analysis at the relatively general level of the current state of the apparatus of pornography across various media in Western capitalist societies, Britain in particular.

Economic Conditions

The economic conditions of the pornographic apparatus are in a very general way shaped by economic relations prevailing in the society as a whole. Since I have confined my analysis to Western capitalist societies, such prevailing relations will be, by definition, capitalist. But capitalism, of course, takes a variety of forms: it may, for example, take in a range of relationships between state and private sectors of the economy. Despite such variations, however, it seems safe to say that pornography is always a province of private enterprise. There are doubtless historical variations in the ways in which the pornography industry fits into the overall economy, variations which will be determined by existing states of the law as it touches on pornography. Thus sectors of the pornography industry might, for example, be a visible (if a pariah) sector of the overall structures of private enterprise, a situation the more likely in times and places where laws surrounding its products are relatively relaxed. This might describe the current situation in Denmark and other Scandinavian countries, for example.

Where, on the other hand, legal proscriptions of various kinds exist and are systematically enfored against the pornography industry, it will tend to become an 'underground' form of private enterprise, a black market. The characteristics of a black market in pornography will tend to be conditioned in turn by the specific terms of the law and the areas within which, and the degree to which, it is enforced.

An instance of this process at work is cited in the Williams Report, in the context of a discussion of self-regulation by the pornography trade. The imprecise terms of current British obscenity laws, together with the fact that these laws give the police powers of search and seizure, has meant that publishers, distributors and retailers of certain 'adult' publications have been unsure of the legal limit of what could be represented in their magazines – that is, what kinds of representations would or would not excite the attentions of police forces in various parts of the country. When police seize material, the trade stands, of course, to lose money. Accordingly, the British Adult Publications Association was formed by a group of publishers, distributors and retailers of sex magazines, with the aim of providing guidelines for members

> of what they considered material unacceptable for this type of publication based on what had been found in certain previous legal proceedings to be obscene or not obscene, and members of the Association agreed to observe these in the magazines they produced and sold from September 1977 (Home Office, 1979, p. 42).

In this instance, in making a public attempt to regulate itself, a section of the pornography industry is asserting that it is a respectable and responsible part of the economy. Such attempts at 'integration' on the part of the pornography trade with the overall structures of private enterprise are the more likely to occur to the extent, first of all, that the product occupies a borderline between what may or may not be regarded as illegal, and secondly and relatedly, that the nature of actual enforcement of obscenity laws – or indeed of the terms of the laws themselves – becomes more relaxed in certain areas. At another extreme, however, sections of the pornography industry dealing in material which is absolutely legally proscribed would be driven underground, and would attempt to keep their very existence concealed from public scrutiny. It is exactly this kind of area where, it has been suggested, organised crime takes an interest in pornography.

The economic conditions of the pornographic apparatus, or more specifically the relationship between the pornography industry and the economy, are formed crucially by the state of relevant laws and their enforcement. Apart from this, other determinants may be at work. These may include the state of certain codes of morality and their political articulation within pressure groups (such as, in Britain, the Festival of Light and, in the USA, Moral Majority). Another pertinent factor with economic implications is technology – in particular at present the availability and cost of mechanical means of producing visual representations. The possibility, for example, of printing colour photographs in large numbers and relatively cheaply must be an important factor in the prevalence and profitability of the 'adult' magazine market. The more recent proliferation in Western societies of home video technology, too, has been instrumental in generating a new, immensely profitable, and virtually uncontrollable area of enterprise for the pornography industry (Parry and Jordan, 1981a).

Legal Conditions

Apart from their role in relation to the structures of the pornography industry, legal constraints may be instrumental in producing social definitions of what is and what is not pornography. This definitional process tends to work in a somewhat tautologous fashion: representations of certain kinds are pornographic if they are proscribed by law, and pornography may be defined as legally proscribed representations of certain kinds. Such reasoning, circular as it may be, does describe in broad terms socially available understandings of what pornography is – given, of course, a legal definition of the 'certain kinds' of representations which are to be proscribed.[2] However, although everyday understandings may be founded on, or may bolster, legal definitions of pornography or obscenity, complete precision in legal definition is in fact impossible. Take, for example, the legal test in the USA of what is considered obscene: representations which, among other things, 'Depict or describe sexual conduct in a patently offensive way' (Home Office, 1979, p. 219). It is evident that since both 'sexual conduct' and 'offensive' cannot be precisely defined before the fact, the test of obscenity must rest finally with the courts. But legal precedent has demonstrated that, even when based on a single set of statutes, judgements as to what is or is not obscene vary from time to time and from place to place. Such variations may furthermore have retroactive effects on the pornographic apparatus itself. The attempts at self-regulation of a section of the British pornography trade, discussed above, illustrate this point quite well: the problem faced by the members of the association concerned was largely definitional – the current state of the law and its enforcement made it difficult to know in advance what kinds of representation were 'obscene' and what were not.

At the same time, the fact that certain representations which are not currently legally proscribed in Britain are still sometimes regarded as pornographic suggests that at any one moment there exist varying and sometimes competing definitions of pornography and obscenity. The legal is simply one such definition, although it may by its very nature assume some kind of privileged status in relation to others. The proposals of the Williams Committee, however, are premised on the liberal assumption that the law, far from being a privileged discourse, can do no more than 'hold the ring' for competing social definitions of pornography. It is significant that the feminist notion of 'forms of feminine visibility' (Brown, 1981, p. 15) exceeds even the Williams Report's liberal terms of definition.

Patriarchal Relations

The economic and the legal, taken together, do not exhaust the conditions of existence of the pornographic apparatus: they cannot, for example, fully explain the textual characteristics of pornography, its codes and modes of address. It seems to me that another, and rather more difficult to specify, set of conditions is also at work here. These conditions are in some sense ideological, but as a description the term 'ideological' is none the less too broad, since both economic and legal conditions have their own ideological components and effects. I have adopted the handy but rather imprecise 'patriarchal' to refer to this set of conditions. In using this term, I am suggesting that although modes of address in pornographic representations in general may be a feature of a patriarchal order, any specification of the pornographic apparatus demands not only a consideration of other structures (economic and legal, for example), but also an examination of the precise character of patriarchal social relations at any particular conjuncture. Among patriarchal social relations might be included, for example, the current state of power relations between women and men, both within the family and outside it, the overall position of women of different classes and races within society, current sexual mores, and codes of conduct governing social and sexual relations between women and men. Patriarchal relations may also set the terms for forms of subjectivity available in the reader–text relations set up by pornography. The instances of the operation of patriarchal relations in the pornographic apparatus considered below take up the issues of social relations and psychic relations respectively.

A common explanation for the fact that increasingly 'extreme' pornographic representations are currently falling outside the scope of obscenity laws and their enforcement in Britain appeals to a notion of increased levels of 'permissiveness' in sexual conduct as a causal factor. However, attention to the operation of patriarchal social relations in their historical specificity indicates that the situation is rather more complex than such an explanation would suggest. The 'permissiveness' argument does not, for example, take account of the fact that there was no law on the British statute book relating specifically to pornographic representations before the passage of the Obscene Publications Act of 1857 – the earlier common law offence of obscene libel did not relate specifically to representations. Thus before the middle of the nineteenth century, pornography could be produced and circulated more or less unchecked by legal sanction, and there is indeed evidence to suggest that a good deal of pornography was in fact available during the period (Marcus, 1969). At the same time, social and sexual conduct between women and men could hardly be regarded as 'permissive': in terms of patriarchal social relations, the period is marked on the contrary by a clear gender separation of social and affective spheres, at least in the middle classes. Given the separation of spheres – within a broader context of social and power relations between the sexes – it might be concluded that the very considerable traffic in pornography took place more or less exclusively on the male side of the gender divide, certainly as far as 'respectable' middle-class women were concerned (and class is clearly an important factor here). This would render pornography in effect invisible both on the female side of the divide and also, as a consequence of the sexual mores of the dominant class, in public. In other words, the differences we may perceive between the situations in Britain today and in early Victorian times as regards pornography may not be as great as is often thought, and may in any case not be totally explicable within the terms of the 'permissiveness' argument. There are, of course, other factors involved in this situation. Changes in the nature of the media in which pornography is produced, for instance – particularly the development during this century of relatively inexpensive visual pornography – will obviously be an overdetermining factor here.

For my second example, I refer to the question of the spectator–text relations set up by contemporary visual hard-core pornography. Writers on this subject argue that there is currently a crisis in representation pivoting on the problematic and disturbing character, for males, of representations of female sexuality. John Ellis, for example, suggests that such representations are potentially subversive of dominant relations of subjectivity, while Paul Willemen's argument is rather that the address of hard-core constitutes an obsessive movement towards a confirmation of the male viewer's phallic power, a movement which is never quite brought off, because gratification cannot in fact be found in pornography (Ellis, 1980; Willemen, 1980). In either case – and the two arguments are not, I think, mutually exclusive – some important conclusions concerning patriarchal relations and the pornographic apparatus can be drawn.

Ellis offers an explanation for representations of sexual violence towards women in pornography in terms of a 'punishment' for the unfathomability of woman's sexual pleasure. Such representations, he argues, try obsessively to get to the bottom of the enigma by their repetitious cataloguing of sexual activities:

> The pornographic film text responds by multiplying instances of possible pleasure by multiplying its little stories of sexual incidents. Either that, or ... it turns upon the object of the enquiry, the woman, and vents its (and the audience's) frustrations at the impossibility of gaining an answer to the question, by attacking her for her obstinate refusal to yield the impossible secret (Ellis, 1980, p. 105).

Willemen explains hard-core pornography in terms of a crisis of male self-confidence, and suggests that the fact that this 'coincides with the growth of the women's movement may well not be merely a coincidence' (Willemen, 1980, p. 61). There may, that is, be a degree of compensatory wish-fulfilment at work in contemporary pornography, a wish for woman once more to be powerless. Taken together, the two arguments offer an interesting explanation, in terms of patriarchal relations, for the current proliferation, and also the increasingly violent nature, of hard-core pornography.

Cinema and Pornography

A consideration of pornographic representations in recent cinema and the place of such representations within cinematic institutions and the pornographic apparatus calls for an examination not only of the conditions of existence, but also of the textual operations and spectator–text relationships, of pornographic film. This is obviously a large project. What I propose to do here is limit it by focusing attention on some films that are situated on the borderline of what may be defined as pornographic, and examine their location within a set of social and ideological parameters. My reasons for choosing 'marginal' representations are threefold. First, for reasons already discussed, certain socially visible representations of women – 'everyday sexism' – are often of more immediate concern to feminists than are the more exotic and less widely available manifestations of hard-core pornography. Second, because of the availability of the kinds of films discussed here through 'mainstream' exhibition outlets, readers of this book are likely to have the opportunity of seeing, or films like them, and thus be in a position to draw their own conclusions. And finally, the very marginality and social visibility of the films I shall be looking at serve actually to problematise them in relation to their conditions of existence. In consequence, they foreground many of the contradictions surrounding certain kinds of representations of women.

I shall be making reference here to three films which involve representations of female sexuality and of sexual violence towards women: *Nea* (Kaplan, Les Films la Boétie, 1976), which was first released in Britain in 1977 under the title *A Young Emmanuelle*; *L'Amour violé* (Bellon, Films de l'Equinoxe, 1977), released in the USA in 1979 as *Rape of Love*; and *Dressed to Kill* (de Palma, Filmways, 1980). But first I will consider some of the conditions surrounding the current reception of films of this kind in Britain. On an institutional level, these include the state of structures of production, distribution and exhibition in the film industry, legal discourses concerning obscenity or indecency in film, and institutions of film censorship. The institutional intersects with the textual in considerations involving the proliferation of certain cycles of films, relationships between legal and other institutional discourses, and the specificity of cinema as a signifying process. Each of the films I will discuss occupies its own space within this complex and interrelated set of determinations.

The specificity of cinematic pornography, as against pornography in other media, is the basis of some important legal distinctions in Britain. Until as recently as 1977, film was excluded from the provisions of the Obscene Publications Act, being governed instead by common law tests of indecency and obscene libel. What this meant in practice was that it was impossible to construct a legal defence of individual shots and sequences in films on the grounds of the integrity or artistic merit of the work as a whole. The law, in other words, was unable to take into account the overall context of isolated representations. However, the fact that the Obscene Publications Act has now been extended to cinema means that the current legal test of obscenity rests on whether or not a film in its entirety has the tendency to 'deprave and corrupt' a significant proportion of its likely audience. This change has significant implications for 'marginal' representations. Film was originally excluded from the provisions of the Obscene Publications Act on the grounds that it was unnecessary for a medium which was already subject to its own censorship (see below) to be covered also by obscenity laws. But the fact that distinctions in legal discourses around obscenity and indecency in film as against other media remained for so long, and indeed still persist, suggests that more fundamental considerations may also be involved. The Williams Committee, for example, argues strongly for the continuation of film censorship, while at the same time recommending that, for the most part, pornography in other media should fall outside the scope of laws on obscenity. The grounds on which the distinction is made are precisely those of cinematic specificity and spectator–text relations in cinema. The experience of seeing a film, the committee argues, is altogether different from that of looking at other published material:

> [T]he close-up, fast cutting, the sophistication of modern make-up and special effects techniques, the heightening effect of sound effects and music all combine on the large screen to produce an impact which no other medium can create (Home Office, 1979, p. 145).

Added to the peculiar power of cinematic address, suggests the committee, is the fact that film is aimed at mass audiences. The notion of a mass audience here seems to imply not so much audience size as the public character of the film-viewing situation. It is implied that film viewing, calling as it does for special premises as well as for public displays and advertisements aimed at attracting passers-by, makes film a socially visible medium. Given the overall thrust of the report's recommendations towards restricting the visibility of pornography, film presents something of a problem. Recommendations for the censorship and rating of pornographic films and for the provision of special 'porno' film theatres are aimed at dealing with this troublesome aspect of pornographic cinema. The recommendation that post-production censorship of films should continue on much the same basis as it currently operates is addressed more immediately to the problem of the impact on spectators of cinematic representations.

Although in Britain local authorities hold legal powers of film censorship, they almost invariably accept the recommendations on individual films put forward by the British Board of Film Censors. The BBFC is a body set up by film trade associations and as such has no legal status, but does command the support of both the film industry and the legally constituted censorship authorities. Producers or distributors who want their films to be exhibited in public cinemas must submit them to the board for censorship. The board in its turn is responsible for conferring various categories of certificate indicating films' suitability to particular kinds of audiences, for recommending cuts, or for refusing certificates. If a film is not exhibited in a public cinema, it does not require a certificate, and thus does not need to be submitted to the censor. Cinema clubs, which must legally have some minimal membership requirements, are free, therefore, to exhibit uncensored films. The censors consequently never see the bulk of hard-core films released in Britain. The films discussed here, however, do not fall into that category.

The legal and censorship institutions, certainly as they relate to films for public exhibition, have retroactive effects on the film industry itself. Film producers tend, for example, to take into account current conventions governing what is or is not acceptable to the censor: thus in the case, say, of a film made for international distribution, several versions may be cut to conform to the predilections of film censors in different parts of the world. It is widely acknowledged, for example, that representations of certain violent acts are less acceptable to censors in Britain than they may be elsewhere. In any one country, therefore, legal and quasi-legal institutions relating to cinematic representations may have certain effects across a range of other institutions, both at home and abroad. For example, the operations of the industry, legal discourses and censorship practices intersect with those of cinematic signification in the development of cycles of films. A film cycle can proliferate quite rapidly from the commercial success of one film, a success which other producers may then attempt to exploit by producing films of a very similar kind: the spate of 'knife films' of the early 1980s is a case in point. The first films in a new cycle may establish the parameters of what is acceptable by in effect testing the censorship institutions: later films in the cycle may then trade off a more or less established set of limits. When it becomes clear that the exploitation of a new cycle is in progress, censors may respond in turn by restricting the limits of what they will accept.

The conditions of the release in Britain of *Nea* illustrate the ways in which film cycles can have their own institutional and textual effects. In this case, the structures of distribution and exhibition – rather than those of production – were instrumental in the situation. *Nea* deals with adolescent sexuality through the story of a young woman, Sybille, who writes an erotic novel. In the course of her writing, Sybille witnesses and experiences various sexual activities. Sybille is represented as having supernatural powers, and it is by exercising these powers that she gets what she wants. *Nea* was made in France by a woman director, Nelly Kaplan: but when the film came to Britain in 1977 it was dubbed and retitled *A Young Emmanuelle*, released with an X certificate (passed as suitable for exhibition only to adults of 18 years and over), and exhibited in cinemas specialising in soft-core pornography. What is of interest here is the fact that a text that was, in intent at least, more of an art house film than soft-core pornography could be transformed from the one into the other by a set of institutional processes. This serves concretely to demonstrate both that text and context operate together in the production of meanings, and also that readings are generated in the conditions of reception of film texts. A causal explanation of these events may be sought on the one hand in the conditions of development of film cycles, and on the other in the current state of institutions of film distribution and exhibition in Britain. *A Young Emmanuelle* was released in the midst of a cycle of sex films with the name 'Emmanuelle' in the title. This cycle was an exploitation of the enormous success of the first of its kind, *Emmanuelle*, which ran continuously in London for several years, and any subsequent film with 'Emmanuelle' in its title was immediately marked, without the necessity for further details, as a sex film. But while this may explain why *Nea* was retitled as it was, it does not account for the fact that the film was taken up in the first place by the soft-core market. Here the explanation lies in the state of art house distribution and exhibition. The small art house market in Britain is virtually the only outlet for certain kinds of subtitled foreign-language films. Consequently, relatively few such films find their way into British cinemas. *Nea*, because of its subject matter, found a different market, but in order to meet the requirements of that market was transformed so as to privilege a particular reading. Perhaps because of the interest generated by Kaplan's work among feminists, however, a subtitled print of the film has now been released in Britain under its original title.

L'Amour violé is similar to *Nea* both in its serious intentions regarding the treatment of sexuality, and also in its inclusion of representations of sexual activity. Like *Nea*, too, it was made as an art house movie and directed by a woman. It has not been released in Britain, but a subtitled print is in distribution in the USA under the title *Rape of Love*. *L'Amour violé* is the story of a victim of a gang rape who decides, against the counsel of her family, her boyfriend and her attackers' relatives, to bring the rapists to justice. Early in the film there is a lengthy sequence depicting the rape itself. This sequence raises important questions for feminist film theory concerning the ways in which, under various circumstances, representations of this kind may be read, even given an overall narrative context in which a rape victim is sympathetically portrayed.[3]

Although *L'Amour violé* itself has not been submitted to the British censors, a film of its kind would probably be passed with an X certificate without cuts. There are at least two reasons for this, which relate to the current legal situation and its consequences for censorship practices. The fact that film is now governed by the Obscene Publications Act permits the censor to take the overall character of a film into account when making a decision. This means that *L'Amour violé* would probably, by virtue of its narrative trajectory, be regarded as a worthwhile film in which a representation of an act of rape is entirely justified: first of all, by the fact that the motivation of the narrative is the act of rape itself, and second in the fact that the victim is sympathetically characterised, and brings the rapists to justice. Depictions of rape and other acts of sexual violence are judged by the censors in terms of their function in the film's narrative, so that certain representations which are regarded as excessive to the requirements of the narrative may be cut. At the same time, some representations involving sexual violence are inadmissible under any circumstances (Home Office, 1979, p. 30). Nevertheless, it is significant that in general it is questions of narrative structure, rather than of spectacle, which govern censorship practices.

The issue of representation of sexual violence towards women is also raised, albeit in a very different way, by *Dressed to Kill*, a film which has been the subject of condemnation by many feminists. Although the violent attacks on women in *Dressed to Kill* are not, as in the case of the rape in *L'Amour violé*, directly sexual, it can be argued that the murder and the attempted murders in the film are narratively motivated by women's sexual fantasies and activities. The murder victim, Kate, bloodily slashed to death in a lift with a cut-throat razor, is doubly marked as 'guilty': first in the immediate sense that just before the murder takes place she engages in a sexual liaison with a complete stranger (who, to reinforce the point about the destructiveness of sexuality, is revealed to be a carrier of VD). Furthermore, as it turns out, Kate is also 'guilty' of having sexually aroused her (male) psychiatrist, whose transsexual female *alter ego* is responsible for the murder. Not only, therefore, are women represented as guilty of being victims: it is in effect also a 'woman' who is guilty of the crime of murder. Women are marked as victims also at the level of the specifically cinematic: this is particularly evident in numerous sequences involving optical point-of-view shots on the film's second would-be victim, Liz (who, significantly, is a prostitute). Because reverse shots are withheld, the source of point-of-view is never explicit. The uncertainty as to the identity of Liz's watcher is thereby rendered highly threatening. Despite all this, however, there is little or nothing in the film that would invite censorship.

Although the version of *Dressed to Kill* shown in Britain and in the USA had several shots cut from it – shots depicting degrees of violence deemed unacceptable – the censors' requirements had nothing to do with the film's misogyny. Apart from outright rejection, which is very unlikely in an instance of this kind, no form of censorship (which in the final instance works only at the level of specific moments in a film) can meet a critique of *Dressed to Kill* which points to a general attitude towards women and female sexuality structuring the film's narrative and cinematic codes. How can patriarchal ideology be censored? The case of *Dressed to Kill* offers a powerful illustration of how the terms of a feminist discourse on forms of 'feminine visibility' can exceed those of dominant legal and quasi-legal discourses, however liberal, on obscenity and pornography.

PART IV

Replacing Dominant Cinema:

Feminism and Film Practice

In the fourth part of this book, I want to move away from issues relating exclusively to dominant cinema and the kinds of questions a feminist perspective might raise for it. In these three chapters, I will look at alternatives to dominant cinema which may be regarded as relevant to a feminist cultural politics. Such alternatives are not necessarily confined to types of cinema whose overt 'content' is informed by a consciously feminist intent on the part of film makers: I will consider also cinema which operates outside the institutional and textual structures of dominant cinema to construct either subject matters, or modes of address, or ways of going about producing, distributing and exhibiting films, or various combinations of these, in ways that might be understood as 'feminist'. I begin, in Chapter 7, by addressing the question of realism — or better, realisms — by examining forms of cinema which, in textual terms, operate in varying degrees within the limits of dominant modes of cinematic signification, while at the same time posing alternatives of other kinds. Such a discussion does call for a consideration of dominant cinema and how it may be informed by feminism, but it also involves looking at a number of film practices which operate, institutionally speaking, outside dominant structures. In Chapter 8, I discuss feminist 'countercinemas' — work on cinematic signification which, in challenging dominant processes of meaning production, may be regarded as exemplary of feminist or feminine 'cinematic writing'. These alternatives are discussed at this point in terms of their textual strategies, although in institutional terms they all also operate outside dominant cinematic apparatuses. Institutions are the central concern of Chapter 9, in which oppositional approaches to film production, distribution and exhibition are examined in relation to the textual practices discussed in the two preceding chapters.

7

Real Women

In opening up consideration of feminism as film practice by discussing variants of cinematic realism, I am perhaps approaching the question in exactly the way it most immediately presents itself to many cinema-goers. If only because one of the principal characteristics of dominant cinema is that it embodies certain forms of realism, most cinema-goers are familiar and comfortable with realism, particularly in its narrative forms. But certain kinds of cinema other than classic narrative – notably documentary – are also frequently regarded as 'realist'. What, then, do different types of realist cinema have in common? The basic shared characteristic of all forms of cinematic realism is their tendency to transparency in representation: what is seen on the cinema screen appears to the spectator to be constructed in much the same way as its referent, the 'real world'. The film, that is, 'looks like' the real world. This is what makes realist films easy to watch and follow: they seem to duplicate spectators' everyday ways of experiencing the world. This realistic appearance is in fact brought about not by a duplication of 'real world' referents but by certain conventions of cinematic signification. All films are coded: it is simply that certain types of film are coded in such a way as actually to seem uncoded. Thus, for example, the codes at work in classic Hollywood cinema (see Chapter 2) operate in certain ways to obscure the processes of meaning construction in which the spectator is constantly engaged. The transparency of realist cinema then consists in the fact that the spectator is seldom actually aware in watching a film that she or he is making meanings: meaning seems to be there already in the film, the spectator's only task being to sit back and take it in. This of course, is one of the pleasures of the classic realist cinema: an address which draws the spectator in to the representation by constructing a credible and coherent cinematic world, which at the same time situates her or him as a passive consumer of meanings which seem to be already there in the text.

While realism can be a defining characteristic of both fictional (the classic narrative, for example) and non-fictional (the documentary film) cinemas, all realist forms have the 'appearance of reality' in common. Cinesemiotics, in tracing the ways in which this transparency is coded, has tended to confine its analysis to fictional narrative cinema. However, it is equally important for our purposes to look at the codes at work in non-fictional realist cinema. The apparently uncoded character of all realist cinema is what lends it its verisimilitude: a certain kind of credibility in relation to the 'real world' is set up, and the spectator undergoes a 'suspension of disbelief'. This process works rather differently with non-fiction than it does with fictional realism. The defining characteristics of fiction as against non-fiction film lie in the dual operations of narrativity and characterisation. In watching a fiction film, the spectator is involved in two forms of identification. One is with the momentum of the narrative itself, from the disruption of a fictional equilibrium which constitutes its beginning, through the movement towards resolution and then final closure. The other identification is with the narrative's central character or characters. In these identification processes, the spectator is in varying degrees, depending on the linearity and economy of the narrative and the representation of central characters in terms of their fictional personality traits, drawn into the world of the film. The operation of the specific cinematic codes associated with fictional realism – continuity editing, close-ups, shot/reverse shot structures and point-of-view shots – serves to reinforce the spectator's identification with a credible fictional world. Although realism as representation does not of course normally lead spectators to confuse the boundaries of the world of cinematic narrative with those of the 'real world', its address – its processes of fictional identification in particular – none the less does set up a kind of credibility that is well described by the notion of suspension of disbelief. The credibility of non-fiction film tends to work rather differently, however. A general point to be made about the realism of documentary as against that of fiction film is that its address typically constitutes an appeal to some kind of empirical conceptual-isation of the visible as 'evidence': if it is on the screen, it must be true

(Kuhn, 1978a). This kind of credibility obviously rests on transparency: the cinematic image constitutes itself as a record of 'reality'. The specificity of documentary forms of transparency is that the image appears to be 'natural' – an unmediated transposition of one reality onto another – as well as 'real' – as setting up, that is, an internally credible film world.

Documentary film thus always makes implicit reference not only to its profilmic event, but also to the 'real world' in general. While this visibility is constituted as 'truth' by the apparent naturalness of the representation, this very 'naturalness' is itself an outcome of the operation of a certain set of cinematic codes. Cinematic signifiers such as monochrome image, apparently haphazard mobile framing (the mark of a hand-held camera), focus shifts, editing which is rather more 'free' than would be the case with fictional cinema, and direct gaze at the camera by protagonists of the film, all currently tend to mark a film as a documentary. Further sets of codes relating to sound may also connote 'documentariness'. Many documentary films have voice-over: a voice from a source outside and apparently 'above' the world of the film speaks a discourse which directs the spectator's reading of the film. The documentary voice-over is typically marked as authoritative, as a metadiscourse which orders the potentially erratic signifiers of image and diegetic sound. In this case, the guarantee of the 'truth' of the film lies in the relationship between voice-over and image, in that the latter may be read as 'illustrating' the former. The notion of the visible as evidence is still at work here, of course, but the specificity of the classic voice-over documentary lies in the fact that the image somehow serves as evidence of the truth of the commentary rather than as direct and visible evidence of events in the 'real world'.

How are feminist concerns and feminist cultural politics actually written into different types of realist films? How are realist modes of representation deployed in dealing with issues of relevance to feminists? It is significant that questions about realism immediately seem to emphasise 'dealing with issues'. This, I would suggest, is a direct outcome of the transparency which marks all forms of cinematic realism. Articulated within a mode of representation that does not foreground its own processes of signification, political issues can stand out clearly. Put in another way, since the 'issues' are played out in the 'real world', it may be argued that they are suitably dealt with in film by translating that world in general, and the issues in particular, into a representation which allows the spectator a freedom directly to 'see' issues as they look, operate, and develop in the 'real world' of everyday existence or political struggle. In a realist fiction film, the spectator's identifications can be quite direct, easy and pleasurable: for a feminist, for example, pleasure may arise in the process of identifying with a strong and independent female character who is able to control the process of the narrative and its fictional events in such a way as to bring about a resolution in which she 'wins' in some way. In documentary, identifications may take place more directly with what is represented in the image, so that, for example, a film about a woman's life and her work as a mother and housewife may bring about forms of recognition in female spectators of themselves or their own everyday lives. The question of the political implications of these forms of pleasure is dealt with in the next chapter: my discussion of feminism and cinematic realism assumes for the moment that their appropriation for feminism can in certain circumstances be productive.

The rest of this chapter is devoted to a consideration of several types of cinematic realism in relation to the questions posed at the beginning of the last paragraph. I shall look at the points of identification, modes of address and subject positionings characteristic of each type, and examine a number of films in some detail. I begin by discussing two variants of fictional realism: first, some recent Hollywood films which may be read as responses to the women's movement on the part of dominant cinema, and, second, socialist realist cinema as it intersects with feminism. In considering the question of non-fictional realism, I shall examine some of the ways in which the textual organisation of feminist documentary films is frequently overlaid by autobiographical discourses.

Hollywood and New Women's Cinema

Since the years of ascendancy of the Hollywood studio system, the industry has undergone many institutional changes which have had a number of implications regarding the textual organisation of Hollywood films. Molly Haskell and Marjorie Rosen have charted shifts in representations of women in Hollywood films which have accompanied these institutional changes (Haskell, 1975; Rosen, 1973) and both writers conclude that during the 1960s Hollywood films became increasingly violent, that women characters were increasingly represented as victims, and that the days of the powerful female star and the 'independent woman' as a character were gone. Haskell offers a sociological explanation for this finding, arguing that: 'The closer women come to claiming their rights and achieving independence in real life, the more loudly and stridently films tell us it's a man's world' (Haskell, 1975, p. 363). The rise of the second wave of feminism, according to this explanation, brought about a backlash effect: the threat posed by the liberated woman was actually contained in films, often by a literal containment, at the level of story, of female protagonists. This might range from confinement within home and family, or in mental institutions, through to containment by various forms of physical violence up to and including murder.

At the same time, however, since the middle 1970s – after Haskell's and Rosen's books were first published – a number of Hollywood films have been made which may be read as indicating an opposite trend. In these films, the central characters are women, and often women who are not attractive or glamorous in the conventional sense. Narratives, moreover, are frequently organised around the process of a woman's self-discovery and growing independence: instances of this genre include *Alice Doesn't Live Here Anymore* (Scorsese, Warner Bros, 1975), *Starting Over* (Pakula, Paramount, 1979), and *An Unmarried Woman* (Mazursky, Fox, 1977). The existence of this 'new women's cinema' might be explained in terms of direct determination: that it simply reflects the growth and influence of the women's movement. On its own, however, such an explanation is perhaps rather one-dimensional, in that it cannot take into account the simultaneous existence of, say, films portraying violence towards women. By what process, in any case, are 'social climates' translated into cinematic signifieds? Given the complexity of the institutional structures of the film industry, not to mention the coded operations of film texts, the relationship between social climates and the content of films is obviously not a simple one. Explaining the coexistence of dissimilar types of Hollywood films calls for an examination of a variety of structures in their historical specificity. For example, if the cinema audience is composed of segmented 'sub-audiences' with different interests, films will address themselves to these various audiences. Thus the 'new women's film' addresses itself in particular to women, even to women with some degree of feminist consciousness, while other film genres will be directed at quite different social audiences.

In what ways do new women's films embody realism, and what is their relevance for feminism? As dominant cinema, their realism rests on the credibility of texts which construct identifications for the spectator on the levels of character and narrative, within a fictional world constituted as coherent and internally consistent. The spectator may, in other words, be drawn fairly readily into the identifications offered by the films. The pleasure for the female spectator of films of this kind lies in several possible identifications: with a central character who is not only also a woman, but who may be similar in some respects to the spectator herself; or with a narrative voice enunciated by a woman character; or with fictional events which evoke a degree of recognition; or with a resolution that constitutes a 'victory' for the central character. The address of the new women's film may thus position the spectator not only as herself a potential 'winner', but also as a winner whose gender is instrumental in the victory: it may consequently offer the female spectator a degree of affirmation. Two questions may be posed at this point, however. First, how do these various identifications operate in relation to one another in the address of film texts? And, second, what are the implications for feminism of a classic realist cinema which is 'affirmative' of women?

These questions are best dealt with by reference to specific films: I shall look at Claudia Weill's *Girlfriends* (1977) and Fred Zinneman's *Julia* (1977), both of which take up a genre popular in the 1960s and the 1970s, the male 'buddy movie'. *Girlfriends* and *Julia* become women's films by virtue of the simple fact that the buddies in these cases are female. A primary requirement of the new women's film is thus immediately met – the central characters are female, and they are sympathetically portrayed. *Girlfriends* goes a step further than this by presenting its main characters as not at all glamorous. The heroines of *Julia* conform much more to the Hollywood 'star' model, however: Lillian Hellman (Jane Fonda) is a famous writer and Julia (Vanessa Redgrave) an obscure but highly courageous revolutionary. The star system is obviously at work here: while the central characters in *Girlfriends* are played by little-known actresses, who play 'ordinary' women, the casting of two world-famous figures – both of them also highly visible as political activists – as the stars of *Julia* has important consequences for the meanings generated by the film. Neither Julia nor Lillian as 'fictional' characters can be regarded as ordinary, and the casting underlines this: the point of identification for female spectators lies not so much with the characters as with the relationship between them.

Both *Julia* and *Girlfriends* may be seen as departing somewhat from the classic realist model in their narrative resolutions. In each film the questions set up by the narrative are not fully resolved by the closure. In *Girlfriends*, in fact, full closure is perhaps impossible, given the nature of the structuring enigmas of the narrative. The story begins with one of the women friends moving out of their shared apartment in order to get married. Ann's departure seems to motivate a series of events in Susan's life, all somewhat unconnected by anything other than the fact of her friend's absence. In the classic narrative model, resolution of this absence would be brought about by the restoration of an equilibrium. Within the trajectory of lack to liquidation of lack (see Chapter 2) which marks variants of this model, resolution in *Girlfriends* might be brought about by the establishment of love relationships for Ann and Susan: either with each other, or with new partners. Although the first option would fit in well with the structural demands of classic narrative, as well as with the powerful Hollywood 'romance' model, its content is excluded by rules, conscious and unconscious, currently governing representations of homosexuality in dominant cinema. But at the same time the second option – re-establishment of equilibrium through the setting up of new relationships – is also ruled out, in this case by the demands on the narrative set up through the characterisations of the two women: it would simply not be plausible. However, although there is a constant movement towards the latter resolution – in Susan's relationship with a rabbi, for instance, and even in Ann's with her husband – it is never quite brought off, partly perhaps because it would undermine the 'buddy' structure that governs the organisation of the narrative. And so, caught in its own contradictions, the narrative cannot be resolved in the classic manner. We are left instead with a relatively open ending: the women's relationship continues to be problematic and contradictory, and yet important enough to be continued. It may be argued, of course, that such an open ending is in fact more 'credible' than any classic resolution which ties all the ends of the narrative together.

Julia, too, possesses a degree of openness, which in this instance operates not so much in the film's resolution as through its entire narrative. This openness is crucially related to the film's articulation of plot and story, and the fact that its discourse is pivoted on memory. The film's enunciation involves at least two layers of memory. First there is the overarching discourse of Hellman's memoir, rendered in the film as her voice-over and as the temporal 'present' of the narrative, and marked by the representation of the writer's relationship with Dashiell

Hammett. Second, there is the memory within the memoir, constituted as the 'past' of the film and marked cinematically as subjective, as Hellman's fantasies and dreams, most of them involving Julia. The two levels are brought together only in those sequences in the film's 'present' when Lillian and Julia meet – in a Vienna hospital and in a station café in Berlin. Since the relationship between the women is largely told discursively through Hellman's narrative point-of-view, and exactly because of its status as memory within memoir, it is relativised. What we see is Hellman's impression of a remembered relationship, doubly marked as subjective. We can therefore read the film in several ways. The openness of *Julia* centres less on the film's closure (which is in any case not entirely inconclusive, in that the past and the present of the narrative are brought together with Julia's death and Lillian's dealing with it in her relationship with Hammett) than on the nature of the relationship between the two women. This is encapsulated in a scene – a flashback, in fact – in which Lillian slugs a drunken male friend for suggesting that 'the whole world knows about you and Julia': that, in other words, the women have a lesbian relationship. The scene may be read in at least two ways: either Hellman's reaction is to the slur on lesbianism implied in 'the whole world's' uncomprehending gossip, or the 'accusation' of lesbianism is itself a slur on the relationship (*New German Critique*, 1978, p. 92). A reading of reviews of *Julia* certainly upholds this suggestion: while most reviewers agree that the relationship portrayed between the women is central to the film (although it might in fact be argued, to the contrary, that the way the Hellman–Hammett relationship is represented, and also its place in the film's 'present', serve actually to enclose and relativise that of the women), there are almost as many opinions as there are reviews concerning the precise nature of that relationship.[1]

The question of openness in these two examples of new women's cinema may be considered in relation to some general formal and thematic shifts within recent Hollywood cinema. These shifts have been regarded as significant enough to constitute a 'New Hollywood Cinema'. The mobilisation in New Hollywood Cinema of certain cinematic codes – zooming, telephoto shots, slow motion and split screen – have, it has been argued, 'destroyed the dramatic and spatio-temporal unity that founded the classical mise-en-scene' (Neale, 1976, p. 117). Another mark of New Hollywood Cinema is a degree of open-endedness or ambiguity at the level of narrative – a defining feature of both *Julia* and *Girlfriends*. Two points of relevance to the question of realism, feminism and the new women's film may be made here. The first is that although New Hollywood Cinema is something of a departure for narrative cinema, it reworks rather than destroys the textual operations of dominant cinema: 'Ambiguity and open-endedness are sustained and articulated *within* the limits of the dominant discourse, within the text. They are not of the kind likely to fracture the unity of position of the reader' (ibid., p. 121, my emphasis).

Second, although the openness of New Hollywood Cinema operates across a range of cinematic genres and narratives, it may be argued that, precisely because of its subject matter, the new women's cinema is particularly prone to such openness. Although feminism and new women's cinema are by no means coterminous, new women's cinema does raise, at some level at least, the question of feminism. Feminism is controversial, however, and it would be problematic for a cinematic institution whose products are directed at a politically heterogeneous audience overtly to take up positions which might alienate certain sections of that audience. Films whose address sustains a degree of polysemy – which open up rather than restrict potential readings, in other words – may appeal to a relatively broadly based audience. Openness permits readings to be made which accord more or less with spectators' prior stances on feminist issues. *Julia* illustrates this point quite well: while lesbians may be free to read the film as an affirmation of lesbianism, such a reading – just as it is not ruled out – is by no means privileged by the text. *Girlfriends* works similarly with regard to the question of feminism. On its release, the film was widely received as charming, warm, amusing and likeable. It was not regarded as threatening largely because, despite its status as a female buddy film, it does not demand a reading as a feminist film. Nevertheless, at the same time, the 'buddy' structure can equally well justify a reading of the film in terms of woman-identification.

The possibility that this kind of openness may actually be a defining characteristic of new women's cinema is pointed out by Julia Lesage, who argues: 'The industry wants to let everybody have their ideological cake and eat it, too. In other words, you'll see deliberate ambiguities structured into almost every film to come out about strong women' (*New German Critique*, 1978, p. 91). Whether or not this process is as conscious or deliberate as Lesage suggests, one of the most significant effects of this ideologically implicated ambiguity must be to buttress the textual and institutional operations of dominant cinema.

Whatever positive identifications it offers to those who choose to make them, new women's cinema cannot in the final instance deal in any direct way with the questions which feminism poses for cinematic representation.

Socialist Realism

Socialist realism (or progressive realism[2]) is often discussed in relation to literature and the fine arts rather than cinema. None the less, the somewhat abstract level at which debates about socialist realism tend to be conducted does permit a consideration of its characteristics as they operate across various forms of expression, cinema among them. Socialist realism was defined by Stalin during the 1930s as 'a true and historically concrete depiction of reality and its revolutionary development'. While such a statement is open to a range of interpretations, it does suggest two basic defining characteristics for socialist realism: first, an adherence to some form of realism ('true ... depiction of reality'), and, second, that representations either deal directly with history or inscribe historical specificity in some other way ('historically concrete'). It is, I would argue, the latter quality which sets socialist realism apart from other forms of realism.

But what, in terms of textual operations, does 'historical concreteness' mean? This question may be approached by examining the nature of the realism inscribed by socialist realism. In debates on art and literature in the Soviet Union during the early years of the revolution, it was suggested that art should not only represent, but also be accessible to, the people (Vaughan-James, 1973). Although no definition was offered of what 'accessibility' might mean in textual terms, a tendency to favour transparent modes of representation was soon in evidence. This tendency was consolidated in official Soviet policy on the arts during the 1930s (Gorky *et al.*, 1977), in which realism was distinguished from naturalism and the latter rejected in favour of the former. The distinction between realism and naturalism turns on historical concreteness and characterisation: whereas both forms involve characterisation, in realism history takes centre stage through characterisation. In other words, historical changes, conflicts and contradictions are rendered textually within developments of consciousness on the part of characters, as well as in their interactions with one another. The dual requirements of characterisation and 'accessibility' mean that narrative is a common setting for these representations. Thus the socialist realist narrative operates on the levels of both character and history, the one encapsulating and representing the other.

From this emerges the concept of 'typification': in socialist realism, characters may be drawn as rounded individuals with their own traits of personality, but at the same time they also function as embodiments of social and historical characteristics. In this way, characters become social 'types' as well as individuals. The representation of reality in its historical concreteness thus takes place through fictional characters who partly operate as types expressive of social groups or classes and historical configurations. This is the fundamental difference between socialist realism and the realism of Hollywood cinema. In the latter, identifications by readers with central characters occur predominantly at the level of individual traits of personality set up by, and expatiated upon within, the narrative. In socialist realism, on the other hand, identification at the level of individual personality traits also, and concomitantly, involves identification with the social–historical situation of the character's 'type'.

The central characters of socialist realist texts frequently embody heroic traits, a quality which has its origins in the influence of revolutionary romanticism on socialist realism. In revolutionary romanticism, art offers a vision of the future which is optimistic, but also aims to be grounded rather than utopian. This optimism is rendered in the revolutionary development of a figure who becomes 'heroic' in the course of that development: hence the 'positive hero' of socialist realism. She or he is represented as a personality having individual qualities, positive and negative, with which the reader may identify. At the same time, the movement of the narrative involves a personal or political development and a growth of insight and strength on the part of the 'positive hero' which enables the character both to attain a degree of political consciousness and also to overcome difficulties and obstacles which are both specific – pertaining, that is, to the fictional individual's personal situation – and general – signifying a broader social/historical situation. Thus the socialist realist narrative, like the classic narrative, involves resolution and closure. However, there are differences between them as regards the narrative processes through which resolution is reached. In the case of classic realism, closure comes about when the structuring enigmas of the narrative have been resolved, probably by the main character or characters, through the deployment of personal qualities – perceptiveness, toughness, cunning, or whatever. In socialist realism this happens too, but the process is overlaid by the intervention of 'history', which – in the guise of typification – is also a point of identification for the reader. The fact that history marches on, as it were, transcending the resolution of any individual narrative, may also mark a potential for openness in socialist realism that does not necessarily exist in classic realism.

What I have said so far applies to socialist realism in any narrative form, and is therefore just as relevant, say, to the novel as it is to cinema. Are there any codes whereby 'socialist realist' meanings are produced in cinema? I would argue that there are in fact no specifically cinematic codes for socialist realism. The codes of narrativity I have mentioned are, of course, not peculiar to cinematic representations. And while it is possible also to identify certain codes of composition associated with socialist realist images – representations of the 'the people' or of working people as a solidary group, 'heroic' low-angle compositions of the people and of the hero, partially silhouetted against a strong light source, for example (see Still 7.1) – this 'heroic' coding also operates across visual forms of socialist realism (such as painting and photography) other than cinema. On the level of the specifically cinematic – codes of the camera, editing, and so on – socialist realist cinema works in much the same way as classic realist cinema. A coherent narrative time and space is set up by means of continuity editing, and sound and image support one another in the construction of a transparent, readable and credible fictional world. This clearly relates in various ways to the demand made of socialist realist texts that they be widely accessible and understandable. Contradictions and developments in character, narrative and history may emerge with as much clarity as possible from a text whose signification process is effaced: from a text, that is, which produces an effect of transparency for its signifiers. Despite similarities between socialist realism and classic Hollywood cinema as regards the articulation of cinematic codes, the consequences of differences on the level of narrative codes are significant to the extent that the address of socialist realism may offer a set of identifications which is not possible in classic realism. Thus for example, the 'people' may recognise itself as a group which inhabits history. Moreover, the presence of history as a component of characterisation may problematise a film's closure to the extent that history may be represented as transcending the fate of the individual hero.

7.1 Salt of the Earth: Esperanza (Rosaura Revueltas)

I have not dealt in any detail with the characteristics of the heroes of socialist realist texts, mainly because I want to consider socialist realism in relation specifically to feminism. I shall do this by looking at an example of socialist realist cinema which constructs women's struggles as a central point of identification: *Salt of the Earth* (Biberman, Independent Productions Corporation, 1953). Clearly, the positive hero of a socialist realist representation may be a woman, and if this is the case, it is possible – though by no means necessary – for her gender to be significant in narrative terms. In other words, an area of development or contradiction worked through at the levels of character and narrative might be women and their position in relation to the 'history' signified by the text. The positive heroine then stands in for all women in a particular situation, so that women are accorded the status of historical subjects.

The central protagonist of *Salt of the Earth* is Esperanza Quintero, a Mexican-American mother whose miner husband becomes involved in a strike (Wilson and Rosenfelt, 1978). The story of the film concerns the increasing involvement of the miners' wives in the strike, their support of their husbands, and their assertion of their own strike demands (especially improved sanitation in the mine-owned houses they live in). The women's involvement culminates in their taking over from the men on the picket line after the union has been served with a Taft-Hartley injunction. Reprisals by the employers against Esperanza's husband Ramon and against the women on the line, and finally an attempt to evict the Quinteros, are dealt with by Anglos and Mexican-Americans, women and men, of the New Mexico community, with a measure of success in relation to the immediate struggle, and with significant success in terms of the working people's solidarity. In that Esperanza's voice-over opens and closes the film and punctuates it at various points between, the story is told from the woman's narrative point-of-view: woman is thus central at the levels of enounced and enunciation. It is Esperanza's discourse, too, which makes explicit the relationship between the particular struggle which is the immediate topic of the film's narrative and the broader historical process. The concrete issues of the strike are not represented as hermetic: broader struggles, it is made clear, transcend this particular story.

The awakening political consciousness of the women of the community is a crucial element, too, of the film's narrative. Some of the contradictions involved in such a process for ethnic minority wives and mothers are concretised in the progress of the relationship between

Esperanza and Ramon. His reaction to her increased activity in the strike, which takes her more and more outside her domestic sphere, ranges from ambivalence to outright disapproval. In a climactic quarrel scene, Esperanza tries to make Ramon understand the woman's position by likening the racism of Ramon's Anglo bosses with his male suprematism at home:

> Do you feel better having someone lower than you? ...
> Whose neck shall I stand on, to make me feel superior? ...
> I don't want anything lower than I am. I'm low enough already. I want to rise. And push everything up with me as I go.

The next scene – in which Ramon goes hunting to escape from his troubles – is, cinematically speaking, the most expressionistic of the film. The uncharacteristic fluidity of the mobile framing and the intensity of Ramon's point-of-view, constructed in sweeping camera movements in a film virtually devoid of point-of-view shots, mark this scene as a climax in the story: at this point, Ramon reaches an understanding of Esperanza's position. His attainment of this degree of consciousness permits a kind of release to take place in the film, which then concludes with a long sequence dealing with the bosses' attempt to evict the Quinteros, and the community's solidarity and collective action in preventing the eviction: 'a single collective act combines a rejection of sexism and racism with resistance against the unadulterated power of the ruling class' (Rosenfelt, 1976, p. 20).

This ending constitutes a resolution of the enigmas set in play by the narrative: not only the question of the strike itself, of course, but also problems of sexism, and to a certain extent also those of racism, within the community, brought into the open by the strike and encapsulated by and played out in the relationships between the film's central characters. At the same time, however, Esperanza's final voice-over suggests that the broader struggles of history will go on, and be worked through, in the lives of her children.

Some of the differences between socialist realism and Hollywood's new women's cinema are brought out in comparing *Salt of the Earth* with a more recent 'working-class' film, *Norma Rae* (Ritt, Fox, 1979). While both films have similar themes – industrial action in a poor American community – and both have women as central characters, the identifications posed by their respective narratives and characterisations are quite different. Norma Rae's success in unionising the Southern textile factory where she works is explained largely in terms of personality traits – her stubbornness, defiance and nonconformity – set up in the early part of the film as pre-existing the struggle over unionisation. After the arrival in town of a (male) union organiser, the narrative becomes focused to a significant degree on the progress of the relationship between Norma Rae and the outsider. In the portrayal of this relationship, there is something of a tension between on the one hand the socialist realist demand that it constitute the site, on Norma Rae's part at least, of a development of political consciousness, and on the other the demands of the classic Hollywood trajectory of romantic love. At the same time, Norma Rae's relationship with her husband, which in a socialist realist narrative would perhaps be represented as a site of struggle around political awareness, is scarcely dealt with at all. The husband's tolerance of Norma Rae's union activities has more to do with steadfast loyalty to his wife than with any development of political consciousness on his part. *Norma Rae*, unlike *Salt of the Earth*, is institutionally and textually a Hollywood film. Although it represents a departure for Hollywood in its portrayal of a strong woman who is not only working class but is also victorious in a class-related struggle, its characterisations are marked by individualisation rather than typification, so that the identifications they pose do not move readily into the terrain of either the social or the historical. Its address consequently operates largely within the limits of dominant cinematic discourse.

Direct Cinema and Beyond

To shift discussion away from fictional realism towards non-fictional realism is to begin opening up the question of a self-consciously feminist film practice operating outside dominant cinema. For a variety of political, technical, financial and organisational reasons, many film makers have, since the early 1960s, taken up and developed a variety of forms of documentary cinema. In considering such film practices, it is virtually impossible to separate the textual from the institutional (see Chapter 9). It is significant, for example, that documentarists working on film have mostly used 16 mm technology (while feature films are usually shot on 35 mm film), and 16 mm technology has, in its turn, been instrumental in informing and legitimating certain documentary film practices. Documentary is in fact often the form of production, most immediately taken up by independent film and video makers, particularly if their practice has social or political objectives. It is significant too that many early efforts in this direction were informed by the technological bases, working methods and textual operations of one particular documentary film practice: direct cinema.

Direct cinema, which had its beginnings in the USA during the early 1960s, is informed by a variant of positivism which situates the film maker as an observer who documents, without in any way interfering with or changing, what is observed. Because the object of observation constitutes the topic of the film, the purpose of this kind of film practice is 'rediscovering a reality that eludes other forms of film-making and reporting ... [It] is a practical working method based on a faith in unmanipulated reality, a refusal to tamper with life as it presents itself (Mamber, 1974, p. 4).[3] Such a philosophy lays great emphasis on the conditions surrounding the shooting of a film. If the observer/film maker is not to manipulate the profilmic event, then her or his presence on the scene should be as unobtrusive as possible. To this end, film crews would ideally be small and equipment minimal. The earliest practitioners of direct cinema consequently made use of – and some of them also developed and refined – the technology of film making in the relatively manageable gauge of 16 mm.

The earliest feminist film makers also for the most part adopted the technologies and working methods of 16 mm. Some of the implications of this choice as regards the institutional structures and social relations of feminist film making are considered in Chapter 9. Many feminist film makers, particularly in the earliest years of self-consciously feminist film practice, also looked to documentary forms. I want to focus here on the textual operations and modes of address characteristic of feminist documentary cinema.

Julia Lesage, in discussing the tendency among the film makers of 'second wave' feminism to adopt documentary as their preferred mode, points to the radical potential of simply putting 'real' women and their lives on the cinema screen without constructing the limited range of images of women prevalent in dominant cinema. Representing 'the ordinary details of women's lives, their thoughts – told directly by the protagonists to the camera – and their frustrated but sometimes successful attempts to enter and deal with the public world of work and power' (Lesage, 1978, p. 507) constituted a significant break with existing cinematic representations of women. Although the working methods, and to a certain extent also the philosophy, of direct cinema were taken up in this kind of feminist documentary, it is significant that both methods and philosophy were appropriated in a rather selective manner, and transformed to meet the requirements of a feminist film practice. These transformations operate across texts to produce certain codes and modes of address which constitute a specific set of signifiers for feminist documentary cinema. By this I mean that certain sets of textual operations have, for various political and historical reasons, become defining characteristics of this type of cinema. These operations may be seen at work in the three films which I have selected as representative examples of feminist documentary cinema: *Janie's Janie* (Ashur, New York Newsreel, 1971), *Women of the Rhondda* (Capps, Kelly, Dickinson, Ronay, Segrave and Trevelyan, 1973), and *Union Maids* (Klein, Reichert and Mogulescu, 1976).

If there is any structural principle governing the organisation of feminist documentary film, it is that provided by autobiographical discourse: 'Film after film shows a woman, telling her story to the camera' (Lesage, 1978, p. 515). Protagonists of these films are women who talk about their own lives, and their autobiographies tend to be organised in the linear manner characteristic of the plots of fictional narratives. The speaker begins her story at a point in her earlier life and works through to her own present and the 'present' of the film. The plot order of the film will usually reflect this linear chronology. This 'consistent organisation of narrative materials', argues Lesage, is structured in a manner analogous to the process of consciousness-raising, and functions similarly in political terms. Lesage takes for granted a degree of transparency in cinematic representation, assuming that its 'truth' will be accepted by the spectator in processes of identification with the 'narrative' trajectory of the autobiography on the one hand and the protagonists and their lives on the other. She also suggests that the contents of the autobiographical accounts which structure the films are, like those brought forward in consciousness-raising, selected and ordered by their subjects.

Given that autobiographical discourse structures feminist documentary films, and if protagonists order their own discourses, then clearly the enunciating voice of these films belongs to the female protagonists themselves. This point is underscored by the fact that voice-over is invariably absent from feminist documentaries. When there is a voice-over, it does not come from outside the diegetic space set up by the film, but is spoken by the subject or subjects of the autobiography. If women, as 'speaking subjects', order the discourse of feminist documentaries, in what ways do such films embody the conventions of direct cinema? To the extent that direct cinema assumes transparency in representation and 'objectivity' on the part of the film maker and/or the camera, enunciation is marked as neutral. This is one reason why direct cinema documentaries never have voice-over of the traditional kind: the image presents itself as standing on its own as evidence of the naturalness of the representation. If the camera is the 'observer', the spectator – by standing in for the look of the camera – also becomes a neutral observer (Kuhn, 1978a). However, although feminist documentary takes up some of the methods and philosophies of direct cinema, it also departs from direct cinema in significant respects. I will discuss this point in more detail through an examination of *Janie's Janie*, a feminist documentary film which may be regarded as in certain respects exemplary of direct cinema.

Janie's Janie is a thirty-minute documentary about a white working-class welfare mother of five children, living in a small town in New Jersey. The film is structured autobiographically by the woman's story of her own past and present life, related in chronological order. The story begins with Janie's accounts of her family of origin, moves through her marriage and separation from her husband, and ends with her attainment of a degree of feminist consciousness and solidarity with other women in the community. With a single exception – a brief sequence of family snapshots – the film image remains relentlessly in Janie's 'present': her story is situated in the context of her current situation as a housewife and single mother. Thus, up to the point in the film when Janie tells of beginning, as she says, 'associating other people with me as far as other people go', Janie is usually shown at home, involved in housework and childcare tasks as she talks about her life. The film is strongly coded as 'direct': for example, by the constant camera movements, zooms and focus pulls attendant on the film makers' attempts to follow Janie's movements around her house. In one sequence, in which Janie is shown ironing while she talks, there is a sudden rapid pan right and a focusing to frame a child about to open the refrigerator just as Janie interrupts her story to scold him (see Stills 7.2 and 7.3). In a later sequence, her talk is repeatedly punctuated by demands for attention from another child. The constant mobile framing, reframing, and movement within the image, together with the rapidity of Janie's verbal delivery, the various ambient sounds, and the children's interruptions, all lend the film a frenetic pace and an urgency evocative of the unremitting pressures on a woman in Janie's situation. In the ordinariness of her story, as in the representation of her

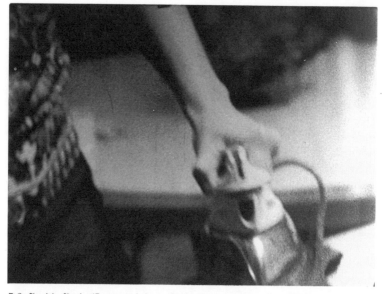

7.2 Janie's Janie: 'I gotta right to be happy, whether I'm doin' wrong or not ...'

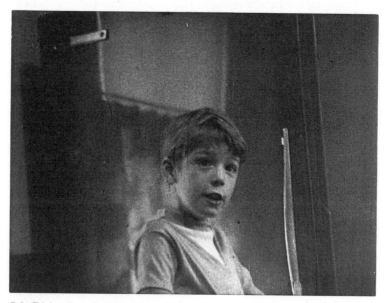

7.3 'Richard ... I told you not to go in and out of that ...'

work in the home, Janie may be seen as a woman whose life is like that of many poor working-class mothers. To this extent, the film offers a set of identifications for women in certain situations, identifications which operate through recognition of Janie's situation. Given the verisimilitude of the cinematic representation, then, the 'truth' of Janie's situation may be accepted, recognised and identified with. Thus although the film deals with only one woman, a spectator–text relationship is set up which permits generalisation from this single case.

Janie's Janie possesses many of the defining textual features of direct documentary, but departs from direct cinema in the structures governing its organisation. Proponents of direct cinema argue that the organisation of a film should be governed by the chronology of profilmic events, or – failing that – by any internal logic which emerges out of these events as they are filmed. The objective, in other words, is to respect the integrity of the profilmic event itself. The ground rules of *Janie's Janie* differ, however, from those of direct cinema, in that it is the chronology of Janie's discourse which governs the 'narrative' ordering of the film. It is the woman, Janie, who tells the story, whose discourse orders the film. While *Janie's Janie* may be regarded as in some respects exemplary of direct cinema, the point at which it departs from that model may be regarded as highly significant in feminist terms. If the film is structured by the autobiographical discourse of its protagonist, then Janie – or rather Janie's story – is in charge. The political implications of the kinds of identifications made possible by this documentary strategy centre on the necessity of naming women's experience, of making the personal political. The 'truth' of a film like *Janie's Janie* is therefore not an absolute truth derived from 'neutral' observation, but a situated truth embedded in a feminist politics founded on an acceptance of the validity of individual experience.

The identifications set up by *Janie's Janie* operate on an individual level, but may be generalised in certain circumstances, in much the same way as individual life stories may be generalised if dealt with in a consciousness-raising group – through the awareness that women have many life experiences in common. *Union Maids* and *Women of the Rhondda* are rather different from *Janie's Janie*, however, in that their autobiographical accounts contain a historical discourse: both films function in part as oral history. Oral history has been instrumental in inserting groups hitherto largely 'hidden from history' – women and the working class in particular – into the mainstream of historical discourse. In representing working-class women talking about events in their own past lives which also have a broader historical reference, *Union Maids* and *Women of the Rhondda* suggest that women can be subjects in history. The credibility of these films rests specifically on the fact that they unite two forms of verisimilitude: a verisimilitude emerging from the transparency of documentary realism itself, and a verisimilitude which comes from the notion underpinning the practice of oral history that there is a 'truth' in accounts of the lived individual experiences of members of certain social groups. This articulation of truth as both visibility and personal experience structures the address of both films. There are, however, significant differences between them as to their representations of relationships between past and present.

In *Women of the Rhondda*, four working-class women talk about the past situation of women in a Welsh mining community, with particular reference to the general strike of 1926. Intercut with direct interview footage of each woman – sitting in her own home and wearing her best clothes – are shots of these same women doing their housework, of miners leaving the pit-head and enjoying their leisure at a working men's club, and of the mining town and its surrounding landscape. The only voices in the film are those of the four women themselves, whose recollections constitute the voice-over for the non-interview sequences. The references to the past, however, are only in the women's spoken discourses: the images exclusively construct the film's 'present'. This sometimes results in a certain degree of irony which operates through the relationship of sound and image. At various points in the film, there is a play on the similarities and differences between women's situations in the past and in the present. For example, when one of the women talks about the laboriousness of housework at a time when a woman had to iron as many as twenty-four shirts a week for the men in the house, the same woman appears on the image track – ironing shirts.

The discourses of *Union Maids*, however, remain more firmly situated in the past. The three women who talk about their youthful experiences as labour organisers in Chicago during the 1930s, like the women of the Rhondda, construct the accounts of their own lives in relation to contemporary public events. Their accounts also constitute virtually the sole spoken discourse of the film. In *Union Maids*, though, the direct interview footage of the women telling their stories is intercut with contemporary representations of the past events they are talking about. It is the address constructed by this intercut material which marks the crucial difference between the two films. *Union Maids* makes use of newsreel, reportage and other film footage, as well as still

7.4 Union Maids: 'We fought the police ...'

7.5 '... I mean, we threw glasses at 'em, and we threw bottles ...'

photographs, all from the 1930s, to 'illustrate' the stories of the three interviewees. At the points when such archival material is intercut, the women's talk functions as a voice-over, and the image stands in evidence of the 'truth' of their spoken discourse. When, for example, Sylvia Woods tells of the police breakup of a sit-down strike at the laundry where she worked with other black women, the footage showing a group of policemen fighting with black women functions as evidence that this sort of thing did indeed happen (see Stills 7.4 and 7.5). In this way, sound and image are mutually reinforcing throughout much of the film. The focus on oral history interviews backed up by evidence in the form of contemporary visual representations unites the different discourses of the film to place its events firmly in the historical past. As a consequence of this, the question of relationships between past and present can be introduced only in the form of direct questions posed by the film makers.

As filmed oral history, both *Women of the Rhondda* and *Union Maids*, in mobilising documentary modes of address in the particular ways they do, validate the place in history of working-class and black women's lives and struggles. In this sense, they give women, and working-class women in particular, the status of historical subjects, thereby taking the 'consciousness-raising' character of the autobiographically organised film documentary one step further. The autobiographical structure common to all three documentary films discussed here, and characteristic of numerous other feminist documentaries, works in conjunction with the transparency of the address of documentary representations to construct their 'real life' protagonists as full and rounded human subjects, as 'real women'. However, this very quality of humanism embodied in non-fictional realism itself forms the basis of a critique of feminist documentary cinema. This critique and some of its consequences in relation to feminist film practice are examined in the next chapter.

8

Textual Politics

The film practices taken up in the last chapter were discussed as examples of realism: as representations, that is, which present an appearance of transparency by effacing the processes of meaning production in their own textual operations. Realism is a feature of dominant cinema, but non-dominant film practices like socialist realism and feminist documentary draw on this transparency both in order to appeal to as wide an audience as possible, and also with the assumption that a politically oppositional message will come across the more clearly to the extent that it is not complicated by 'noise' from foregrounded textual operations. Such a cultural politics is grounded in an assumption that meanings – even politically oppositional meanings – exist already in society, that human subjects are already formed for such meanings, and that representations can operate as neutral vehicles for conveying those meanings from source to recipient.

Other approaches to cultural politics may, however, take different positions as to the nature of meaning. The construction of meanings may, for example, be regarded as an ongoing process of texts and reader–text relations which may work in some respects independently of the operations of other social formations. Such a stance on signification suggests that in the moment of reading, recipients of texts are themselves involved in producing meanings, even if – as in the case of realism – they are not aware of the fact. To the extent that the signification process is effaced in realist representations, it is argued, realism perpetuates illusionism, the notion that, in the case of cinema, what is on the screen is an uncoded reflection of the 'real world'. Illusionism may then be regarded as an ideological operation, on at least two grounds: first, that the concealment of processes of signification through codes of transparency mystifies both the spectator and the signification process by setting up a view of the world as monolithically preconstructed 'out there', and, second, that spectator–text relations characteristic of realist representations – identification and closure, for example – position their reading subjects as unitary and non-contradictory, and thus as neither active, nor as capable of intervention, in the signification process. These critiques of illusionism may underpin a cultural politics which takes textual signifiers to be a legitimate area of intervention. If illusionism is a feature of certain textual practices, then it may be challenged on the level of the text by means of non-realist or anti-realist strategies and modes of address.

The present chapter is devoted to a consideration of what might be termed 'anti-illusionism' in cinema, and to anti-illusionist film practices as they touch on feminism. From this point of view, then, I will address the question of feminist countercinema. Countercinema may be defined as film practice which works against and challenges dominant cinema, usually at the levels of both signifiers and signifieds. Although it may challenge the institutional practices of dominant cinema too, my concern here is primarily with the text. Considerations relating more specifically to institutions of countercinema are dealt with in Chapter 9.

As textual practice, countercinemas attempt to challenge and subvert the operations of dominant cinema. Before proceeding to an examination of some approaches to and examples of countercinema, therefore, I will briefly look at features of dominant cinema which countercinemas (feminist or otherwise), may set out to challenge. I have already touched on the argument – and the reasoning behind it – that the effacement of processes of signification in dominant cinema is an ideological operation. The question of how this ideological operation works in cinema may be dealt with by considering how codes in dominant cinema work to construct certain kinds of spectator–text relations. For example, classic narrative codes structure relations of spectator identification with fictional characters and also with the progress of the narrative itself. By means of these identifications, the spectator is drawn into the film, so that when the questions posed by the narrative are resolved by its closure, the spectator is also 'closed', completed or satisfied: in cinema, this partly operates through the 'binding-in' process of suture. In documentary forms of film realism,

closure, completion and unity are brought about through identification with the coded self-presentation of the 'truthfulness' of the
representation, as well as through identification with, or recognition
of, real-life protagonists on the screen.

But what kind of relationship might there be between the practices of
countercinema and those of feminism? It could be argued, for
example, that there is nothing specifically feminist about challenging
the modes of identification and subjectivity set up by dominant
cinema. If this is the case, where does feminism enter into countercinema? In answer to this question, I will point to two interrelated
arguments on behalf of feminist countercinema. The first is premised
on the notion that all forms of illusionism are ideologically implicated,
while the second focuses more specifically on the forms of pleasure
generated in the relations of specularity set up by dominant cinema,
classic Hollywood narrative in particular.

In her 1973 pamphlet *Notes on Women's Cinema*, Claire Johnston
argues that 'It has been at the level of the image that the violence of
sexism and capitalism has been experienced (Johnston, 1973a, p. 2). In
other words, the image constructs a specific set of signifiers (as distinct
from those, say, of the written word) for constructing the world-views
of a society which is both patriarchal and bourgeois. The ideological
discourse of dominant cinema, certainly at the level of the film image, is
therefore seen as sexist as well as capitalist. The specificity of the
'patriarchal' nature of the film image is at this point analysed in terms
of Lévi-Strauss's anthropological argument about woman's status as
'sign' in relations of exchange between males (Cook and Johnston,
1974), while the bourgeois character of dominant cinema is associated
with the mystification involved in the naturalisation of operations of
signification by the surface appearance of transparency of meaning.
The task of constructing a feminist countercinema, according to this
argument, involves first of all 'an analysis of the functioning of signs
within the discourse' (Johnston 1973a, p. 3), and then a subversion of
this discourse by means of anti-realist or anti-illusionist textual
strategies. What is at stake here, then, is a deconstructive countercinema whose project is to analyse and break down dominant forms as
they are embedded in bourgeois and patriarchal ideology.

Following the early work of Johnston and Cook, feminist film theory
began to turn its attention away from a concern with the film text as an
autonomous set of formal operations and towards the question of
spectator–text relations in cinema. Here, particular regard was given

to relations of looking and their psychic inscription. Laura Mulvey's work on the look and cinematic representations of women (see Chapter 3) was an important development in this area, and in it Mulvey also argues for the creation of new forms of pleasure in cinema. Given her argument that the codes of dominant cinema 'and their relationship to formative external structures must be broken down before mainstream film and the pleasure it provides can be challenged' (Mulvey, 1975, p. 17), Mulvey is clearly also advocating a deconstructive counter-cinema. Her suggestion is that in such a countercinema the 'voyeuristic–scopophilic look' can be broken down in certain ways. However, although Mulvey's analysis appears to arrive at a prescription for film practice rather similar to Johnston's – deconstruction – her concern with the psychic structures of subjectivity opens up possible new areas of work for feminist countercinema. As well as shifting the debate from a consideration of the film text as an autonomous set of formal strategies, towards a notion of interaction between spectator and text, Mulvey's analysis also raises the questions of specularity and gendered subjectivity. Although the consequences of this for feminist film practice are not explicitly addressed in her article, crucial questions are implicitly raised, in that the issue of gendered subjectivity poses in turn that of a specifically feminine film language and its potential for feminist countercinema.

The discussion which follows is structured around the argument that oppositional textual practices in cinema which may be regarded as of relevance to feminism fall roughly into two categories. The premisses grounding each correspond more or less with those underlying the respective analysis of Johnston/Cook and Mulvey. I say more or less, because the film practices I shall be examining have not for the most part arisen in any immediate or determined sense from the theories with which I associate them. Although I would maintain that certain types of theorising have been important in shaping feminist film practice, the influence is rarely either one-way or direct. In any case, any identifiable influences emerge as much from the ways in which films may be read as from the intentions of their makers. Thus although in this case theory and practice are in important respects interrelated, it is neither possible nor desirable to map the one immediately and unproblematically onto the other. The two areas of textual practice discussed here, then, are constituted on the one hand by a counter-cinema grounded in the deconstruction of dominant cinema, and on the other by a form of cinema marked as more 'other' to dominant cinema, as 'feminine writing'. Although it will be clear that these two areas of practice do have certain things in common, I believe their differences permit a consideration of some crucial developments and prospects for feminist countercinema. I shall therefore deal with them separately.

Deconstruction

As the term suggests, deconstructive cinema works by a process of breaking down. On one level, the object of the deconstruction process is the textual operations and modes of address characteristic of dominant cinema, the aim being to provoke spectators into awareness of the actual existence and effectivity of dominant codes, and consequently to engender a critical attitude towards these codes. Provocation, aware- ness and a critical attitude suggest in turn a transformation in spectator–text relations from the passive receptivity or unthinking suspension of disbelief fostered by dominant modes of address to a more active and questioning position. Deconstructive cinema aims therefore to unsettle the spectator. But there is more at stake in deconstructive cinema than simply a challenge to the textual operations of dominant cinema. After all, many forms of avant-garde and experimental cinema may be read as doing just this, without – except in the very broadest sense – being defined as deconstructive. The distinguishing mark of deconstructive cinema, as against other non-dominant or anti- dominant forms, is its recruitment of the spectator's active relation to the signification process for certain signifieds, or areas of substantive concern. The distinction between form and content may help clarify this point: deconstructive cinema, it can be argued, is not definable simply by its formal strategies. Departure from the formal conventions of dominant cinema may be a necessary condition of deconstructive cinema, but it is certainly not a sufficient one. Deconstructive cinema departs from dominant cinema in its content as well as in its form: it speaks from politically oppositional positions or concerns itself with subject matters commonly ignored or repressed in dominant cinema. But although oppositional content is necessary, it is not a sufficient condition of deconstructive cinema, either. Deconstructive cinema, then, may be defined by its articulation of oppositional forms with oppositional contents. If deconstructive cinema thus defines itself in relation to dominant cinema, it is not a static entity, because its character at any moment is always shaped, in an inverse manner, by dominant cinema. Deconstructive cinema is always, so to speak, casting a sideways ·look at dominant cinema. The term 'counter-cinema' – which is in fact often understood to be synonymous with deconstruction – conveys this sense of conscious opposition very well.

It can be helpful to compare the operations and political objectives of deconstructive cinema with those of the 'epic' theatre associated with Bertolt Brecht. Epic theatre departs from more conventional theatrical forms in that, for example, narratives may be fragmented and subject to interruptions, characters may not be presented as psychologically rounded, narrative time may not be linear, and so on. The effect of these epic devices is to render impossible the kinds of spectator identification typically set up by 'realist' theatre. The analogy between epic theatre and deconstructive cinema is grounded, in fact, in the anti-illusionist stance and strategies of distanciation common to both. As Walter Benjamin says of epic theatre, it

> advances by fits and starts, like the images on a film strip. Its basic form is that of the forceful impact on one another of separate, distinct situations in the play. The songs, the captions included in the stage decor, the gestural conventions of the actors, serve to separate each situation. Thus distances are created everywhere which are, on the whole, detrimental to illusion among the audience. These distances are meant to make the audience adopt a critical attitude (Benjamin, 1973, p. 21).

It is clear from this that the effect of this epic form derives from the spectator–text relations it constructs. Formal devices are justified only to the extent that they evoke distanciation rather than involvement, a critical attitude rather than passive receptivity.

Therefore although both epic theatre and deconstructive cinema are often discussed in terms of their formal strategies – sometimes, in fact, to the extent that forms are fetishised – these strategies are important only in relation to their consequences for the address of the representation – the film or play – as a whole. The impact of epic or deconstructive representations thus arises in direct relation to the challenge they offer the operations of dominant strategies. The importance of the contextual specificity of deconstructive strategies is emphasised here mainly because my discussions of particular films will focus on their formal attributes, which seems a regrettable, but perhaps unavoidable, consequence of singling out individual texts for atten-tion. It is important to stress, therefore, that the films I discuss as examples of deconstructive cinema acquire their deconstructive force in the final instance only from their context: only in their relation, that is, to the contemporary state of dominant cinema and to their place in the history and institutions of non-dominant cinematic forms. The films I shall look at here are *One Way Or Another* (*De Cierta Manera*) (Gomez, ICAIC, 1974) and *Whose Choice?* (London Women's Film Group, BFI, 1976). Both of them deal with fairly well-defined and circumscribed topics, and draw upon and articulate, while at the same time also challenging, certain conventions of narrative and documentary realism.

One Way Or Another deals with the problem of 'marginalism' in post-revolution Cuba. Marginalism is the culture of poverty associated with the urban slums and shanty towns of pre-revolution days, areas marked by high levels of unemployment and delinquency, poor educational provision, violence and economic poverty. The integration of 'marginal' populations into the wider society is regarded as a priority and a problem for the revolution. The film investigates the contradictions – both personal and social – involved in the integration process by examining some of the effects of, and causal links between, certain cultural features of marginalism. It is because of its concern with tracing the relationship between the personal and familial and other social structures that *One Way Or Another* may be regarded as a film which prioritises feminist issues and political perspectives: although it does this, of course, within the terms of a broader concern with the effects of a socialist revolution. The problem of contradictions between marginal culture and the revolution present the film not only with its analytical project, but also with the problem of accessible cinematic forms for that project. The project and the problem are dealt with by the film's mobilisation of two discourses: a story which has many of the qualities of a socialist realist narrative, and a documentary with voice-over.

The narrative discourse is focused primarily on the progress of a loving relationship between Mario, a worker living in a marginal district, and Yolanda, a teacher of middle-class origins drafted into a school in the area. In the socialist realist manner, the narrative discourse 'traces how the internal dynamics of a single personality, family or love affair are related to the larger social processes of the revolution' (Lesage, 1979, p. 21). But at the same time, it does not construct the kinds of identification typical of socialist realist modes of address, primarily because the narrative is articulated with another, and very different, discourse: that of documentary realism.

Throughout the film, there are sequences of documentary with voice-over commentary, which address the problem of marginalism from the point-of-view of a distanced, if sympathetic, social observer. Thus for instance, following immediately on the pre-credit and credit sequences is a documentary sequence showing the demolition of some city slums and the reconstruction of the area, with a voice-over which explains that elimination of the slum conditions has not resulted in the disappearance of certain features of marginal culture. In this way, the notion of contradictory relations between social formations and an analytical approach to such contradictions are established within both the signifiers and the signifieds of the text. The film takes up two different conventions of cinematic realism, but in combining them in certain ways undercuts the spectator–text relations which would be set up by each one on its own. This type of deconstruction works by means of its direct reference to dominant cinematic codes, setting up, through familiarity with such codes, certain expectations in the spectator. These expectations are then cut off because the film offers no single internally consistent discourse.

Examples of distanciation in the discourses of *One Way Or Another* may be cited with reference to some of the formal strategies associated with epic theatre. For example, the interaction of narrative and documentary discourses in the film works in a similar way to the separations and 'fits and starts' of epic theatre. During a sequence in which Mario and Yolanda exchange confidences about their past lives (see Still 8.1) Mario confesses that he once seriously considered becoming a *ñañigo*, a member of a male secret society. At this point, the narrative is cut off by an intertitle: 'Abacua society – documentary analysis' – followed by an account, with documentary footage and voice-over, of the history of these secret societies and their roots in and connections with marginalism (see Still 8.2). The first concern at this point is with a description and analysis of one of the ways in which marginal culture still persists after the revolution. At the same time, however, this documentary interlude is marked as functioning analogously to a flashback (Mario's), for afterwards the narrative discourse resumes where it left off, with Yolanda telling Mario the story of her own background – her marriage, divorce and current independence.

Epic theatre is characterised also by an undercutting of identification with fictional characters, in that psychologically rounded representations are refused. While epic interruptions will in themselves function to cut off spectator identification with characters, there is

8.1 *One Way Or Another*: fiction – Mario and Yolanda

8.2 *One Way Or Another*: documentary – Abacua society

another Brechtian device associated specifically with this form of distanciation – 'acting as quotation'. Instead of inhabiting and 'becoming' their characters, actors will, as it were, stand in for them in the distanced mode of 'quoting' characters' words. Although in *One Way Or Another* much of the acting is in fact quite naturalistic, it does take on some of the features of 'quotation' but usually through cinematic, rather than dramatic, means. The first documentary sequence, for example, which ends with a reference to education in the marginal areas, is immediately followed by a close-up of a woman talking directly to the camera in lip-synch, *cinéma vérité* style, about her work as a teacher. It subsequently transpires that the woman is Yolanda, who actually belongs to the fictional part of the film, but at this point her discourse is marked as 'documentary' by its codes and context. This has the effect of cutting off identification and relativising the acting in later sequences.

How do these distanciation devices serve the analytical project of *One Way Or Another*? In the first place, the distanciation itself tends to force the spectator into an active relation with the text, opening up the potential for questioning and analysis. The different discourses, moreover, are put together in such a way as to integrate analysis at the levels of signifier and signified. Halting Mario's talk about being a *ñañigo* with a descriptive 'aside' about Abacua society serves both to complete the reference and also to unpack the wealth of social, cultural and historical meaning encapsulated by it. The interaction of narrative and documentary codes, then, underscores the substantive sociological analysis. The enunciating discourse of the film as a whole thereby privileges an analytical approach to its signifieds.

Whose Choice? constructs similar modes of address in its treatment of the issues of contraception and abortion. The film operates in a relatively complex manner, by presenting its material as three discourses – information, interviews and narrative. In the interviews, two women detail the current situation in Britain as regards abortion and present a number of arguments in favour of 'a woman's right to choose'. The film also includes documentary footage of the June 1975 National Abortion Campaign demonstration in London. Added to – and transformed by – the documentary/informational aspects of these two discourses is a fictional narrative about a young woman's attempt to obtain an abortion. This third discourse is marked also by some of the distanciation devices characteristic of epic theatre, in particular lack of characterisation and narrative interruptions. The address of the film is constructed not only severally by its three discourses, but also as a whole by the ways in which the discourses are articulated together. There is little rigid separation in terms of the overall organisation of the film between elements of narration, information and interview, for example. Throughout, one discourse leads into, or is interrupted by, another – once more in the Brechtian manner.

Like *One Way Or Another, Whose Choice?* takes up familiar realist forms, and then deconstructs them by means of fragmentation and interruption, thereby transforming the spectator–text relations which would be privileged by each discourse on its own. This transformation marks a move away from identification, involvement and suspension of disbelief and towards a more active and questioning attitude to the processes of signification of the film and to its areas of concern. If *One Way Or Another* deconstructs the conventions of Hollywood and socialist realist narrative and traditional documentary, *Whose Choice?* offers a challenge to the kinds of documentary address commonly associated with the agitational/political film. The intended consequence of these deconstructive strategies is to open up space for active intervention on the part of spectators in the meaning production process, to subvert the completion and closure of meaning proposed by dominant cinema, and thus to offer spectators the opportunity to consider their positions on the issues at hand through their own processes of active reading, questioning and discussion. The oppositional character of the forms of expression of deconstructive cinema thus ideally works in conjunction with its matters of expression. *One Way Or Another* presents itself as oppositional on a fairly general level – as an example of Third World cinema and as dealing with problems arising in a developing and revolutionary society. Its treatment of the personal and the familial underscores this oppositionality, for these concerns have frequently been repressed even in revolutionary cinema. *Whose Choice?* deals with a topic which is either repressed in dominant discourses or, if not actually repressed, treated from different political perspectives: the film may be regarded as oppositional by virtue of its treatment of contraception and abortion from a feminist standpoint.

Feminine Voices

A concern shared by feminist representations of many kinds and across all media is an intent to challenge dominant modes of representation.

This concern is premised on the notion that in a sexist society, women have no language of their own and are therefore alienated from culturally dominant forms of expression. This permits a feminist politics of intervention at the levels of language and meaning, which may be regarded as equally applicable to the 'language' of cinema as it is to the written and spoken word. A politics of this kind can have two aspects: it may on the one hand challenge the dominance of certain forms of signification, and on the other move towards the construction of new, non-dominant, forms. The latter, of course, includes the former, but also goes further by posing the possibility of a specifically feminist or feminine language. Deconstructive cinema, in taking up and breaking down dominant forms and matters of expression, operates predominantly as a challenge to dominant cinema. I want now to look at some signifying practices which may be regarded as moving beyond the modes of expression privileged within patriarchal ideology. The distinction between the deconstruction of existing forms of representation and the creation of new ones is to some extent one of degree rather than of kind. In the first place, deconstruction may be regarded as an important – and perhaps even a necessary – step towards more radical forms of rupture. And in any case, in a situation where certain forms of representation are culturally dominant, alternative forms – however radical and regardless of their actual textual operations and modes of address – will always tend to be construed as a challenge to dominant forms. It should be emphasised, then, that the films discussed in this context may also be read (and indeed most of them have been read) as examples of deconstructive cinema.

The issue of a non-patriarchal language immediately raises the question of the relationship between such a language and feminism. Although it is clear that the question of women and language could not be raised in the ways it has been without the impetus of feminist politics, the nature and provenance of such a language remains rather more problematic. Posing the question of a women's language may be a feminist act, but are we talking here about a feminist language or a feminine language? If the question is of a feminine language, where does such a language come from? I have already discussed certain theories of femininity and language developed by feminist writers and theorists (see Chapters 1 and 3), and will not repeat the arguments here, save to reiterate that they are grounded in theories of female subjectivity as constructed in and by language. To this extent, then, the concern is with feminine language rather than feminist language. And although the possibility of feminine language could not even begin to be raised were it not for the existence of feminist politics, the converse is not necessarily true. This point has to be borne in mind in any consideration of the possibility of 'authentic' forms of expression for women, and it is certainly at issue in 'feminine writing' in the cinema.

Arguments on the question of feminine writing suggest first of all that certain texts privilege relations of subjectivity which are radically 'other' to the fixity of subject relations set up by dominant forms of signification, and, second, that the 'otherness' of such texts is related to, or emerges from, their articulation of feminine relations of subjectivity. This is perhaps the crucial point of distinction between deconstructive texts and feminine texts. Whereas the former tend to break down and challenge the forms of pleasure privileged by dominant texts, the latter set up radically 'other' forms of pleasure (in Roland Barthes' term, *jouissance*, or bliss). The possibility of such 'other' forms of pleasure in cinematic representations is raised in Laura Mulvey's theoretical work (as well as in her film practice, as co-director of *Riddles of the Sphinx* in particular). If the pleasure of dominant cinema draws on narcissistic and fetishistic scopophilia, Mulvey argues, any alternative approach needs to construct forms of pleasure based in different psychic relations (Mulvey, 1975). A suggestion by Claire Johnston that a feminist film practice should aim at 'putting ... the subject in process by textual practice' (Johnston, 1976, p. 58) indicates moreover that what is at stake here is a feminine cinematic writing, a cinema of *jouissance*.

Certain film practices of the 1970s may in fact be read as developments in this direction, and in this context, I shall look at four specific examples: *Thriller* (Potter, Arts Council of Great Britain, 1979), *Lives of Performers* (Rainer, 1972), *Daughter Rite* (Citron, 1978) and *Jeanne Dielman, 23 Quai du Commerce, 1080 Bruxelles* (Akerman, Paradise Films/Unité Trois, 1975). My argument is that these films share a discourse which sets up the possibility of sexual difference in spectator–text relations by privileging a 'feminine voice'. They pose the possibility of a feminine writing which would construct new forms of pleasure in cinema. The areas through which the 'feminine voice' speaks in these films include relations of looking, narrativity and narrative discourse, subjectivity and autobiography, fiction as against non-fiction, and openness as against closure.

Thriller is structured around a rearrangement of narrative discourse in dominant cinema by the instatement of a woman's questioning voice as the film's organising principle. The film is a reworking of the opera *La Bohème*, which is about a doomed love affair between a poet and a young seamstress: the woman finally dies of consumption. *Thriller* is told from the narrative point-of-view of Mimi, the tragic heroine, whose interrogatory voice-over pervades the film. The enigma set up by the film's narrative is the question of how and why Mimi died, the investigator ('I') being Mimi herself. By its recruitment of investigatory narrative structure and first-person voice-over, *Thriller* at once draws upon, parodies, challenges and transforms the narrative and cinematic codes of the Hollywood film noir. The female victim adds a twist to the reconstruction of her own death not only by telling the story herself, but also by considering causes for the unhappy romance and death of a young French working woman of a kind – social and historical conditions, for instance – that could not possibly enter the universe either of operatic tragedy or of the private investigator of film noir.

Lives of Performers is also, on one level, a reworking of the conventions of popular narrative genres. The film is subtitled 'a melodrama', and the narrative conventions it draws on are those of the 'backstage romance'. In thirteen long sequences, it tells the story of the relationships between a man and two women, a triangle. The characters, however, are 'playing' themselves – they are real-life performers in the group of dancers working with the film maker, Yvonne Rainer. The film departs quite radically from dominant conventions of film narrative in its ordering and structure, and in the freedom with which it articulates elements of fiction and non-fiction. The plot, for instance, proceeds by leaps and bounds punctuated by runnings on the spot – by ellipsis and accretion, in other words. Rainer says of her films: 'For me the story is an empty frame on which to hang images and thoughts which need support. I feel no obligation to flesh out this armature with credible details of location and time' (*Camera Obscura*, 1976b, p. 89). The story of *Lives of Performers* is told with so many asides that we never quite get to the end or the bottom of it. There is no resolution. The asides are the accretions, and the accretions are so many that they seem to call forth gaps elsewhere in the story, as if to make up for lost time. The first sequence shows the performers, whose lives the melodrama is about, in rehearsal for what turns out to be a real-life Rainer performance. An intertitle – 'all at once our tension vanished' – leads into the next sequence, in which the three star performers 'recall', as voice-over, their first meeting, with still photographs of Rainer's dance piece 'Grand Union Dreams' on the image track. These recollections are punctuated at points by the film maker's explanations of what is going on in the photographs. Where does the 'real' end and the 'fiction' begin? The subsequent cinematic rendering of the romance is interrupted wherever 'other concerns' seem more important – by a disquisition on acting, for example ('The face of this character is a fixed mask'), or a direct question to the spectator about the problem of character identification ('Which woman is the director most sympathetic to?' asks one of the women in the triangle, looking directly into camera). The narrative of *Lives of Performers* has its own logic, then, but it is not that of the enigma-resolution structure of classic narrative. Nor does it construct a closed and internally coherent fictional world: on the contrary, it opens itself up at numerous points to intrusions from the 'real world'.

What does this heterogeneous narrative voice imply for spectator–text relations? It is clear that none of the subject relations posed by classic narrative is at work here: identification with characters is impossible, and there is no narrative closure. The narrative processes of ellipsis and accretion offer, on the contrary, the possibility of pleasures other than those of completion. first, in moments of accretion (for example, during a long single-take sequence with virtually static camera, in which one of the performers dances a solo), the spectator has the option of pleasurable and open-ended contemplation of an image which constructs no particularly privileged viewpoint. The ellipses offer the possibility of a rather different pleasure, that of piecing together fragments of the story – the active pleasure, that is, of working on a puzzle. The interpenetration of fictional and non-fictional worlds and the lack of narrative closure set up a radical heterogeneity in spectator–text relations, and finally refuse any space of unitary subjectivity for the spectator. The textual practice of *Lives of Performers* may then be regarded as a 'putting in process of the viewing subject'.

As part of its articulation of fiction and non-fiction, *Lives of Performers* includes, at times, discourses readable as autobiographical. The second sequence of the film, mentioned above, examplifies this, and the autobiographical concern becomes more apparent in Rainer's next film, *Film About A Woman Who ...* (1974). *Daughter Rite*, Michelle Citron's film about mother–daughter and sister–sister relations, is even more pervasively autobiographical, but whereas in Rainer's films the would-be autobiographical material is somewhat distanced – it may be told in the third person, 'she' instead of 'I', or characters may be substituted for one another – the discourse of *Daughter Rite* seems more immediate and intimate: the autobiographical voice of the film, for example, is always the same and always speaks in the first person. Splitting in the film's discourse arises elsewhere, however, in the relationships between sound and image and in the juxtaposition of the film's different sequences. The film as a whole proceeds by alternations between sequences of 'journal discourse' in which a woman (the film maker?) talks about her relationship with her mother, and sequences – marked cinematically as 'direct' documentary – in which two sisters act out their relationships with one other and with their absent mother. In the 'journal discourse', the image is composed of 8 mm home movies, presumably of the speaker's childhood, optically printed on 16 mm, and slowed down, looped and replayed.

In the last chapter, I discussed the autobiographical structure which is common to many feminist documentary films, and argued that the combination of autobiographical material with documentary codes permitted identification on the part of female spectators with the women in the films. *Daughter Rite* may be read as both drawing on and critiquing the autobiographical structures of these earlier examples of feminist film making (Feuer, 1980). The directness and universality of the experience remains, particularly in the daughter's voice-over. But the film nevertheless adopts a quite complex and critical stance on the question of the 'truthfulness' of autobiographical and documentary discourses. This is evident first of all in the sound/image relationship of the 'journal' sequences. The daughter talks about her relationship with her mother by referring to events in the daughter's childhood. At the same time, the home movie footage, in depicting childhood scenes, may be read as 'illustrating' the voice-over. The magnification and graininess of the image and its slow movement and repetitiousness suggest also a close scrutiny of the past for clues about the present. The irony is that however hard the image is examined for clues, it cannot in the end deliver the goods. The assumption that sound and image support one another is a trap. The spectator has to draw her own conclusions about, for instance, the laughing and smiling mother of the family world of the home movies – a world where the sun constantly shines and whose inhabitants are always on holiday – and the pitiful mother talked about on the soundtrack who 'works so hard to fill her empty hours'. The film's critical position in relation to autobiography, too, works in the articulation, the one interrupting the other, of the 'journal' with the 'sisters' sequences. The latter scenes, despite their 'documentary' appearance, actually tread a borderline between fiction and non-fiction, as becomes apparent in the increasing unlikeliness of some of the situations acted out in them. The uncertainty evoked by this play of fiction and non-fiction may remain until the end of the film, when it is revealed in the credits that the 'sisters' are in fact actresses.

Although at one level the articulation of the different discourses of *Daughter Rite* works to produce distance in the relation between spectator and text, the film is difficult to read purely as an example of deconstructive cinema. The distanciation, if such it is, is not that of the critical spectator of the Brechtian film. The subject matter and the intimacy of the address of *Daughter Rite* draw the spectator closely into the representation, in effect replicating the pain and ambivalence of our hostile and loving feelings towards those to whom we are closest, our mothers in particular. At the same time, its discourses open up space for an involved but critical approach to those feelings, a kind of detached passion. Moreover, if only by virtue of the kinds of issues it deals with, the film constructs an address which acknowledges sexual difference as crucial in the signification process. Male and female spectators will surely read this film differently. At the same time, the representation clearly constructs no unitary subjectivity for spectators of either gender. *Daughter Rite* appears to offer a relationship of spectator and text in which distanciation does not necessarily ensue from gaps between discourses, although an actively critical perspective might.

Jeanne Dielman ... also invites a distanced involvement, but of a rather different kind. This 3½-hour long narrative film is a document of three days in the life of a Belgian petit-bourgeois widow and mother. Her movements around her flat, her performance of everyday chores, are documented with great precision: many of her tasks are filmed in real time. Jeanne's rigid routine includes a daily visit from a man – a different one each day – whose fees for her sexual services help maintain her and her son. The man's visit is slotted neatly between Jeanne's preparations for dinner and her son's arrival home. Every shot in the film is photographed at medium distance from its subject, with static camera mounted at about five feet from the ground. Many shots also work as autonomous sequences – a whole scene unfolds in a single take. There is thus none of the cutting back and forth characteristic of classic narrative. There are no reverse shots, match cuts or cut-ins, for example, and camera point-of-view maintains a relentless distance from the action. These cinematic elements of *Jeanne Dielman* ... function to establish the rhythm and order of Jeanne's repetitive household routines, the woman's means of maintaining control over her life. By the afternoon of the second day, the narrative has set up a series of clear expectations as to what Jeanne will do and when. At this point something (an orgasm with her second client?) provokes disorder in Jeanne's highly structured world, and a series of parapraxes ensues. Jeanne forgets to comb her hair when the client leaves, she burns the potatoes, she leaves the lid off the tureen where she keeps her earnings. Erupting into Jeanne's ordered routine, and disrupting the expectations set up for the specator by the cinematic representation of that routine, these tiny slips assume enormous and distressing proportions. *Jeanne Dielman* ... can in some respects be read as a structural/minimalist film (like Michael Snow's *Wavelength*, for example), in that the nature and duration of the representation call on the spectator to work out the structures governing the film's organisation, and thus eventually to predict what will happen next. Any disruption of these expectations can then seem quite violent. It is established, for instance, that Jeanne 'always' gets up in the morning before her son, puts on a blue robe and buttons it meticulously from top to bottom. On the third day, however, she misses a button, a slip which is immediately noticeable and assumes great significance – but the enunciation of the film nevertheless ensures that it is no more nor less significant than Jeanne's final 'slip', the murder of her third client.

Jeanne Dielman ... may be regarded as important in several ways for the question of feminine writing in cinema. Of particular significance are the qualities of the cinematic image and the relations of looking which it sets up. In the first place, the very fact that the film shows a woman doing housework sets *Jeanne Dielman* ... apart from virtually all other fiction films. Domestic labour has probably never been documented in such painstaking detail in a fiction film: for example, one sequence-shot about five minutes in length shows Jeanne preparing a meat loaf for dinner on the third day. The positioning of the camera in relation to the profilmic event at the same time constructs the representations of the woman's routine work as 'a discourse of women's looks, through a woman's viewpoint' (Bergstrom, 1977, p. 118). Chantal Akerman, the film's director, has said that the relatively low mounting of the camera corresponds with her own height and thus constructs a 'woman's-eye-view' on the action. More important, perhaps, is the refusal to set up privileged points-of-view on the action by close-ups, cut-ins and point-of-view shots. The relentless distance of the camera's (and the spectator's) look and the duration involved in representations of Jeanne's activities mean that 'the fact of prostitution, the visualisation of the murder, in some respects evens out into equal significance with the many conventionally less important images: Jeanne peeling potatoes; Jeanne kneading raw minced beef into a meat loaf' (ibid., p. 116). Finally, the refusal of reverse shots in the film entails a denial of the 'binding-in' effect of the suture of classic cinema: the spectator is forced to maintain a distance in relation to both narrative and image, constructing the story and building up narrative expectations for herself. The familiarity of Jeanne's tasks and the precision with which they are represented, combined with the refusal of suture, serve to free the look of the spectator while also, perhaps, shifting it towards the attitude of 'passionate detachment' that Laura Mulvey speaks of.

These four films – *Thriller, Lives of Performers, Daughter Rite* and *Jeanne Dielman* ... – hold out the possibility of a 'feminine language' for cinema, by offering unaccustomed forms of pleasure constructed around discourses governed either – quite literally – by a woman's voice, or by a feminine discourse that works through other cinematic signifiers. What I am suggesting is that although part of the project of feminine writing in cinema is obviously to offer a challenge to dominant modes of cinematic representation, its procedures for doing so go beyond deconstruction, in that their references to dominant cinema are oblique rather than direct. There are other differences, too, between deconstructive cinema and feminine cinematic writing. First, if it is accepted that feminine writing privileges heterogeneity and multiplicity of meanings in its modes of address, then it will have a tendency towards openness. The deconstructive text seems to work rather differently, however, in that although it too refuses the fixed subjectivity characteristic of classic spectator–text relations, meanings are limited by the fact that the various discourses of the text tend to work in concert with one another to 'anchor' meaning. Thus although the spectator may be unsettled or distanced by epic interruptions, 'acting as quotation', and so on, each of the fragmented discourses will tend to work in a common direction – in terms, certainly, of their matters of expression. It is perhaps no coincidence that both the examples of deconstructive cinema discussed here have highly circumscribed and predefined subject matters. The different discourses of the text may address these topics in different ways, but in the end there is a degree of overdetermination in the signification process. The space for active participation in the viewing process is opened up by the different modes of address of the discourses structuring the text, as well as by the ways in which they are articulated together. If, for example, *Whose Choice?* presents different discourses around its central concerns, those discourses when taken together constitute the film's subject matter in a particular way, so that the act of reading tends to be directed at differences of position and point of view on contraception and abortion between, say, the medical profession, the ordinary woman who requires an abortion, and feminists. It may therefore be concluded that deconstructive cinema can be tendentious (see Chapter 1), while at the same time allowing the spectator the space to negotiate her or his own position, but always in relation to a specific set of issues. If this is indeed the case, then a feminist deconstructive cinema is possible: feminist, that is, in its textual operations and matters of expression, and also feminist in intent.

I would argue, on the other hand, that tendentiousness and feminine cinematic writing do not necessarily go together. If the 'femininity' of a film emerges in the moment of reading, then clearly the intentions of its producers are not necessarily either here or there. This is well illustrated in the case of *Lives of Performers*: although there is some uncertainty as to whether or not Rainer is actually a feminist (Lippard, 1976; Rich, 1977), it does seem clear that when she made *Lives of Performers* she did not consciously intend any specifically feminist input, either as 'form' or as 'content'. And yet the film has been widely taken up by feminists. This suggests two things: first, that a text may be feminist, or of interest to feminists, without being tendentious, and, second, that non-tendentious texts may be seized as feminist in the moment of reading. Rainer's films were made in the milieu of the New York avant-garde art scene, whose practices at the time generally had little connection with feminist politics. Rainer's films have, however, subsequently been taken up within other cultural milieux, notably among feminists, and read as being of feminist interest. The context within which such films are received is therefore obviously crucial for the meanings they can generate.

But this is not the whole story. It would surely be wrong to suggest that signifiers, even in 'feminine' film texts, are completely free-floating: there are limitations to openness. Certain feminine film texts are not regarded as feminist simply because, by pure chance, they have been interpreted as such by certain audiences. Each of the films discussed here draws on certain matters of expression which, although not necessarily speaking feminist issues directly, may be regarded as doing so tangentially. Again, Yvonne Rainer's films usefully illustrate the point, precisely because Rainer's stance on feminism might problematise her films for those who want to claim them as feminist in intent. Ruby Rich, for example, argues that Rainer's films are central to feminism, not because of any intentionality on the part of the film maker, but because of the narrative conventions they take up and the modes of address they construct (Rich, 1977). The 'backstage romance' of *Lives of Performers* refers to a film genre that, in classic cinema, has been both attractive to and manipulative of women – the melodrama. The film offers both a pleasurable reworking and an ironic undercutting of this genre. The other three films I have discussed here similarly draw on, criticise and transform the conventions of cultural expressions traditionally associated with women: *Thriller*, the melodramatic story of doomed love, *Daughter Rite*, autobiography and the 'family romance', and *Jeanne Dielman* . . ., the family melodrama.

If deconstructive cinema sets up the possibility of an active spectator–text relation around a specific set of signifieds, and if feminine cinematic writing offers an openness of address in combination with matters of expression in relation to which spectators may situate themselves as women and/or as feminists, then clearly a feminist countercinema is not simply a matter of texts or 'form plus content'. In different ways and in varying degrees, the moment and conditions of reception of films are also crucial. The question of feminist countercinema is by no means exhausted by a discussion of feminist or feminine film texts: it has, in the final instance, to be considered also in terms of its institutional conditions of production and reception.

9

The Production of Meaning and

the Meaning of Production

Feminist countercinema is not a matter simply of a set of films which embody matters of expression and/or formal strategies that may challenge those of dominant cinema, or which construct a specifically 'feminine' cinematic language. Although feminist countercinema may obviously be any one or all of these things, this is by no means the whole story. In the last chapter I raised the interconnected questions of tendentiousness and spectator–text relations, and suggested that in feminist countercinema, meanings are constructed not only through the internal operations of texts, but also in their relations of production and reception. What I am suggesting is that as signifying practice, feminist countercinema must be conditioned by its institutional formation, just as dominant modes of cinematic representation, as I argued in Chapter 2, are formed in and by certain institutional apparatuses. The differences between dominant cinema and feminist countercinema lie precisely in the consequences of the dominance of the one as against the oppositional character of the other. Put simply, the logic of dominant cinematic institutions works in the final instance towards the production of dominant meanings. Dominant institutions of film production, distribution and exhibition cannot, for the most part, accommodate alternative or oppositional textual practices: the local Odeon is not the place to look for countercinema. This raises some important questions of political practice for all forms of oppositional cinema, feminist and otherwise: how to deal with the difficulties first of all of actually getting films made, and then of getting them to audiences, or of getting audiences to films. Questions of textual address, conditions of reception, and suchlike remain rather academic so long as films are not even made, or when they are, if the opportunities for exhibiting them remain severely limited.

The question of institutional structures is therefore crucial to all oppositional film practices, which face many problems in common. Feminist countercinema is no exception. Since institutional structures of cinema form the conditions under which films are, or are not, made and seen, they may be regarded as an important area of intervention for a politics of representation. There are basically two possible approaches to such politics: one, to work on dominant structures by attempting to open them up to new matters and forms of expression, and, two, to build oppositional institutions independently of dominant cinema. Although the two approaches are not necessarily mutually exclusive, oppositional cinema has for a variety of reasons – having to do mainly with the monolithic character of the institutions of dominant cinema, their economic *raison d'être* and the hierarchical character of their production relations – tended to work towards building its own alternative structures. My discussion in the present chapter will for the most part – although not exclusively – reflect this tendency. I begin by considering some issues and problems common to all forms of oppositional cinema, and then proceed to examine the questions of production, distribution and exhibition in relation specifically to feminist film practice.

Practitioners of what I have, in a general way, been calling countercinema or oppositional cinema formed the constituency of the Independent Film Makers' Association (IFA), a body set up in Britain in 1974 to promote 'an area of film-making which is not recognised by even the liberal sector of the industry': that is, to promote work which was 'aesthetically and politically innovatory in form and content'.[1] Because the IFA was instrumental in drawing attention to the relationships between structures of production, distribution and exhibition, and the ways in which film texts produce meanings differently in various contexts – the concerns precisely of the present chapter – I shall discuss its practices in some detail. The association's objective was to intervene in these structures and contexts by promoting certain kinds of signifying practice in cinema. The notion of 'independence' taken up by the IFA included, but also went beyond, independence from the structures of the film industry. The film practices which the association supported emerged independently of the structures of finance and production relations of dominant cinema, but they were also 'independent' in terms of textual strategies and modes of address. In the discussion which follows, I adopt the IFA's definition of independence.

The objective of the IFA was not so much to tackle the film industry as to foster various contexts in which independent film practices might have some opportunity to develop. This included, for example, the lobbying of organisations which provided, or might in future provide, financial support for independent film production. However, pressing for films to be produced, although obviously necessary, is not in itself sufficient for the construction of a social practice of cinema. The culturally marginal status of all non-dominant forms of cinema often means that audiences for them do not already exist, but must in a sense also be produced. The IFA recognised the potentially active role in this context of constituencies, apart from film makers themselves, concerned with the production of meaning in cinema. These included those involved in teaching or writing about film and others working with audiences, whose practices might inform the reception and reading of films. Consequently, at its 1976 annual general meeting, the IFA resolved to include in its brief: 'all those who are involved in the production of film meaning – that is, not only independent producers, but also exhibitors, film teachers, critical workers and film technicians' (Curling and McLean, 1977, p. 107). Despite the fact that the membership of the IFA took in feminist film makers, teachers and critics, the relationship of the association's practices to a specifically feminist countercinema was not necessarily either immediate or unproblematic. None the less, I would argue that, to the extent that feminist film practice is – to use the IFA's term – a social practice of cinema, the work of the association was pertinent to it. And indeed the IFA's inclusive approach to the question of meaning production seems particularly relevant to any discussion of feminist cinema. Moreover, feminist film practice shares many of the problems faced by independent cinema in general – notably the cultural marginality which manifests itself in problems of production funding and of making films available and accessible to audiences through distribution and exhibition.

Production

Film production is clearly an indispensible prerequisite to any other work on cinema. But production can embrace a range of activities and practices which may have a variety of implications as regards the nature and reception of film texts. Here I will focus on two areas of particular significance for feminist film practice, past, present and future: these are, on the one hand, material conditions of production in the form of both production finance and film-making technology, and, on the other, relations of production – the ways in which film makers work with each other and with their subjects to produce films. As regards the material conditions of film production, feminists have in general drawn on funding sources, techniques and technologies common to all oppositional or independent film practices. Working methods may, however, be informed by a more specifically feminist politics. The material conditions and relations of production peculiar to feminist cinema may have repercussions – not all of them straightforward or obvious – on the nature of feminist film texts and the ways in which they are received by audiences.

Making films is a costly activity, and few film makers have sufficient personal resources to fund anything other than the simplest of productions. Most film makers have consequently to seek outside backing for their work. In the film industry in capitalist societies, production costs are met by private investment made by individuals or corporations in the hope of a financial return if a film turns out to be commercially successful. Independent film makers are not as a rule in a position to secure investment capital, however, and therefore have to turn to sources whose object is not necessarily profit. These may include charitable trusts, arts foundations, government bodies with remits in the field of cinema or the arts, special interest groups, educational institutions, and so on. Relationships between funding agencies and film makers may vary from the patron–client model practised, for instance, by many private and state arts foundations in the USA and by the Arts Council of Great Britain in their funding of 'artists' films', to a situation in which the funding agency takes on more of a producer role, as in the case of the British Film Institute (BFI) Production Board.

Independent producers of feminist films are on the whole dependent on the same funding sources as independent film makers in general, and must compete with many others for the limited funds available. Funding is a perennial problem for independent film makers, and most films are made on low budgets, their producers often remaining unpaid for much of their labour. Most independent film makers support themselves and subsidise their own productions by other paid work –

teaching, say, or working in the film industry. Until the late 1970s, for
example, British Film Institute Production Board funding for independent cinema covered only the cost of materials, hire of equipment and
wages during the shooting of films: planning, scriptwriting and editing
and postproduction work were done largely in film makers' own time.
The London Women's Film Group production, *Whose Choice?*, for
example, was funded by the BFI Production Board with a grant of
around £1,700. This small budget was supplemented by sums
obtained from various other sources, including fees from rentals of the
group's other films. *Whose Choice?* took nearly eighteen months to
complete, and for much of that time the film makers worked on it,
unpaid, in their spare time.

In Britain, the second major state body promoting certain kinds of
independent film work is the Arts Council of Great Britain, which has a
funding category for 'artists' films' – for films, that is, made by
individuals already established as artists in one medium or another.
This brief tends to privilege certain types of film making – avant-garde
or experimental film, perhaps, rather than countercinema as it has
been defined here. Nevertheless, the concerns of a specifically feminist
countercinema may coincide with those of avant-garde cinema to the
extent that film language is a topic of investigation for both. Certain
kinds of feminine 'writing' in cinema may consequently be regarded as
falling within the definition of the 'artists' film'. Sally Potter's *Thriller*,
which was in fact funded by the Arts Council, is a good example of this.
The film is 'experimental' in the sense that it constitutes an
investigation of cinematic narrativity, and since Potter had previously
been a performance artist, her film could be seen as operating within
the terms of the Arts Council's funding policy. The relative openness of
the feminine text permits its concerns to be categorised, under certain
circumstances, as sufficiently similar to those of avant-garde cinema to
attract funding from a state body whose brief is subsidy of the arts.

As far as production finance is concerned, feminist film making has
thus, according to the nature of its intervention, to insert itself into the
institutional spaces available to independent cinema in general.
Depending on the policies of funding bodies, this will have consequences for the nature of films produced. In Britain, there exists no film
funding body, state or private, devoted specifically to the promotion of
feminist films, or even to films by women; whereas in Australia, for
example, a Women's Film Fund was set up by the Federal Parliament
in 1976, under whose auspices several films have now been produced

(Stern, 1978). The Australian situation seems, however, to be unique. Elsewhere in the world, the position is shaped very much by the relative prominence of state and private funding organisations. In the USA, for example, where private foundations are much more active as sponsors of films than in Britain, a somewhat uneven situation appears to obtain. Whereas funding agencies in the arts, say, will tend to operate a *laissez-faire* patron–client model in their relations with film makers, other sponsors may exert tighter control over film makers and their work.

Technology was also instrumental in the emergence and growth of independent feminist cinema, indeed of independent cinema in general (Johnston, 1975d). For reasons largely of cost and 'expertise', film production in the 35 mm gauge used within the industry is not an activity in which many people have the opportunity to engage, particularly if they want to make films which are different from the products of an industry whose principal *raison d'être* is financial return. Film making in the cheaper and more manageable gauge of 16 mm, however, made film production a much more widely available undertaking. Since the early 1960s it has been technically possible to shoot 16 mm film with synchronous sound in relatively poor lighting conditions, with lightweight equipment and a crew of no more than two people. This partly explains why the earliest independent film makers of second-wave feminism took up the technology of 16 mm production. Moreover, women have traditionally experienced, and continue to experience, great difficulty in obtaining training and positions in certain areas of production within the film industry, which means that few in any case have acquired the skills to deal with 35 mm production.

Claire Johnston has suggested that: 'alternative film-making on 16 mm opens up the possibility of *different conditions of production* which are particularly important for feminists today who are attempting to develop a feminist cinema' (Johnston, 1975d, p. 1, my emphasis). And indeed the women who, in the early 1970s, took up 16 mm technology to produce feminist films also adopted some of the working methods associated with 16 mm production, often developing approaches consistent with their feminist politics. I have described (see Chapter 7) how 16 mm film technology was developed hand in hand with a particular type of documentary cinema – direct cinema – and that, partly as a consequence of this, early feminist film making was largely documentary in form. There are, of course, other reasons for the early adoption of documentary forms on the part of feminist film makers, notably their commitment to put 'real women' on the cinema screen.

Some feminist film makers in the early 1970s were committed also to campaigning around forms of discrimination – confinement to low-paid, low-status jobs in particular – experienced by women working in the film industry (Association of Cinematograph, Television and Allied Technicians, 1975). The working practices of such film makers might be seen as a challenge to the hierarchical production relations of the industry, in which women are usually relegated to the lowest positions. These practices might include attempting to make film-making skills more widely available to women. The London Women's Film Group, for example, was formed in 1972 'to disseminate women's liberation ideas, and for women to learn the skills denied them in the industry' (LWFG, 1976, p. 59). Members of the group shared skills and worked collectively at all stages of production, not only in order to learn from each other, but also because of a principled feminist commitment to collective work. The commitment to collective work among film makers could extend to the subjects of their films, too, particularly where the techniques and conventions of direct documentary were taken up.

The specificity of feminist documentaries, I have argued, lies in their autobiographical character, and in their organisation around the discourses of the women appearing in them. The prominence given the subjects of these films has two aspects. It may operate first of all through the text itself, to the extent that its overall structure is governed by what protagonists have to say about their own lives. This is true of all three of the documentaries discussed in Chapter 7, but is perhaps most evident in *Union Maids*. Second, the influence exerted by the subjects of films might also be extra-textual. *Janie's Janie*, for example, charts the development of feminist consciousness of one woman, and this development structures the organisation of the film. However, it appears that the film-making process was in itself instrumental in inducing some of the changes and developments undergone by Janie (Kaplan, 1972, p. 39). Feminist film practice may therefore privilege both collective working methods on the part of film makers, and also a degree of participation and control on the part of the actual subjects of films – on the levels both of the film-making process and also of the organisation and structure of the final film.

To the extent that it has adopted collective and participatory working methods, feminist film practice shares in and contributes to a broader tradition within independent cinema, a tradition which arises from a rejection of the production practices of the film industry, with their highly developed divisions of labour and hierarchies of power and authority. The oppositional production relations I have described are, in other words, not confined to feminist film making. Nor, conversely, is all independent feminist film practice founded on collective and participatory working methods. The collective/participatory model is founded in a critique of industrial production relations which is premised on notions of film making as a form of labour. The proponents of such a critique would therefore tend to regard themselves as workers attempting a radical or prefigurative transformation of dominant relations of production. Another variant of independent film making which has a long history of its own, however, sets individual self-expression against the alienation and lack of personal autonomy characteristic of industrial relations of production. This notion of self-expression underpins most film practices defined as 'artistic' or avant garde, where film makers have typically worked on their own with simple and inexpensive technology. In this 'artisanal' mode of production, the film maker has total control over her or his work – but at the cost of cultural marginality. It is significant, however, that investigations of cinematic language and representation have abounded in this area.

What is the relevance of an artisanal mode of production to feminist film practice? First of all, low investments of money and 'professionalism' have meant that avant-garde cinema has historically been much more open than the film industry to women: indeed, the history of avant-garde cinema includes a number of women – Germaine Dulac, Maya Deren, and Joyce Wieland among them – who are acknowledged to have made significant contributions (Mulvey, 1979). Second – and perhaps rather more contentiously – it has been argued that the concerns of a cinema of self-expression, 'with its emphasis on the personal, the intimate and the domestic' (Cook, 1978b, p. 53), are of particular significance to women and, to the extent that these areas represent 'the submerged discourse of the domestic', to feminists also. Feminist film practice which draws on the notions of artistic freedom and self-expression that underpin much avant-garde cinema may, however, embody a certain contradiction: between on the one hand the individualism inherent in the concept of self-expression and on the other the social character of feminist politics. In some circumstances this contradiction can actually be quite productive, for it permits of a combination of bold and innovative approaches to cinematic representation with matters of expression which have a relatively broad social relevance and may possess a degree of immediacy for audiences.

Examples of feminist film making that constitute a move towards feminine or non-patriarchal cinematic 'writing' may be considered as in some respects working from, while at the same time also transforming, the concerns of avant-garde cinema. *Daughter Rite* is a good illustration of this: the film draws on the intimacy of the diary form, frequently regarded as a 'feminine' mode of expression, and its topic is, of course, the close personal relationships of the nuclear family. Moreover, in its use and reworking of 8 mm home movie footage, the film makes reference also to the artisanal modes of production characteristic of avant-garde cinema. The point at which *Daughter Rite* constitutes a transformation, a movement beyond the avant-garde tradition, however, is the point at which the personal vision of the diary and the home movie may be generalised as an experience shared by many women. The 1980s saw something of a shift within feminist film practice away from collective and participatory ways of working and towards more individualistic approaches. This change in working methods began with a move away from the documentary forms dominant in the early 1970s and towards the kind of work on cinematic representation which I have characterised as feminine writing. The distinction in feminist film practice between collective/participatory and artisanal working methods is thus clearly of some significance as regards the kinds of films produced.

Distribution

Production, crucial though it is, constitutes only one moment in the process of meaning production in cinema. If meanings are produced at the point of reception, then films in order to signify must actually be seen. Film makers, however, seldom have the time or the resources to ensure that their films are seen by more than a very few people. Making films available for exhibition calls for work mediating between the points of production and reception: this work is the province of film distribution. A distributor holds and maintains prints of films, publicises them, takes bookings and rents them out to exhibitors. A certain proportion of booking fees received for a film is then returned to its producer, according to the terms of the contract between producer and distributor. Returns on the distribution of films are a source of income for film makers which may be ploughed back into new productions.

Although distribution is invariably a prerequisite of exhibition in independent cinema as in dominant cinema, each has its own institutions of distribution, in which work is handled in different ways and according to distinct political and administrative principles. First of all, commercial distributors handling 'mainstream' films will rarely, if ever, also deal with independent films. Although there are a variety of fairly obvious reasons for this, I should like to emphasise one point in particular: the question of audience. There is at present no mass audience for independent cinema and no large-scale theatrical outlets for its exhibition. However, for many films of this type there already exist small and often very dedicated audiences; while at the same time, in view of the cultural marginality of independent cinema, film makers and distributors may also be keen to create new audiences for their films. Work with audiences – either making sure that films reach existing constituencies, or building up new audiences – is therefore a priority for independent film distributors in a way it rarely is for commercial distributors. The work of independent distribution consequently often overlaps into the area of exhibition. A distributor may, as a matter of policy, offer programming advice to exhibitors, say, or put exhibitors in touch with film makers who are willing to discuss their work with audiences. Although I shall attempt to confine discussion to distribution, some of what I say will inevitably reflect this tendency to interpenetration between structures of production, distribution and exhibition in independent cinema. I shall examine structures of independent film distribution as they relate specifically to feminist film practice, with particular reference to two organisations working in this field in the USA and in Britain respectively: New Day Films and Cinema of Women.

New Day Films had its beginnings as a distributor of feminist films in 1971, when two American film makers, Julia Reichert and Jim Klein, decided to deal with the distribution of their film *Growing Up Female* themselves. When Reichert and Klein were joined by two more film makers, New Day became a co-operative distributing films made by its members, films broadly defined by them as feminist, as demonstrating, that is, 'a feminist consciousness in one way or another. It has to deal with a feminist issue . . . .' (Lesage *et al.*, 1975, p. 22), while at the same time having a sufficiently wide appeal to be successful also with audiences outside the women's movement. The membership of the New Day co-operative expanded, and by 1982 the group had upwards of twenty films on its list, including *Union Maids*, of which the founders of New Day were co-directors.

Cinema of Women (COW) was set up in 1979 as an offshoot of Cinesisters, a group of women involved in film production who met regularly as a means of combating isolation at work and to provide mutual support. They also viewed and discussed feminist films. COW therefore had closer links with the women's movement than New Day, a difference which was reflected in the British group's approach to the politics of feminist film practice.[2] As it became increasingly apparent to Cinesisters that a large number of feminist films were simply not available for exhibition, six members of the group decided to set up an autonomous women's collectively run distribution organisation specialising in such films. COW's list soon included films made in Britain and elsewhere by feminist film makers. Both *Thriller* and *Daughter Rite*, for instance, were distributed by COW. The policy of COW was to handle feminist films made by women: films, that is, which in the view of the collective 'speak from the position of a woman and/or seek to disrupt the social, political and economic domination of women by men' (Hicks, 1980, p. 22). The efforts of the group were directed also at building up audiences for feminist films outside cinemas as such – in schools and colleges, women's groups, tenants' associations and trade unions, for example.

New Day and Cinema of Women both operated in a situation in which independent films are not as a rule handled by commercial distributors. While there do exist, both in Britain and the USA, distributors specialising in non-dominant cinema, from educational films and documentaries through to avant-garde and experimental films, organisations of this kind tend to regard themselves as specialist or perhaps 'alternative', rather than as oppositional, organisations. Thus although some of them may, under certain circumstances, be prepared to handle some kinds of countercinema, they will usually treat it in the same way as the rest of the films on their lists, films which may well be aimed at audiences or viewing situations in which oppositional cinema might not be readily acceptable as such. This in fact was one of the reasons why the founders of New Day decided to distribute their own films: they and the film makers who subsequently joined the co-operative felt that, even if they could secure distribution for their films within existing organisations (Emmens, 1975), in the hands of such organisations the films would probably not reach the audiences for which they were intended. They suggested that 'film-makers should distribute their films, particularly political film makers, in order to know their audience, complete the process. Making the film is just the first part' (Lesage *et al.*, 1975, p. 22). Both New Day and COW claimed to be able to maintain a degree of personal contact with their clients, by providing information on films and advice on programming: indeed COW in certain cases also arranged for film makers to be present at screenings of their films. Apart from this concern to foster relationships with audiences, independent distribu-tion may permit some degree of control on the part of film makers over the conditions of reception of their work, something which is in most cases impossible through commercial outlets.

Control by independent film makers over the distribution of their films may be exerted at several levels. These range from interventions within existing distributing organisations which are sympathetic to independent cinema, through the formation of distributors specialising in certain areas of independent cinema, to companies actually run by independent film makers. These forms of organisation within the field of independent distribution are not, however, without contradictions, many of which centre precisely on the question of control by film makers over their work. For example, conflicts arising between the IFA and the BFI over the terms under which the BFI was distributing films made by association members were in part related to the kinds of control over the product exerted by the distributor as against the film maker. And in fact one of the impulses for the formation of COW was dissatisfaction with the practices of existing oppositional distributors handling feminist films, some of which also distributed sexist material or permitted feminist films to be screened in sexist contexts: thus although most of the makers of the films distributed by COW may not have had any day-to-day influence in the work of the organisation, its political objectives were aimed at ensuring that films would not be used in ways which might be regarded by feminist film makers as undesirable.

Independent distribution, it seems, may offer film makers a degree of control over their work: first by actually providing an outlet for that work, and then in that, in working through a distributor, a film maker may direct her or his work towards particular audiences and may even be able to maintain some direct contact with those audiences. But what, given my earlier arguments concerning intentionality and the independent effects of texts and modes of address in meaning production, are the consequences of the conscious aims of film makers? While film texts may generate meanings independently of the intentions of their producers, many film makers are none the less committed, for one reason or another, to securing specific readings for their films. Such a commitment may be of particular relevance in relation to films intended as political interventions – to tendentious films (see Chapter 1). Film makers may have a political investment in certain interpretations of their films, and thus seek to delimit readings. One of the points at which the film maker may intervene in the production of meaning is in distribution, where she or he can be instrumental, at the very least, in directing a film towards specific audiences.

However, the very institutional structures of independent distribution may also have effects for signification. COW's dissatisfaction with the practices of non-feminist independent distributors concerning feminist cinema is a case in point. If feminist films are rented to 'inappropriate' clients or exhibited in a sexist context, then it is likely that they will be read differently than when exhibited in situations more acceptable to many feminists. On a more general level, the specific contexts in which films are exhibited will have effects on the readings of those films. This point highlights once more the significance of structures of distribution for both the servicing of, and also the creation of new audiences for, independent cinema. Distribution provides a point of contact with structures and contexts of exhibition, and exhibition contexts in turn inform relations between film texts and spectators, and therefore the ways in which films are read.

Exhibition

I have already mentioned the importance for independent cinema of work with audiences, in that audiences for oppositional films have often to be actively solicited. Given this, structures and contexts of exhibition must constitute an important area of intervention within independent film practice. This is particularly the case where independent films, in offering a challenge to textual operations of dominant cinema, may work in rather unexpected ways for audiences. A film which operates to unsettle spectators and push them towards an active approach to reading may come as a refreshing surprise.

However, it may equally well seem so completely 'other' by comparison with the easy involvement fostered by the modes of address of dominant cinema as to come across as difficult, boring, or even meaningless. It is pertinent here to point to a distinction between the spectator – as the subject positioned within processes of cinematic signification (see Chapter 3) – and the audience as a social group (Stern, 1979–80). A film may, through the modes of address it constructs, privilege a certain kind of spectator–text relationship. This, however, is no guarantee that every member of every audience for that film will react to it in precisely this way. 'Audience' may have a broad range of connotations, which may include – but is not necessarily limited to – a notion of the spectator as a component of the cinematic apparatus (Neale, 1980, p. 46).

The distinction between spectator and audience has potentially far-reaching political consequences for independent cinema. The 'other' character of much independent work may render it unpalatable at first sight. At the same time, however, if the future of a social practice of cinema depends upon the construction of new audiences for certain kinds of films, the reactions of actual audiences, particularly as these reactions depart from whatever spectator–text relations may be privileged by films' textual operations, need to be negotiated. This is why work with audiences is regarded as a priority for independent cinema. The objective of working with audiences is to effect some transformation in the passive receptivity characteristic of spectator–text relations in dominant cinema, rather perhaps than simply to create another mass audience for a different kind of film. Work with audiences might therefore involve active efforts to make films available for distribution, to ensure that they are exhibited, and – to the extent that they may work in unexpected or unfamiliar ways – to render them accessible to audiences and to generate debates around cinematic representation. Three overlapping sets of practices – those of distribution, exhibition, and film theory and criticism – constitute this work with audiences. I shall look at each in turn as it intersects with feminist film practice.

Independent distributors are aware that they must take an active stance in relation to their constituencies if they are to ensure that their films reach certain kinds of audience, people who are not regular cinema-goers in particular. Hence their commitment to the provision of guidance to exhibitors, and their stress on the importance of bridging the gap between film makers and audiences. When New Day Films was first formed, for example, attempts were made to contact groups, such as trade unions, with which many distributors would not normally be in regular touch. The nature of access by independent film makers to public television in the USA has in fact meant that some of New Day's films have reached quite large audiences: *Union Maids*, for instance, has been broadcast nationally on PBS at least twice. Cinema of Women's interventionist approach to the politics of feminist cinema led it to adopt a practice pioneered by its predecessors in the London Women's Film Group: providing speakers or notes for teachers or group leaders in order to facilitate and encourage discussions around its films.

The practices of independent distributors around work with audiences obviously intersect with those of exhibitors of independent films. Exhibitors, however, also face their own problems: among them, that of suitable venues is paramount. Most commerical film theatres do not, particularly outside metropolitan areas, deal with independent film. Art houses will sometimes handle certain films of this kind, particularly films which – like Chantal Akerman's, for example – may be assimilated to European art cinema. Art house exhibition, however, has implications for the ways in which films are received, in that art cinema as a genre and an institution proposes its own conventions of reading films. Other types of film theatre may attempt more actively to work with audiences for independent cinema. This is the practice, for example, of some of the Regional Film Theatres subsidised by the British Film Institute with the objective of promoting the exhibition of non-commercial films outside London. Films may be programmed as seasons, and other activities – publications, courses, discussions, and so on – set up in conjunction with exhibition (Neale, 1980). Independent exhibitors may extend this practice by opening up control over programming and related events to groups within the local community.[3] Wherever exhibition is dealt with in these ways, the relations of consumption of films characteristic of dominant cinema are shifted somewhat. At the same time, however, some of the forms of subjectivity proposed by the apparatus of dominant cinema may remain in operation so long as films continue to be exhibited in conventionally designed cinema auditoria. If, then, 'The intensity of the desire for visual pleasure which film embodies is considerably amplified in conventional cinemas' (ibid., p. 55), an independent film practice premised on a challenge to dominant relations of spectator and text must come to terms with the potential consequences for the social audience of the screening of oppositional films in conventional viewing situations. In other words, independent exhibitors' work with audiences – discussions, publications, courses and the like – may in some measure have to operate against the effects of relations of subjectivity constructed by the cinematic apparatus.

The position is different, however, where screenings take place in venues other than film theatres – in classrooms or in community centres, say. Non-theatrical exhibition sets up its own spectator–text relations, and the expectations of audiences may be adjusted accordingly. They may, for example, come prepared to take a more active approach to film viewing. Non-theatrical exhibition is of particular importance for independent feminist film practice, because a large potential audience for feminist films exists among women who rarely visit film theatres, and who would certainly not normally consider going to see films in non-commercial cinemas: 'Feminist films ... belong to a political movement and need to be seen other than in independent cinema. They need to be seen in women's organisations, trade unions and community groups' (Hicks, 1980, p. 22). In contexts such as these, the accepted rationale for screening films is usually to generate discussion, and this attitude will obviously have consequences for the ways in which films are received by audiences. On the other hand, to the extent that many of the contradictions surrounding relations of subjectivity and pleasure in cinema are not raised by non-theatrical exhibition, it tends to sidestep rather than attack the important issue of the forms of pleasure generated by the apparatus of dominant cinema.

Whatever the exhibition context, critical and theoretical practices can be instrumental in informing audience response to films. These practices are of particular significance wherever screenings are accompanied by discussions, say, or form part of a course. This was the rationale for the Independent Film Makers' Association's inclusion of film teachers and critical workers within its brief: such groups, it was argued, were just as much involved in the production of meanings in cinema as were film makers, distributors and exhibitors. What, then, is the relevance of critical and theoretical work on cinema to a feminist film practice? In answering this question, I will examine three interrelated points of intervention in feminist cinema by critical/theoretical practice, and consider some problems and contradictions, and also some possibilities for future developments. The areas of activity I will consider are: the relationship between feminist film criticism and the women's movement; the appropriation of certain films to a body of feminist cinema; and the construction of a critical/ theoretical language adequate to developments in feminist film practice.

Feminist film criticism straddles on the one hand film theory as it is generated in educational institutions, magazines, and suchlike, and on the other the diverse political practices of the women's movement itself. The relationship is not always free of contradiction, for the perspectives, politics and needs of the two sets of practices do not always coincide. However, since a feminist film practice which prioritises work with audiences obviously requires contact with its constituency, there is clearly some coincidence of interest. Feminist films may, according to their character, be instrumental in consciousness-raising or in publicising specific campaigns, or may operate more generally to affirm certain forms of feminist consciousness or to constitute oppositional cultures for women and/or feminists. The most immediate point of contact between feminist film criticism and the women's movement is a servicing relationship through which the actual existence of feminist films is made known: for example, popular feminist magazines usually carry regular film reviews. Feminist film critics have also been active in organising screenings, courses and discussions centred on certain film practices.[4]

Feminist film criticism may, moreover, through practices of reading and textual analysis, be instrumental in recontextualising instances of classic cinema by appropriating them for a feminist perspective on cinematic representation (see Chapter 4). In this way mainstream films can be transformed by oppositional readings, and even come to acquire new and unexpected interest and pleasure for feminists. A similar process may take place also with independent cinema, in that critical work, by advancing readings of certain films, may not only bring these films to the attention of feminist audiences, but may even at times be instrumental in ensuring that films are put into circulation. Chantal Akerman's film *Jeanne Dielman . . .*, for example, was acquired for 16 mm distribution in Britain by an independent distributor probably largely as a result of the interest generated around the film among feminist critics and audiences. This occurred within an overall political context in which independent cinema, although small-scale and marginal, is relatively well organised. At the same time, in the USA – where independent film culture is more fragmented – *Jeanne Dielman . . .* did not find a distributor, despite the attention it received from feminist critics there (Kinder, 1977; Loader, 1977; Perlmutter,

1979). Possibly the only context in which Akerman's films might find an institutional outlet in the United States is in the art house field – with the implications for their reading which I have already indicated – or possibly within the avant-garde, where they will be lost to most feminist audiences.

Lives of Performers is a similar case in point. This film was taken up by feminists, in some measure at least as a consequence of the attention given it by feminist critics in Britain and the USA. *Lives of Performers* and *Jeanne Dielman* ... – both, I have argued, feminine texts – are relatively open as regards the meanings they generate. They can, in other words, be read in a variety of ways, and one of the crucial determinants of their reception must be the institutional context within which they are positioned. Thus while *Jeanne Dielman* ... might in certain contexts be read as an art house movie or as a structural/ minimalist film, *Lives of Performers* might be seen as exemplifying a certain form of avant-garde cinema. The appropriation of both films for feminist cinema ensures that certain limits are placed on the range of meanings available from them. This has come about – in part at least – through the work of feminist film criticism.

As part of its practice, feminist film criticism is called upon to develop critical and theoretical language to deal with various kinds of independent feminist cinema. This is the province of the film theory developed through the teaching of courses on women and film or feminism and cinema, through festivals or seasons of screenings devoted to feminist cinema (Johnston, 1980; Stern 1979–80), and through writings in the field of film theory and criticism as they relate to feminism. Theory produced in these contexts may also inform subsequent film practices. In Britain at least, where film theory is less highly institutionalised within the academy than in the USA, there has been a relatively close – and sometimes highly charged – relationship between the institutional practices of feminist film theory on the one hand and feminist film making on the other. While theory has been productive as regards film making, and vice versa, and while there is some acceptance of the argument that theorists are engaged in the production of film meaning, the situation is none the less not without its contradictions. Some of these stem from a perennial problem besetting any theory which aims to be grounded, while at the same time constructing concepts adequate to oppositional or innovatory signify-ing practices: that of accessibility. The problem is compounded where film is concerned to the degree that feminist film practice seeks to

revolutionise dominant modes of cinematic representation and spectator–text relations; for the results of such a practice may at times appear
unfamiliar or difficult to understand. The question of accessibility thus
arises in relation both to film texts themselves and also to critical and
theoretical work around those texts. However, given the central place
occupied by questions of language and signification in feminist politics
in general, and the challenge to dominant modes of representation
posed by feminism, it is, I believe, important to work towards the
construction of feminist theories of cinema which are neither theoreti-
cist nor unduly alienating (Kuhn and Wolpe, 1978a; Stern 1979–80),
but which are at the same time adequate to their objects and purposes.

The institutional practices of film production, distribution and
exhibition intersect at the point of meaning construction, operating in
specific ways in individual film texts. The particular institutional and
textual practices which constitute independent feminist cinema also
operate in conjunction with various other practices, notably those of
feminist politics. These formations and interrelations are often
contradictory, and are certainly constantly changing. In this situation,
meanings generated by films are conditioned by a series of textual and
contextual operations. In some circumstances, textual operations may
be more instrumental than contextual operations in producing
meanings, while in other cases the process may work the other way
about.

PART V

Postscript

In this postscript I consider some of the many changes that have come about in feminist film theory and practice since Women's Pictures *was first published in 1982. I also reassess the relationships between feminist theories and feminist practices of cinema, and between feminism, cinema, cultural politics and knowledge. In Chapter 10 I present a critical overview of the main strands of a decade's developments in feminist film theory, extending and critiquing some of the discussions in the original* Women's Pictures, *and offering some suggestions for future directions. In Chapter 11, I consider in depth three key issues of contention within feminist film theory: the question of female spectatorship in cinema; the theoretical issues at stake in a debate around a historical film genre aimed specifically at women audiences, the Hollywood woman's picture of the 1930s and 1940s; and a series of appropriations from psychoanalysis to feminist film theory of the idea of femininity as a masquerade. Finally, in Chapter 12 I take up some of the issues dealt with in Part Four, tracking changes since the early 1980s – at the levels of both film texts and institutional contexts – in feminist practices of cinema and in the connections between these and feminist film criticism and theory. In an epilogue to this closing chapter, the question of the politics of feminist knowledge, discussed in Chapter 1, is re-examined in the light of today's conditions.*

10

Bent on Deconstruction

In the years since *Women's Pictures* was first published, feminist film theory has flourished – to the extent that it has become a keystone of the discipline of film studies and the locus of developments at the very cutting edge of contemporary film theory. Since parts II and III of this book were written, feminist film theory has continued its exploration of the relationship between classic Hollywood cinema and 'woman', or 'the feminine'. While this has entailed losses as well as gains, the gains have been considerable. The conceptual and methodological sophistication of feminist film theory has increased enormously: it has challenged the very paradigms it recruited from film theory, forcing fresh questions onto the critical agenda and opening up entirely new territories for exploration. If my discussion here of the recent evolution of feminist film theory is structured more or less chronologically, this is largely for convenience of exposition: no suggestion of any teleology of 'progress' is intended. On the contrary, given that feminist film theory has repeatedly returned to a particular range of issues, its development is perhaps better described as a series of circles or spirals than as a straight line.

The early 1980s saw the rise within feminist film theory of a tendency which, following the lead taken by Laura Mulvey in her essay 'Visual pleasure and narrative cinema' (Mulvey, 1975, reprinted in Mulvey, 1989b), sought to found a specifically feminist metapsychology of cinema. The objective was to investigate the ways in which the cinematic apparatus operates psychically – at an unconscious level, that is – to produce meanings and modes of spectatorial subjectivity organised around sexual difference. Variants of psychoanalytic theory were appropriated in this quest. However, this move – although influential – did not go unchallenged. In the first place, the value of psychoanalytic theory and its utility in feminist practices of film theory and criticism were, and indeed continue to be, subjected to question. Second, the notion of film spectatorship itself became a focus of intense debate and controversy among feminist film theorists.

The psychoanalysis question had been a bone of contention within film theory well before feminism began to make its mark in the field. And despite Juliet Mitchell's arguments on behalf of a feminist interest in psychoanalysis (Mitchell, 1974), it was a point of dispute also within feminist social theory. Meanwhile, the efforts of those (male) film theorists who, around the early to mid 1970s, were attempting to recruit certain forms of post-Freudian thought to their quest for a metapsychology of cinema (see, for example, Metz, 1975) were themselves hardly calculated to inspire feminist enthusiasm. None the less, the idea of the cinematic apparatus embodied in Christian Metz's metapsychology of cinema is still helpful in understanding the psychical workings of cinema spectatorship, and especially of cinema's peculiar fascinations and pleasures (see Chapter 3).

But Metz's picture is painted in the very broadest brushstrokes, permitting of no distinction between types of cinema and modes of spectatorship. This monolithic quality extends to sexual difference: notwithstanding the centrality within psychoanalysis of questions of sexuality and sexual identity, the Metzian paradigm of the cinematic apparatus remains extraordinarily blind to sexual difference (Penley, 1985; reprinted in Penley, 1989; Rose, 1986).

The feminist project of introducing sexual difference into theories of the cinematic apparatus failed, however, to avert dissension. Psychoanalytic film theory is open to criticism on a number of grounds. Accusations of elitism abound – not only because of the notorious impenetrability of the language of the Lacanian version of psychoanalysis favoured in many explanations of cinematic subjectivity, but also because of the scent of orthodoxy which haunts the entire psychoanalytic enterprise.

Criticisms aimed more specifically at the theoretical grounding of cinepsychoanalysis point to its universalism and its ahistorical nature; to its failure to distinguish between modalities of spectatorship on grounds other than sexual difference; to its idealism; and to its complicity with the sexism inherent in the ideas of castration and the Oedipus complex – in particular of the Lacanian version in which the phallus stands as symbol of the organisation of language-as-difference, and thus of meaning and representation in their entirety (Jacobowitz, 1986; Pribram, 1988).

As a consequence of this controversy, feminist film theory appears to have divided itself into pro- and anti-psychoanalysis camps, with significant consequences for developments in the field since the early 1980s. Theorists who continue to find the psychoanalytic paradigm useful in understanding the apparatus of cinema have persevered in exploring questions of vision, identification, desire and pleasure in relation to sexual difference.

In Laura Mulvey's 'Visual pleasure and narrative cinema', these questions are broached within the terms of the psychical processes of voyeurism, fetishism and narcissism, which Mulvey argues construct sexual difference in the relations of vision embodied in the Oedipal moment: the lesson about having or not having the phallus is premised exactly on *seeing*. The logic of this argument is that the cinematic apparatus organises the unconscious processes associated with the Oedipal moment.

This has been the starting point of several lines of enquiry in psychoanalytic feminist film theory, among the most promising being explorations of fantasy, masochism, and castration. In psychoanalytic terms, the subject of fantasy may occupy multiple and shifting sites of identification, simultaneously and/or consecutively, in relation to the content, the *mise en scène* and the narration of the fantasy. As a component of the cinematic apparatus, fantasy offers a complication of the metapsychology of spectatorial fixity implicit in theories of the look based around the mechanisms of voyeurism, fetishism and narcissism (Cowie, 1984).

Fantasy is also at stake in considerations of masochism as a psychical component of cinematic identification. The concept of masochism permits the admission to consideration of fantasies associated with the pre-Oedipal rather than the Oedipal stage, thus offering a model of cinema as capable of producing meaning and pleasure without the mediations of castration, sexual difference and feminine lack. This circumvents some of the theoretical difficulties associated with the implicit maleness or masculinity of the Mulveyan look.

Gaylyn Studlar has advanced a psychoanalytic model of cinema spectatorship based upon Gilles Deleuze's revision of Freudian theories of masochism (Deleuze, 1971): Deleuze emphasises the psychical implications of the infant's fascination with the all-powerful mother of the pre-Oedipal period. Studlar treats masochism both as the grounding of a film aesthetic and as a metapsychology of cinema, a psychic process governing the production of cinematic meaning and pleasure. She finds her exemplar *par excellence* of the masochistic aesthetic in cinema in the films Josef von Sternberg made in collaboration with Marlene Dietrich, which Studlar believes 'bear an amazing formal and psychoanalytic resemblance to Deleuze's description of the masochistic aesthetic in literature'. The 'formal relations of masochism located by Deleuze . . . also enable classic narrative cinema to produce visual pleasure' (Studlar, 1985, p. 5). In the masochism scenario, visual pleasure is produced through a spectatorial positioning of submission (see also Silverman, 1988b; Studlar 1984; Studlar, 1988).

If the question of castration, with its spectres of penis envy and lack, has been an area of particular difficulty as far as feminists and feminist film theorists are concerned, a focus on masochism gets around the problem simply through shifting attention onto the pre-Oedipal period. But what then happens to sexual difference in the cinematic apparatus? And is it tenable to eliminate the figure of the castrated woman (Lurie, 1981–2), or even of the phallic woman, from psychoanalytic feminist film theory on the grounds purely of the political unpalatability of the idea?

The value of psychoanalytic film theory, however, goes beyond its usefulness in the construction of a metapsychology of cinema, as the discussion of psychoanalytic textual analysis in Chapter 5 indicates. Psychoanalysis offers a set of protocols for cultural reading and interpretation, for an analysis of culture which takes cultural products, such as film texts, and subjects them to symptomatic readings. When undertaken from a feminist standpoint, such interpretations can reveal a great deal about the place of the feminine in the Unconscious of a patriarchal society. Barbara Creed is one of a small number of feminist film theorists who have attempted to shed light on this question by tackling head-on the tough issue of castration. In a study of the 'monstrous-feminine' in the horror film, she argues that woman figures in patriarchal culture not only as castrated, but more significantly as potentially castrating – as a terrifying reminder of death, suffocation, the void (Creed, 1993).

While these extensions and developments of psychoanalytic feminist film theory have been under way, another and different – though in some respects related – set of questions emerged within feminist film theory. Once again, Laura Mulvey's 'Visual pleasure' essay – which by the early 1980s had become a constant point of reference, ritualistically invoked – was the point of departure: as noted in Chapter 3, by proposing that the implied, or ideal, spectator of classic Hollywood cinema is male (or, more subtly, that pleasure in looking is a masculine prerogative, or that cinematic address works to constitute the spectator as male or masculine), Mulvey had opened up the question of female spectatorship in dominant cinema.

At this point, feminist film theory's project of exploring the relationship between dominant cinema and 'the feminine' began to confine itself to a rather circumscribed set of questions centred upon the 'problem' of female spectatorship in cinema: Is looking an inherently masculine activity? Are there specifically feminine ways of looking, and if so what are they? What is at stake in women's pleasure in dominant cinema? Does dominant cinema allow any space at all for women's pleasure? 'Is the gaze male?' (Kaplan, 1983).

The quest for female desire and feminine subjectivity, and the project of introducing female or feminine modes of spectatorship into the Mulveyan paradigm of the look, were prominent features of feminist film criticism during the early to mid 1980s (see, for example, Doane, 1982; Mayne, 1985; Walker, 1984). The search for the female spectator – as against the endeavours of the feminist reader 'against the grain' (see chapters 4 and 5) – aims to bring to light the potential for female pleasure which might already be present in culturally dominant representations.

At this point, feminist film theory began to seek a definition of the female spectator as distinct from the male 'bearer of the look'. In its more nuanced versions, this debate sought to avoid essentialism – the reduction of sexual difference to anatomical attributes – by looking at sexual difference rather than at gender, and at modes of address – at feminine or masculine subject positions, that is – as against female or male spectators (Kaplan, 1986). But in most of the early to mid 1980s debates around female spectatorship, the 'female' or the 'feminine' is regarded as a homogeneous category, of interest because of its difference from the male or the masculine norm (for its 'otherness') rather, perhaps, than for its intrinsic qualities. In other words, psychoanalytically grounded feminist film theory of this period was dominated by a model of female spectatorship defined in terms of its difference from male/masculine spectatorship, and treated as internally undifferentiated.

At the same time, a view was gaining ground that dominant cinema might be capable of offering openings for the play of 'authentic' feminine subjectivities, rather than necessarily suppressing them or constructing them as 'other' in relation to a patriarchal norm. This position emerged not so much from feminist work on cinema as from feminist studies of other popular cultural forms. In an early study of television soap opera, Tania Modleski had put forward the view that mainstream cultural forms might in certain circumstances speak to and for the feminine – and do so without any prior ideological unravelling of the sort proposed by feminist 'reading against the grain'. In other words, popular culture can have something positive to offer to the 'ordinary woman' as well as to the feminist cultural deconstructionist (Modleski, 1982; see also Radway, 1984). The premiss here is that certain popular genres – romantic fiction, television soap opera, the Hollywood woman's picture, for example – offer a safe haven to the female imagination.

After the mid 1980s, this debate surfaced in feminist film theory in the form of a growing interest in 'films for women' or 'women's genres' – as opposed, that is, to an interest in images of women, say, or in feminist cultural or textual readings (Brunsdon, 1986). In a long-running debate in *Cinema Journal* about the 1937 Hollywood film *Stella Dallas* (see Chapter 11), the theoretical preoccupations of the moment are fully exercised. The focus of debate remains, as before, classic Hollywood cinema, but with feminist film theorists now looking for films and genres with special appeal for women. What they came up with was the Hollywood 'woman's picture'.

The woman's picture, which flourished in the 1930s and 1940s, is commonly regarded as a subtype of the Hollywood melodrama, a genre which, by the 1970s, had already attracted the attention of pre-feminist film critics and theorists (see especially Elsaesser, 1972, reprinted in Gledhill, 1987). As in the Hollywood melodrama, the woman's picture's characteristic themes involve moral dilemmas and conflicts associated with sexuality, home and family in a bourgeois milieu. The woman's picture differs from melodrama in terms of its rhetoric, however:

> The women's [sic] picture is differentiated . . . by virtue of its construction of a 'female point-of-view' which motivates and dominates the narrative, and its specific address to a female audience (Cook, 1983, p. 14).

From this it can be inferred that any 'feminine' space constructed by the woman's picture is born of a liaison between an enunciation which proposes a feminine spectatorial position and a textual address which constructs a female audience. This move towards a positive evaluation of popular 'gynocentric' genres – or of one such, at least – served to broaden the female spectatorship paradigm to take in, along with female spectator-in-the-text, the 'social subject', the woman in the cinema audience. In the same move, though, some knotty problems of conceptualisation and methodology were also introduced.

In the first place, the woman's picture appeared to offer ample scope for a characteristically psychoanalytic investigation of its enunciative modes. Does the woman's picture, we might ask, offer a specifically female or feminine position to the spectator, or does *every* relation of spectatorship in dominant cinema fall under the sway of Hollywood's 'objectification' of women? Does the woman's picture offer some space for the free play of the feminine, or does it simply document a troubling of patriarchally defined modes of subjectivity centred upon the figure of the woman (Doane, 1987)? What is the relationship between the modes of subjectivity proposed by the woman's picture and the female audiences to which these films were marketed? How does the woman in the cinema audience, as a social subject, negotiate meanings which might be proposed in the rhetoric of the film text (Gledhill, 1988)? How does the woman's picture orchestrate emotional responses in the women in the audience (Gledhill, 1987)?

One consequence of taking the Hollywood woman's picture of the 1930s and 1940s as exemplary of popular 'films for women' is that the question of the historical cinema audience immediately presents itself. What responses did these films evoke when they first appeared? To what extent do readings made in the 1980s shed light upon the question of historical film reception? How in any case can we know what the responses of audiences of the 1930s and 1940s were? The question of historical as against contemporary readings and responses was at the heart of the *Cinema Journal* debate on *Stella Dallas*, and was eventually to emerge as part of a much broader attack upon the notion of the female spectator as homogeneous and undifferentiated. At the same time, though, concern with the historical female audience, especially the audience for Hollywood cinema, has inspired important new feminist work in the institutional history of cinema.

Taking up an earlier strand of investigation in cinema history (Allen, 1980; Eckert, 1974, reprinted in Gledhill, 1991; Eckert, 1978, reprinted in Gledhill, 1991), feminist film historians working in the USA have recently undertaken research which draws upon a very wide range of historical source materials (studio production records, pressbooks, local newspapers and women's magazines, for example, as well as films) to enquire into the specifics of cinema's address to past American audiences. Many of these historians concern themselves especially with cinema's appeal to women as consumers of fashion, beauty and lifestyle products (Gaines and Herzog, 1990; Herzog and Gaines, 1991, LaPlace, 1987; Ohmer, 1990; *Quarterly Review of Film and Video*, 1989). At once theoretically informed and rooted in empirical research, this feminist historiography of cinema is a promising growth area in feminist film studies (*Camera Obscura*, 1990). Meanwhile, some 'ethnohistories' of historical female audiences based on oral history and other direct audience research, though fewer in number and more troubled by methodological and practical difficulties, are being undertaken in Britain (Stacey, 1993a; 1993b; Taylor, 1989).

The project of investigating film spectatorship from the standpoint of the female audience, historical or contemporary, is part of a broader ethnographic aspiration which has entered film studies under pressure from research in the reception of contemporary popular media other than cinema – of television especially, but also of popular literature (Ang, 1985; Radway, 1984). The bulk of this research has been undertaken under the umbrella of cultural studies, a discipline which operates on the premiss that meanings and their production together constitute culture; and that these are indivisibly linked to social structures and thus can only be exhaustively explained in social and social-historical terms.

Since the late 1980s, cultural studies has had a profound impact upon feminist film studies, particularly in the USA. This is largely because its emphasis on the social and cultural aspects of the uses of popular media – as against film theory's stress on the internal organisation and rhetoric of cultural texts – seems to offer a model of popular culture as potentially redemptive, or as a site of cultural resistance. The popular media audience posited by cultural studies is rather different in nature from the cinema spectator constructed by film studies, however. If the latter is ongoingly produced or formed in the activity of spectatorhip, a process which may involve the Unconscious, the former's relationship with the medium is charac-terised by conscious acts of negotiation or resistance. These latter responses are shaped by pre-existent membership of certain social categories – gender among them – and by the fact that the audience comes to the act of reception already in possession of a range of knowledges and cultural competences.

In the context of an emphasis on the social as against the psychical aspects of spectatorship, feminist film theorists have been forced to question not only the degree to which response, as opposed to address, may be inferred from a text alone; but also whether sexual difference is the only, or even the most important, factor in processes of signification (Waldman, 1988). The notion of sexual difference as a modality of spectatorship had, as I have suggested, been an advance on the undifferentiated spectator of the theory of the cinematic apparatus (see Chapter 3). But the concept of the female spectator of psychoanalytically based feminist film theory, being unequipped to deal with lines of difference other than gender, itself now began to be seen as inadequately nuanced (see Chapter 11).

Feminist film theory's turn to cultural studies has inspired fresh approaches to its object, cinema, and opened up some hitherto unexplored areas of investigation. Among these is a foray into ethnographic work with contemporary black women filmgoers (Bobo, 1988) and some theoretical work on race and spectatorship (*Discourse*, 1986–7; Doane, 1991b; Trinh, 1992). The African-American cultural theorist bell hooks is not alone in pointing out that feminist film theory's concept of the female spectator has both occluded differences *between* female spectators and homogenised the activity of spectatorship:

> Despite feminist critical interventions aimed at deconstructing the category 'woman' which highlight the significance of race, many feminist film critics continue to structure their discourse as though it speaks about 'women' when in actuality it speaks only about white women (Hooks, 1992, p. 123).

However, while some research has also been directed at non-white women, and also at lesbians, as cultural readers (Ellsworth, 1986; Straayer, 1984), there appears to be less concern in studies of the reception of films inspired by cultural studies to document or theorise differences of either social class of age.

Current work on variations within female audiences distinguishes itself from the mainstream of feminist film theory – and indeed from the mainstream of cultural studies – in several significant respects. Distancing itself not only from the solipsism of the spectator produced in interaction with the film text, but also to some extent from the idea of pre-existing cultural competences brought to bear on media reception, this work stresses the agency of subcultures – as 'interpretive communities' – in reading and reception. In drawing attention to subaltern subjectivities and subcultural readings, it also reopens the issue of alternative or oppositional practices of cultural production: can there be a black cinema, or a 'queer' cinema, for instance, that addresses sexual difference in conjunction with these other positionalities or identities? (Bad Object-Choices, 1991; *Screen*, 1988). Such work embodies a degree of political purpose and urgency that is now virtually absent from the straight, white, middle-class mainstream of feminist film studies.

But to what extent is 'identity' at stake here, theoretically or politically? To the degree that they emphasise the shifting and provisional character of all subjectivities, these emergent critical and cultural practices assume feminist film theory's anti-essentialist mantle: in a recent discussion of lesbianism and film spectatorship, for instance, Christine Holmlund enjoins the necessity of remaining aware of the 'diversity, variability and tenuousness of the ... identities and identifications that structure viewing and other social practices' (Holmlund, 1991, p. 165).

Given this insistence on the multiple and fluid nature of spectatorial positioning – one may be, and/or be constructed as, simultaneously female and black and gay, say – the future for feminist work on film spectatorship would appear to lie in micronarratives and microhistories of the fragmented female spectator rather than in any totalising metapsychology of the subject of the cinematic apparatus. Such a radically non-essentialist prospect sits rather neatly alongside the tenets of postmodernist thought. As identities fragment, differences abound, and political allegiances proliferate, so the unitary, the universal, (female) cinema spectator disappears – along with all the other inclusive categories and grand narratives – into the dustbin of intellectual history.

Over the past decade or more, feminist film theory has forced new questions around representation onto the critical agenda, growing considerably in theoretical sophistication in the process. Nevertheless, opportunities have certainly been missed. The key area of concern for feminist film theory has largely remained the relationship between cinema and 'the feminine'. 'The feminine' is now increasingly treated as a social, as much as a psychical, category; and regarded in both respects as much more complex and heterogeneous than was once acknowledged. But cinema is still overwhelmingly conceived exclusively in terms of dominant cinema. And there lingers a feeling that feminist film theory is bent on the intellectual equivalent of a blinkered headlong gallop up and down a single narrow and well-worn track. Do broader avenues wait close at hand to be explored?

This view may be no more than an expression of what Constance Penley – referring specifically to demands repeatedly made upon psychoanalytic feminist film criticism with which it is epistemologically unequipped to deal – has called the 'what if?' school of feminist criticism (Penley, 1988, p. 2). But if rehearsing the past failures of feminist film theory is a rather pointless exercise, it might be rather more helpful to slow the gallop down to a trot, take off the blinkers and survey the wider scene. What follows is a consideration – claiming neither exhaustiveness nor rigour – of some areas hitherto little explored by feminist film theory, with an implicit recommendation that an exploration could prove rewarding.

This book devotes considerable attention to the formal characteristics of classic Hollywood cinema – narrative structure, narrative viewpoint, and specifically cinematic codes (Chapter 2) – arguing that rigorous formal textual analysis is a *sine qua non* of a feminist analysis of dominant cinema. It allows us to ask, for example, how 'woman' as a structure or narrative function operates within the textual organisation of films; and forces the activity of reading to address itself carefully to the structure and rhetoric of texts. Formal textual analysis of this sort has its limitations, and certainly does not tell the whole story. But it can act as a brake upon some of the more speculative excesses of text-based criticism, and constitute a useful heuristic device and an accessible point of entry to feminist criticism. It is perhaps a little unfortunate, then, that feminist film theory has rarely made systematic use of formal textual analysis. Perhaps it was left behind in the rush to psychoanalysis in the wake of the 'visual pleasure' debate?

Another rather underdeveloped area of feminist film studies is work on historical female authorship in cinema. In the original *Women's Pictures*, this issue is sidestepped on the grounds that women's cinema and feminist cinema are not the same thing. Another difficulty, in the present context especially, relates to the concept of authorship itself, which, as indicated in the Introduction to this book, had already had a chequered history within film theory well before feminism came on the scene. Even accepting that a film's main author is usually its director, what implications as regards the organisation of a film text and the meanings it produces does the gender of the director have? And if authorship in cinema is considered in terms of textual structures rather than of a director's artistic decisions or intentions, to what extent can it be assumed or argued that social femaleness produces or entails some thematic or even structural femininity in a film text? And how much does it matter if a woman director was non-feminist, or even anti-feminist?

Because of its commitment to anti-essentialism, feminist film theory has tended to shy away from such questions, and indeed – notwithstanding Claire Johnston's and Pam Cook's pioneering feminist work on the Hollywood director Dorothy Arzner (Cook, 1975; Johnston, 1975b; see Chapter 5) – from the whole subject of female authorship. Cook and Johnston subjected Arzner's *oeuvre* to an ideological reading directed at its figuration of 'woman' as a narrative function; and concluded that the films contain an internal, unconscious, critique of patriarchal ideology, readable through the transgressive nature and disruptive function of female desire in their narratives. This analysis fails, however, to address the question of whether and how textual transgression in films directed by a woman is connected with the director's gender.

A key difficulty in debates on female authorship in cinema remained unresolved, therefore; and in fact the question of authorship disappeared from feminist film theory's agenda for many years, to surface again only recently in new feminist work on 'women's cinema'. Writing in 1989, Lucy Fischer asks, in anti-essentialist vein, where the feminism (assuming there is any) in a particular work is to be located: in the author's intentions? in its content? in the audience's response? (Fischer, 1989). Not only can contemporary considerations of women's cinema like Fischer's not avoid addressing the question of authorship, in tackling the issue they must also take on board the theorisations of female spectatorship, reading and reception developed in feminist film theory since the 1970s.

Dorothy Arzner remains a key reference point for current considerations of historical female authorship in cinema. This has partly to do with Arzner's status as the only female director working regularly in Hollywood during the studio years. An attention to her work thus sits well with feminist film theory's preoccupation with classic Hollywood cinema. However, Arzner re-emerges also in the context of current debates on sexual preference and spectatorship and in the context of the birth of new, 'queer' criticisms and cinemas (Bad Object-Choices, 1991; Mayne, 1990; Mayne, 1991). To the extent that Arzner is now being reclaimed for her lesbianism (a question which did not arise at all in earlier feminist considerations of her work), the spectre of essentialism haunts this project, too; and the issue of whether queerness resides in authors, in texts, in audiences, or in readings remains in the air.

The challenge posed to feminist film theory by the problem of authorship is well worth facing, however. Feminist studies of female 'auteurs' have tended to be rather limited in range, focusing predominantly on directors whose work either fits into feminist film theory's existing concerns, or is readable within the terms of a recognisable contemporary feminist agenda. Directors whose work is problematic for feminists – in its themes, say, or in its representations of women (Lois Weber, Ida Lupino and Lina Wertmuller are examples) – have received relatively scant attention.

A further area of potential development for feminist film theory stems from the fact that feminist metapsychologies of cinema have been thought exclusively in terms of very specific psychoanalytic models of the human subject. These emphasise the centrality of certain unconscious processes in the formation of cinematic subjectivity, along with the role of vision and looking; and (especially in feminist film theory deriving from Lacanian psychoanalysis) the operation of language and semiosis in the production of sexual difference as a key attribute of the meaning-producing subject of cinema. With the exception of a few critiques of the centrality in feminist film theory of paradigms of looking (Silverman, 1988a) thought in relation to the Oedipus complex (Studlar, 1985), this particular metapsychology remains virtually unchallenged.

However, certain questions trouble this paradigm, especially to the degree that film theory foregrounds the centrality of language in spectatorial subjectivity. It is apparent, for example, that cinema often engages emotions or proposes emotional responses. The tears evoked by the melodrama and the woman's picture have been explained, for example, in terms of the genre's characteristic modes of narration and textual address (Gledhill, 1986; Neale, 1986; see Chapter 11). But can every emotional engagement with cinema be understood in terms of textual rhetoric, or even of metapsychology? Can such engagements be explained within the terms of apparatus theory? Would they be better accounted for by cultural studies-style explanations framed in terms, say, of prior knowledges and cultural competences? Or is there some excess, something that goes beyond all of these explanations? If so, how might it be theorised?

Feminist metapsychologies of cinema have largely failed, too, to engage with the question of experience. The very notion of a specifically female domain of experience smacks of essentialism and threatens to evacuate the Unconscious – a fact which undoubtedly goes some way towards explaining this lacuna. Nevertheless, feminist politics – including many interventions in feminist *cultural* politics, some feminist films among them – has repeatedly insisted upon the importance of women's experience in a cultural climate in which the female point of view is undervalued or subordinated.

A film like Michelle Citron's *Daughter Rite* (see Chapter 8) derives much of its meaning and impact from its evocation of experiences shared by many (though not, of course, by all) women: experiences centring upon daughterhood and mother–daughter relations. The same might also be said of maternal melodramas – woman's pictures like *Stella Dallas* which address the question of maternity from a female point-of-view within the context of dominant cinema. But how is a response that might be named 'recognition' to be theorised? Does such a response go beyond language? Are unconscious processes involved? Is it admissable even to conceive of a relation to cinema unmediated by language, by semiosis, by the Unconscious?

There does exist a paradigm which possibly offers a way into exploring affect and experience in film spectatorship: phenomenology. The goal of phenomenological philosophy is to describe pre-reflective experience: experience, that is, which is neither verbal nor literary. According to Vivian Sobchack, a phenomenological film theory would aim to 'describe and account for the origin and locus of cinematic signification and significance in the *experience* of vision as an embodied and meaningful existential activity' (Sobchack, 1992, p. xvii, my emphasis; see also Deleuze, 1986; Deleuze, 1989). However, phenomenological philosophy has been critiqued by feminist philosophers on the grounds of its devaluation of gender (Sobchack, 1992, pp. 149–50); and it remains as yet unclear whether a metapsychology of cinema grounded in phenomenology would be capable of meeting the demands that feminism would make upon it. Nevertheless, more than one feminist film theorist has suggested that an encounter between feminist film theory and phenomenology might well prove productive (Koch, 1985; Studlar, 1990b; see also Judith Butler, 1988).

Some of these tentatively proposed new directions are explored further in Chapter 12, in the context of a discussion of some recent films; while some implications of current and possible future directions in feminist film theory for a cultural politics of feminist knowledge are taken up briefly at the end of that chapter.

11

Three Case Studies

The Spectatrix

The female spectator (as against the feminist reader-against-the-grain) made only the briefest appearance in the original *Women's Pictures*, where it is thought fully within the terms of semiotic and psychoanalytic film theory: as a moment, that is, in the process of cinematic signification. With hindsight it seems odd, given the book's insistence upon treating cinema not merely as an apparatus of meaning production but crucially also as a social and economic institution, that the spectator as 'social subject' is so conspicuously absent from the original *Women's Pictures*. Soon afterwards, however, I made some progress with this problem in an essay which explored the spectator–audience dualism. In this essay I took two popular 'women's genres' – the woman's picture and the television soap opera – as pretexts for considering the theoretical and methodological issues at stake in the debate around female spectatorship (Kuhn, 1984). At the time the essay was written, this debate was concerned primarily with liberating female desire and pleasure from the clutches of the Mulveyan paradigm: but it seemed to me that in the haste to effect a heroic rescue, intellectual rigour was being elbowed aside. A confusing conflation of female spectatorship, as a set of modalities of subjectivity proposed by the operations of film texts, with the female 'social subject', the woman in the cinema audience, was taking place.

What does the fact that certain popular genres are aimed at, and consumed with pleasure by, women as *audiences* suggest about the nature of women's identifications, engagements and pleasures as *spectators?* It seemed to me necessary to clear the ground for tackling this question, by distinguishing not only between the categories 'audience' and 'spectator' but also between the modes of conceptualisation and methods of investigation associated with each: sociological and cultural studies on the one hand as against semiotic and psychoanalytic film theory on the other. In the quest to understand what is at stake in women's genres and their reception, I argued, a methodological rapprochement between the two, not a conflation was called for.

The difficulty here, however, was in some measure political as well as conceptual. Some of the critiques of the Mulveyan model of spectatorship were fuelled by unease with psychoanalytic film theory: to this extent they were actually a demand for attention to 'real' women's responses to films rather than for any revision of psychoanalytic conceptualisations of the spectator. Nevertheless, the assumption persisted that all the parties involved in the debate on female specatorship were talking about the same thing. No doubt the very term 'female spectator', handy shorthand though it might be, perpetuated confusion: for while 'female' suggests an already gendered social category (an audience), 'spectator' implies an ongoing production of sexual difference through signification and representation.

When, several years on, the female spectatorship problematic came under attack for failing to address itself to distinctions other than sexual difference, a similar confusion ensued. The newly proposed modalities of difference – race, social class, age and sexual preference were most frequently invoked – are more readily conceived as social than as psychical or social–psychical categories. The immediate consequences of this were twofold: first of all, psychoanalytic film theory was excoriated for failing to deal with phenomena that are in fact outside its scope (see, for example, Gaines, 1988); and, second, cultural studies – apparently better equipped to handle the new dimensions of difference – was set up as the saviour (Gaines and Herzog, 1990). However, in the headlong rush away from the spectator-in-the-text towards the social subject, an indispensable component of psychoanalytic models of cinema spectatorship stood in danger of being lost: the unconscious aspect of the pleasures, identifications and fascinations evoked by cinema.

In 1989, when the journal *Camera Obscura* published a special issue on 'The Spectatrix' (*Camera Obscura*, 1989), feminist film theory, certainly in the USA, appeared to have become preoccupied by the female spectatorship debate to the virtual exclusion of all else. Sixty contributors, feminist film theorists based for the most part in US academic institutions – with a smattering of voices from elsewhere – had submitted, by invitation, short discussion papers on their understandings of and views on the state of the debate within film studies and television studies about the 'female spectator'. In addition, four writers from outside the USA had contributed in-depth essays on the state of the debate in their respective countries. In their introduction, issue editors Janet Bergstrom and Mary Ann Doane outline the main points emerging, evincing some exasperation with certain aspects of the debate. '[I]t is easier', they say, 'to point to the need to "take other differences into account" than it is to arrive at satisfactory methods for doing so' (Bergstrom and Doane, 1989, p. 9).

They also signal the confusion attending what they evidently regard as a somewhat obsessive quest for the true nature of the female spectator:

> [I]n 1989 the female spectator has become a fractured concept, activating a host of conflicting and incompatible epistemological frameworks, circulating around what could be seen as entirely different objects of study (p. 12).

Perhaps the *ennui* that Bergstrom and Doane identify as a feature of contemporary feminist film theory is a consequence of such loose thinking? Or perhaps, as they also suggest (see also Doane *et al.*, 1984, p. 4), it is in some way associated with the successful academic institutionalisation of feminist film theory, in the USA at least, over the past ten years or so? And perhaps, relatedly, it accompanies a disappearance of political purpose, a loss of impulse to ask about the sorts of knowledge feminist film theory is seeking, and the uses of the knowledge sought?

The *Stella Dallas* Debate

In 1984, *Cinema Journal* published an essay by Linda Williams on the 1937 King Vidor film *Stella Dallas* (Williams, 1984, reprinted in Gledhill, 1987). This remake of a 1926 film directed by Henry King, based upon a novel by Olive Higgins Prouty, is counted among the best-known and best-loved examples of the woman's picture. Often derogatorily dubbed 'three-handkerchief movies' and 'women's weepies', when Williams's essay was published the woman's picture was set to undergo a rehabilitation at the hands of feminist film theorists seeking to come to terms with the undoubted attraction exerted by certain types of dominant cinema on female audiences.

The Stella of the film's title is a working-class woman whose marriage to upper-class Stephen Dallas comes gradually adrift, leaving their daughter Laurel in the care of Stella, a devoted mother who none the less seeks a little innocent fun in life. As the adolescent Laurel starts moving in the smart set, her mother's vulgarity and social ineptitude become increasingly apparent. Stella, realising that she is holding her daughter back, sends Laurel – under the pretext of rejection – to live with her father and his second wife. The final scene of the film shows Stella standing alone on a dark, rain-soaked pavement gazing raptly through the window of the Dallases' grand house at the glittering spectacle of her daughter's wedding within (see Still 11.1).

Linda Williams opens her discussion of *Stella Dallas* by considering alternative readings of this famously tearjerking closing moment: to what extent does Stella's renunciation of Laurel constitute an unbearable sacrifice, to what extent a triumph of successful mother-hood? Upon such questions hang issues of central concern for feminist film theory, and indeed Williams treats *Stella Dallas* and the differing responses it evokes as an occasion for taking a fresh look at feminist thinking on feminine subjectivity and female spectatorship in cinema.

Taking issue with the view that dominant cinematic apparatuses of looking construct the spectator as male or masculine, Williams advances the argument that there are in fact openings within dominant cinema for the play of feminine forms of subjectivity, if only because certain types of cinema demand specifically female 'reading competences'. The argument here is grounded not in the internal operations or the address of certain film texts or genres *per se*, but in their presumed engagement with the world beyond the text, specifi-cally with aspects of women's everyday lives and of their social and cultural competences.

In this context, Williams is particularly interested in competences associated with mothering. Taking up Tania Modleski's argument concerning women's readings of daytime soap operas on US television (Modleski, 1982), she suggests that it is not a question of one reading as against another, but rather that women's identifications may be multifold: indeed that women – like mothers called upon to attend simultaneously to the often conflicting demands of children, work and home – are, as it were, culturally programmed to adopt a double, even a multiple, vision. 'The female spectator is in a constant state of

11.1 Stella Dallas: the closing scene

juggling all positions at once' (Williams, 1984, p. 19). For Williams, this juggling is an objective correlative of women's uncomfortable and contradictory position within patriarchy; and it explains how women may be interpellated by – find an ideological niche within – dominant cultural forms. To this extent, Williams is shifting the ground of debate on female spectatorship in cinema onto the terrain of the social and cultural contexts of reception and away from that of the film text.

The debate which this essay provoked in subsequent issues of *Cinema Journal* reveals much about the central issues at stake in feminist film theory in the mid 1980s. The protagonists engaged first of all with the problem of female spectatorship and the status of various readings of *Stella Dallas*, notably of its closing scene. Implicit in their arguments is the idea that the female spectator might herself be as heterogeneous as the socio-culturally conditioned identifications which, according to Williams, she is capable of making. Not only should a distinction be made between the 'hypothetical' or implied spectator and the 'historical subject' (Kaplan, 1985); an identity cannot be assumed between a feminist reading of *Stella Dallas* in the 1980s and the responses of female audiences of the 1930s (Petro and Flinn, 1985).

Her respondents acknowledged Williams's project of shifting the ground of debates on female spectatorship away from the psychoanalytic terrain of the cinematic apparatus and the spectator–text relationship and towards a concern with 'female social experience', and agreed that such a move could open up fresh debates within feminist film theory. Nevertheless, the advice was not actually taken; and the conceptual and methodological distinctions between spectator and audience embryonic in all the contributions remained unexplored. Nor was Williams's allusion to the significance of popular genres 'for women' taken up in the manner in which she had posed it, although a contribution by Christine Gledhill did attempt to turn the discussion towards a consideration of Hollywood melodrama as a genre of special import for feminist criticism (Gledhill, 1986).

Gledhill points to the argument that a central component of the 'melodramatic imagination' across all of the popular media in which it manifests itself is its articulation of struggles within the social, cultural and ideological *status quo* (in relation specifically to Hollywood melodrama, it has been suggested that these struggles pivot upon contradictions around sexuality and familial relations). In this sense, Gledhill suggests, melodrama functions aesthetically neither on the side of the realism commonly associated with classic Hollywood cinema nor on that of the modernism informing various avant-garde cinemas and political countercinemas. Melodrama, she says, constitutes an intermediate term in the realism–modernism dualism, as a popular genre neither fully complicit with dominant cinema nor, in the vein of countercinema, seeking a complete rupture with it.

Gledhill proceeds to explain melodrama's tearjerking qualities in terms of its textual address, its rhetoric: tears come in the gap between the spectator's privileged knowledge of what is going on produced by the narration (the 'view behind' discussed in Chapter 3) and fictional characters' circumscribed and flawed understandings of their own circumstances. The spectator grasps the character's plight, knows – unlike the character – that it has come about through some insignificant misunderstanding or misrecognition, and weeps because all the ensuing suffering could so easily have been avoided – 'if only . . .'.

This contribution, while not losing sight of the socio-cultural dimension of audiences' relations to popular cultural forms, returns the debate to a rigorous consideration of the operations of both text and genre. But the specific rhetorical features of the women's picture, and of *Stella Dallas* in particular, are not looked at. And the question of the circumstances under which cinematic address might engage social subjectivities – especially those relating to gender – is lost sight of, along with the suggestion, implicit but undeveloped in earlier contributions to the *Cinema Journal* debate, that 'female spectatorship' is itself not necessarily a culturally, socially or historically – let alone a psychically – unitary concept.

The issues at the heart of the debate on *Stella Dallas* were, and remain, of crucial import for feminist film theory, and participants in the debate should not be criticised if they failed to resolve them. Indeed, it is perhaps in its very lack of resolution that the *Stella Dallas* debate stands as a test case for feminist film theory. From it, several important points emerge. The debate touches on some of the varied ways in which the 'female spectator' is conceptualised within feminist film theory; and by beginning to peel away some of the layers of meaning embedded in that concept, prepares the ground for subsequent theoretical and methodological debates and distinctions.

In the process, it raises the question of the status of variant readings of film texts, especially of readings by women and by feminists; and, in advancing the idea of female reading competences, it complicates semiotic and psychoanalytic understandings of the spectator–text relationship, introducing a socio-cultural dimension not only to the question of spectatorship (Williams; Kaplan; Petro and Flinn) but also to that of the text itself (Gledhill). It is refreshingly open about a problem that besets contemporary readings of classic Hollywood cinema: namely that of the historical audience, of whether and how we can gain access to the responses of a film's first audiences. It prefigures a concern that was soon to move to the top of feminist film theory's agenda: the question of the function, and address, of popular culture – specifically of certain genres within mainstream cinema – in relation to female spectators and audiences. And if at this point the debate assumes a basically unitary female spectator, it is in this very failure that the impossibility of such a spectator becomes, with hindsight, obvious.

The Masquerade and its Vicissitudes

Throughout the 1980s, female spectatorship was a site of unremitting preoccupation for feminist film theory, though after the middle of the decade attention to historically popular forms of cinema 'for' women and historical audiences did offer some relief from the frustrating subtleties and confusions of the female spectatorship debate. At the same time, during this same period discussions concerning the nature of femininity itself, notably of the idea of femininity as a 'masquerade', surfaced and resurfaced several times – appropriately enough, always in a fresh guise.

The concept of the masquerade, as it has been appropriated to feminist film theory, has its origin in a paper by the English Freudian analyst Joan Riviere that was first published in 1929. Riviere coined the concept in the course of the intense debates concerning the nature of femininity and its psychical organisation that took place within the psychoanalytic community between the wars. Her paper, drawing on clinical material from one of her analysands, an American professional woman with intellectual inclinations, offers itself as a contribution to an understanding of the Oedipus complex in women (Judith Butler, 1990; Heath, 1986). In her professional life, Riviere's patient would often behave in an 'ultra-feminine' manner in the presence of male colleagues: Riviere characterises this behaviour as putting on a 'mask of womanliness to avert anxiety and the retribution feared from men' (Riviere, 1986, p. 35). What remains unclear in Riviere's discussion, however, is whether there is some 'authentic' femininity lying behind the mask, or whether femininity is to be regarded in itself as a masquerade.

Despite – or possibly because of – this uncertainty, the idea of the masquerade has been taken up in a number of recent considerations of femininity as a psychical attribute. It has also periodically informed debates within feminist film theory. In this latter context it was first referenced in 1975 in an essay by Claire Johnston on a 1951 Jacques Tourneur film, *Anne of the Indies*, whose plot hinges on sexual disguise: the hero is a woman masquerading as a (male) pirate. Johnston treats this masquerade as a form of 'trouble in the text'. It is, she implies, the key to a structural reading of the film's narrative – which is disturbed, even ruptured, by the masquerade: the masquerade, she argues, 'opens up, in phantasy, the possibility ... of a bi-sexuality beyond the determinations imposed by culture and the classic text' (Johnston, 1975e, p. 41).

Anne of the Indies, in other words, is treated as belonging to that group of films that at first sight seem to function fully within the dominant ideology, but which on closer inspection reveal themselves as fractured by internal ideological contradictions (Comolli and Narboni, 1971; see Chapter 5). In this instance, the locus of contradiction is the uncertainty about sexual difference embodied in the film's narrative device of sexual disguise. The masquerade, then, becomes a pretext for a feminist ideological reading of a classic Hollywood text.

After a lengthy absence, the concept of the masquerade resurfaced in 1982 in an essay by Mary Ann Doane. Doane's use of the term is rather different from that of Claire Johnston, to whose intervention she does not refer. The term 'masquerade' is here deployed in the service of theorising female spectatorship: Doane's essay is in fact a contribution to the metapsychological debate current in the early 1980s concerning the status of the female spectator within the cinematic apparatus. Doane defines femininity as a closeness, or presence-to-itself, embodied in the nature of the female look: '[f]or the female spectator there is a certain overpresence of the image – she *is* the image' (Doane, 1982, p. 78; see also Doane, 1988–9). Her conclusion is that over and above a simple identification, *pace* Mulvey, with the masculine position of bearer of the look, the only positions offered within the cinematic apparatus for the female spectator – 'the masochism of over-identification or the narcissism entailed in becoming one's own object of desire' (p. 87) – are embodiments of this nearness.

But to the degree that femininity can be a kind of performance, the idea of the masquerade offers a way out of this cul-de-sac, says Doane. It offers a space of distance from culturally normative modes of femininity, and thus also the opportunity of taking a critical distance from the image. Doane's project is to theorise female spectatorship within the terms of psychoanalytic film theory, to produce a metapsychology of cinema which emphasises the centrality of looking in the cinematic apparatus; and she uses the masquerade as shorthand for a modality of subjectivity produced in and through vision. To this extent, Doane's essay follows from and also develops the paradigm advanced by Laura Mulvey (in Mulvey, 1975).

The masquerade has recently made another reappearance in feminist film theory, and once again in new clothes. Along with a questioning of the notion of a unitary female spectator has come an increased emphasis on the processual, ongoing, multiple, and often contradicatory, identifications that constitute feminity. Joan Riviere's paper can arguably be read as suggesting that femininity is defined by a greater inauthenticity or alienation than masculinity – a view elaborated upon (though from a philosophical standpoint very different from Riviere's) by Simone de Beauvoir in *The Second Sex*.

However, it can equally well be suggested that Riviere's notion of the masquerade embodies a potentially emancipatory potential, in that if femininity is indeed something that is 'put on' in all senses – an act, a mask, a costume – it can by the same token also be taken off. This introduces a degree of fluidity into gender identity – or into femininity at least. Such a view grounds an anti-essentialist understanding of gender as performance, as produced in acts that in fact constitute the gender they appear to express (Judith Butler, 1990). Such a notion of 'gender performatives' has been taken up in some recent work in feminist film studies, which makes implicit or explicit reference to the idea of the masquerade (Kuhn, 1985b; 1988; Studlar, 1990a).

In an introduction to a recent collection of essays (Gaines and Herzog, 1990), Jane Gaines contends that the idea of the masquerade offers new ways forward for feminist film theory. Returning to Claire Johnston's *Anne of the Indies* essay, Gaines points to the idea of femininity as performance implicit in a certain reading of the masquerade; she stresses the particular utility of this idea in readings of films which, in foregrounding the contingency of the relationship between the body and gender, challenge notions of gender identity as fixed and unitary. At the same time, however, Gaines implies that performativity may inform the activity of spectatorship itself, producing fluid modalities of subjectivity for the spectator:

> [T]he masquerade paradigm has been filled out at the liberatory end of the spectrum and many more critics are now considering the radical possibilities of what might be called spectatorial crossdressing (Gaines and Herzog, 1990, p. 25).

From its earliest recruitment to the cause of ideological analysis, through attempts at constructing a feminist metapsychology of cinema, to a deployment at the service of conceptualising the 'gender performatives' of postmodern feminist thought, the idea of the masquerade – appropriately chameleon-like – has traced a passage through all the major developments of a feminist film theory whose quest above all is for the grail of anti-essentialism.

12

The Wild Zone

In pursuing the intricacies of debates within feminist film theory over
the past ten years or so, there is perhaps some danger of losing sight of
the fact that film theory's *topos* is in the end cinema, not film theory.
Film theory needs cinema: many, however, might contend that cinema
can get along quite well without film theory. It is also worth recalling
that feminist film theory could not have come into being without
feminist politics. The rise of second-wave feminism made it possible –
indeed urgent – to ask questions about representations across all
media, cinema included, and so to make demands upon film criticism
and theory which would previously have been inconceivable.

The demands were twofold. In the first place, the new feminist
consciousness inspired a fresh look at Hollywood cinema, at its often
unflattering portrayals of women and its tendency to privilege a
masculine world-view. Feminist critiques of Hollywood generated a
renewed energy in film criticism, a reorientation in film theory, and
oppositional readings as a form of feminist activism. Second, an
activism at the level of production is embodied in demands for
alternatives of various kinds: for contemporary mainstream cinema to
offer more positive images of women and in general to be receptive
towards feminist criticisms of its record in this respect; for more women
and more feminists to become involved in the making of films; and,
most radically, for new sorts of films, altogether different from those in
the mainstream in content, language and methods of production.

Because it took feminist cultural politics and the necessity of feminist
cultural activism as its point of departure, the central concern of the
original *Women's Pictures* was not feminist film theory *per se*, but rather

the relationship between feminism and cinema (Chapter 1). Although the nature and the conditions of existence of this relationship have altered markedly since the early 1980s, the dual model of activities or activisms of reading on the one hand and of production on the other continues, I believe, to offer a key to the rather different state of affairs that prevails in the 1990s. To what extent, and in what ways, have feminist practices of film criticism and theory impacted upon feminist practices of film production – and *vice versa*? How much light does feminist film theory shed upon women's contributions to film making, both historical and contemporary? What indeed is the connection, if any, between female authorship in cinema and feminist practices of cinema?

It is sometimes pointed out that feminist film theory has privileged classic Hollywood cinema as an object of analysis; and also that it has endorsed a rather limited range of feminist alternative cinemas. This state of affairs, it is contended, has to do with feminist film theory's favoured paradigms: most notably its preoccupation with the 'look', and in general with modes of cinematic identification and subjectivity grounded in vision. One of the consequences of this is that feminist film theory has tended to overlook certain types of cinema. Even the category 'dominant cinema' is larger than the output of Hollywood during the studio years, for instance; paradoxically, to privilege this output in oppositional practices of criticism is in effect to assent to Hollywood's own claims to cultural domination.

If this is indeed the case, feminist film theory constructs its object, cinema, rather narrowly: with the consequence that at the levels both of reading and of production it tends not only to sideline certain sorts of cinema, but when it does actually deal with them deploys inappropriate critical tools. Areas in which feminist film theory, as a practice of interpretation, has encountered particular difficulties include: silent cinema, contemporary mainstream Hollywood cinema and other national mainstream cinemas on the Hollywood model; art cinema; Third World cinema; and even some forms of avowedly feminist cinema, most notably feminist documentary.

Redressing this imbalance would call for a thoroughgoing reorientation of feminist film theory. Short of this, the questions concerning feminist film practice addressed in chapters 7, 8 and 9 may be amplified by looking at a number of recent films, some of which sit more comfortably than others within the feminist canon. By considering films that illuminate or are illuminated by recent critical and theoretical debates, or which in one way or another constitute a challenge to feminist film theory, an assessment of the current state of the relationship between feminism and cinema may be attempted.

A number of these films also stand as exemplars of the significant changes in the conditions of existence of feminist independent cinema that have taken place since the early 1980s. For even at an institutional level it is no longer possible to conceive 'the production of meaning and the meaning of production' in quite the way that they are conceived in the original *Women's Pictures*. In the first place, it is decreasingly possible now to insist upon a qualitative break between dominant and alternative cinemas: if at their extremes these categories do remain distinct, changes in the industrial conditions of existence of different types of cinema have coincided with a considerable degree of formal or textual merging or overlap in the middle ground.

The year 1982 saw the launch in Britain of a new departure in television, Channel Four. Through its initiatives in film financing and its programming strategies, Channel Four has not only changed the face of British independent film making – of distribution and exhibition as well as of production – but has also transformed the structures of financing and exhibition of 'small films' and art cinema, both within and outside Britain (Auty, 1985; Lovell, 1990). At the same time, in a Thatcherite and post-Thatcherite climate of public sector cutbacks, sources of financial backing for non-commercial film production, distribution and exhibition have shrunk; and feminist initiatives have been among the first casualties.

For example, in 1992, after the withdrawal of its British Film Institute subsidy, and because in an increasingly commercialised climate an overtly feminist commitment became counterproductive, the feminist film distributor Cinema of Women (COW), which had been set up in 1979, closed down operations to merge with its sister organisation, Circles (Circles, also formed in 1979, specialised in women's experimental film and video and in historical films of feminist interest). Cinenova, the new distribution company formed from the merger, advertises itself as 'promoting films by women' and no longer subscribes to an activist politics of exhibition in the way its predecessors had aimed to do:

> [T]he restructuring of arts funding and the transition from feminism to what can be loosely termed postfeminism effectively undermined the basis on which COW and Circles rested (Knight, 1992, p. 186; see also Merz and Parmar, 1987).

It might also be argued that such changes are symptomatic of a loosening of political ties between on the one hand a feminist film theory that proposes an activism of reading and on the other a feminist film practice that aims to intervene, through strategies of exhibition, at the level of meaning production.

At the same time, the past decade has seen transformations in media production and exhibition technologies that underscore these changes in the independent cinema sector, and indeed have had significant repercussions for cinema in general. The spread of domestic video-casette recorders and the growth of the video film rental market have impacted considerably upon contexts and modes of reception and exhibition of films of all kinds. Not only are oppositional practices of independent exhibition of the sort discussed in Chapter 9 no longer feasible; it also becomes decreasingly tenable to treat film viewing as if it always takes place in a darkened auditorium with a large screen and a film projection apparatus. Moreover, developments in video technology and the spread of relatively inexpensive home video equipment offer new opportunities to avant-garde artists and others who might previously have turned to Super 8 mm or 16 mm film as a working medium. Feminist experimental work in time-based media is just as likely – perhaps more so – today to use video technology as film; and indeed there has been a burgeoning of feminist video production in recent years (Mulvey, 1989a; see also Mulvey, 1979).

Finally, as popular media – most notably music videos – now draw freely on non-narrative, anti-realist languages and on formal strategies characteristic of avant-garde cinema and video, general levels of media literacy have increased. This development will surely demand a reframing of the issues surrounding feminist 'textual politics'. For all these reasons the films discussed below are not usefully regarded as belonging to the hard-and-fast categories 'dominant' or 'oppositional' cinema. They are more appropriately seen as ranged over a continuum, with contemporary Hollywood cinema at the one textual and institutional extreme, and overtly feminist experimental and avant-garde productions at the other.

The Accused; The Color Purple; Thelma and Louise

In Chapter 7, several Hollywood films are discussed under the heading 'Hollywood and new women's cinema'. Films like *Alice Doesn't Live*

Here Anymore, one of a cycle of 1970s pictures with themes of female self-actualisation and independence; and *Julia*, an exploration of female friendship, fit the classic definition of the woman's picture, in that a female point-of-view motivates and dominates their narratives and they are directed predominantly at female audiences. What emerges as distinctive about the 1970s version of the Hollywood woman's picture, though, is its openness, its polysemy: these films can accommodate a range of readings, including feminist ones. This has to do not only with the ways in which stories and characters are handled in these films, but also with their formal organisation as texts; and most especially with their appropriation of certain codes and conventions of art cinema, a genre whose defining characteristics include, precisely, narrative ambiguity and absence of closure.

Feminist critics of a sociological persuasion have drawn attention to a number of recent big-budget, expensively promoted, Hollywood films – such as *Basic Instinct* (Verhoeven, 1992), *Fatal Attraction* (Lyne, 1987) and *Presumed Innocent* (Pakula, 1990) – featuring central female protagonists who are in varying degrees demented, sexually voracious, sexually violent, castrating or murderous. For wreaking general havoc, these women eventually receive punishment – often of a highly excessive nature – for their transgressions. Even if, punishment notwithstanding, such films may offer women audiences vicarious identification with fictitious females who refuse to be nice girls, they are not in any definition of the term 'woman's pictures'. Indeed, many critics regard them as part of a wider cultural backlash against feminism.

On the other hand, a number of films have emerged from Hollywood during the 1980s and 1990s that do, in some measure at least, enunciate a feminine point-of-view, construct female characters as narrative agents and points-of-identification, and offer resolutions that might be regarded as positive. Films like *The Accused* (Kaplan, 1988), *The Color Purple* (Spielberg, 1985) and *Thelma and Louise* (Scott, 1991) raise interesting questions about the ways in which the Hollywood woman's picture, as a mainstream genre, is continuing to transform itself.

Of these three films, *The Accused* is perhaps furthest, in formal terms, from the woman's picture in the accepted definition of the term. Based on an actual case, it tells the story of a working-class woman's struggle to bring to justice the men who have gang-raped her in a bar. Sarah Tobias (Jodie Foster) is assisted – with scant enthusiasm at first – by

1 *The crime*
   a. Prologue: Kenneth Joyce's telephone call; Sarah's escape
   b. Reporting the crime: Sarah's medical examination and statement
2 *The case: phase one*
   a. Rapists identified and charged
   b. Katheryn does a deal
   c. Sarah's anger; her transformation
3 *The case: phase two*
   a. Katheryn's renewed quest; the solicitation charge
4 *The trial*
   a. Sarah's story and Joyce's reluctance
   b. Joyce's story: FLASHBACK
5 *After the trial*
   a. Awaiting the verdict
   b. Guilty verdict announced

Figure 12.1 *The Accused*: a segmentation of the plot

Deputy District Attorney Katheryn Murphy (Kelly McGillis); and in the film's climactic courtroom scene the rape is portrayed in flashback through the testimony of one of the bystanders, Kenneth Joyce (Bernie Coulson). A segmentation of *The Accused* (see Figure 12.1) reveals that the film's plot is structured in certain respects as a classical investigative narrative: the 'truth' of events in the bar is withheld through the simple device of having the story begin after the rape has taken place. The opening scene (Segment 1a) establishes, offscreen, the 'villainy' that sets the plot in motion, and introduces the central character, Sarah. It also hints at the key role Kenneth Joyce will play in the denouement. In terms of narrative agency, the character Katheryn functions in some ways similarly to the detective figure of the investigative narrative.

However, *The Accused* departs from the conventions of the investigative narrative in that the plot is driven not by desire to find out 'whodunit', but by the question of whether and how Sarah, presented unequivocally as the victim of a brutal rape, can obtain justice. This narrative quest is interwoven with the story of the relationship between the two female protagonists, Sarah and Katheryn, and the turning point – in both the relationship and the quest for justice – comes at the structural dead centre of the film (Segment 3), when Katheryn is won over to Sarah's side and decides wholeheartedly to pursue her attackers.

In its organisation of plot and story time in relation to narrative viewpoint, there are interesting parallels between *The Accused* and an earlier Hollywood film bearing marks of both the woman's picture and the investigative narrative: *Mildred Pierce* (see Chapter 2). In both films the 'truth' of a crime is sought through procedures of legal interrogation: in a police station in the 1940s film, in a courtroom in *The Accused*. In both, central female protagonists attempt to tell their stories, their own version of events. But their accounts are in both instances relativised by those of male characters: the detective in the earlier film, Kenneth Joyce in the later one. A key difference, though, is that in *Mildred Pierce* the detective's flashback reveals Mildred's story to be untrue; in *The Accused* the veracity of Sarah's account of the rape is confirmed by Joyce's flashback of the rape scene.

Thus, if the enunciator of *The Accused* is arguably in the final instance Kenneth Joyce – in that a distance from the experience of the rape is proposed in its being recounted through his eyes and not Sarah's (Segment 4b and Stills 12.1 and 12.2) – Sarah is in the end vindicated by Joyce's account of events. It is this which makes possible a positive resolution for her. Aside from this, the female-bonding subplot – the gradual development of mutual respect between Sarah and Katheryn – adds a flavour of the new Hollywood women's picture to the film.

Some feminist critics have suggested, however, that notwithstanding Sarah's victory and Sarah's and Katheryn's growth in maturity and consciousness in the process of bringing it about, *The Accused* does in the end sanction a patriarchal point-of-view in an enunciation that in effect silences Sarah's voice through Joyce's validation – as 'the hero rescuing the "damsel in distress" and the stand-in for the audience' (Fleck, 1990, p. 55) – of her experience. But if this film proposes such an identification for the implied spectator through its textual address, how might a social audience of women respond to it?

The Accused is one of very few contemporary films to have been subjected to the kind of enquiry capable of producing a convincing answer to this question. In the course of research designed to assess the emotional impact of graphic displays of sexual violence upon women viewers (Schlesinger *et al.*, 1992), *The Accused* was shown, along with a number of television programmes with sexually violent content, to several groups of British women. These groups were mixed in terms of social class and ethnicity, but divided according to their actual experience of sexual violence. In all groups, the majority found the film compelling and believable, and even of educational value. But they did not regard it as entertaining, and expressed reservations about the

12.1 *The Accused*: Kenneth Joyce's courtroom testimony motivates ...

12.2 ... a flashback, through his eyes, of the rape

acceptability of using rape as a subject for an entertainment film. These viewers' identifications with characters and narrative events were in fact rather complex; and while some respondents felt that Sarah was presented as in some measure culpable in her rape, there was none the less '[u]niversal identification with the situation of the rape victim' (p. 163).

Respondents were also sensitive to the significance of the placement of the rape scene towards the end of the film, recognising its impact at that point as 'the product of cinematic artifice'; many thought the scene was potentially exploitative and should not have been included. Some also raised the questions of gender and viewing context in relation to responses to the film, suggesting that male viewers might be more prone than women to a 'she asked for it' type of response, and even perhaps to derive some sexual gratification from the explicitness of the rape scene.

Besides not being narratively motivated by a female point of view, *The Accused* was not marketed as a woman's picture, but rather as a social problem film, its supposed seriousness guaranteed by its basis in fact. A key feature of the social problem genre is that it must always negotiate exploitation and social concern, with the one in the end usually eclipsing the other. The responses of the participants in the study by Schlesinger *et al.* suggest, too, that the female bonding subplot of *The Accused* risks becoming submerged by the sensationalism of the rape narrative; which in turn might well divide viewers along lines of gender.

A gender gap is evident in responses to Steven Spielberg's adaptation of Alice Walker's prize-winning novel *The Color Purple*, certainly by black audiences in the USA, among whom the film provoked some controversy on its release in 1985. *The Color Purple* is very much a woman's picture in the classic mould, with the added twist (so far as mainstream popular culture is concerned) that the central protagonist is a black woman, the downtrodden Celie (Whoopi Goldberg), who is raped by her stepfather and forced into a cruel marriage. Black male reviewers denounced the film for its portrayal of black men as unremittingly brutal and violent, for its failure to address issues of class, and for its representation of black family life as degraded. Black feminist critics responded by defending the film, and Alice Walker's novel, on the grounds of its celebration of sisterhood between black women (Cheryl Butler, 1991).

In an ethnographic study of African-American women's reception of *The Color Purple*, Jacqueline Bobo distinguishes between responses to a novel with a limited readership and those of the mass audience for a film produced as 'a commercial venture … in Hollywood by a white male according to all of the tenets and conventions of commercial cultural production in the United States' (Bobo, 1988, p. 93). Many who saw the film will not have read Alice Walker's book. Black feminists who defended the film, however, would certainly have been aware of the changes that took place in the transition from novel to film: the latter's emphasis on Celie's story at the expense of that of her politically and ethnically aware sister Nettie (Akosua Busia), a missionary living and working in Africa; the downplaying of the lesbian aspect of the redemptive love between Celie and blues singer Shug Avery (Margaret Avery); the mellowing with age of Celie's harsh husband; and the virtual loss – in the very nature of the cinematic as opposed to the novelistic signifier – of the first-person voice of Celie's (and indeed of Nettie's) letters, and especially of the changes in Celie's voice that mark her gradual move towards self-respect and confidence.

Despite such 'dilutions', the women who took part in Bobo's study (it is unclear how many were familiar with the novel) generally responded positively to the film, most especially to Celie's eventual triumph over adversity. Many, too, were moved to defend Alice Walker against negative criticism. The film was a significant event in these women's lives, if only because of the complete absence hitherto in mainstream culture of any portrayal of black women from both a female and a black standpoint: 'Finally, somebody says something about us,' rejoiced literary critic Barbara Christian (Bobo, 1988, p. 101). In their responses to *The Color Purple*, Bobo's interviewees had negotiated productions of self incorporating simultaneously both an ethnic and a gender identity, a composite identity embodying a distinctive notion of sisterhood as a key component (see Still 12.3). Such a commitment to sisterhood, too, grounds black women's defence of Alice Walker, and gestures towards a site of significant difference between black and white women at the levels of subjectivity and identity formation.

In Ridley Scott's female-buddy/road movie *Thelma and Louise*, Thelma (Geena Davis), an attractive dimwit married to a boring carpet salesman, and Louise (Susan Sarandon), a streetwise, over-worked coffee-shop waitress, take off for a weekend away from their responsibilities. They soon run into trouble: when Louise shoots dead a man who has attempted to rape her friend, the women go on the run, encountering numerous adventures on the road to Mexico, their

12.3 'Sister heart': the young Celie with her sister Nettie in *The Color Purple*

12.4 Thelma and Louise: popular feminism and intertextual reference

sanctuary. By the time the police catch up with them at the edge of the Grand Canyon, their experiences on the road have changed them so much that neither feels she could possibly return to her former life. As Thelma says, 'Something's crossed over in me.' Rather than surrender, they drive over the precipice.

On its release, *Thelma and Louise* provoked heated debate about its feminist credentials, and a number of critics pointed to its resemblance to *Butch Cassidy and the Sundance Kid* (George Roy Hill, 1969). Both films are buddy–romance adventure stories of outlaws on the run, and both end with the fugitives' deaths. In both, too, the vicissitudes of the road promote bonding, while at the same time providing plentiful heterosexual markers to show there is nothing 'suspect' about the buddy relationship (see Still 12.4). The twist in *Thelma and Louise*, of course, is that the outlaws are women. But does a gender-bending genre movie a feminist film make? In textual terms, *Thelma and Louise* offers a variety of possible answers to this question – all of which appear to reduce to two basic points.

First of all, while it might be contentious to argue that *Thelma and Louise* is an explicitly feminist film, it is certainly a film that would be inconceivable without feminism. After all, the fictional event that motivates the narrative is a 'date rape'; and date rape is a practice that had not even been named before second-wave feminism placed the issue of force in sexual relations firmly within the sphere of the average cinema-goer's cultural competences. In this sense, *Thelma and Louise* appeals to 'popular feminism' – a type of feminism that does not name itself as such but which none the less takes for granted issues and ideas put on the agenda by feminists (Stuart, 1990).

Second, critical discussions of the film repeatedly point to its self-referential and, relatedly, to its polysemic qualities. *Thelma and Louise* is highly conscious of its own generic quotations, and addresses the spectator as equally competent in the codes and conventions of media language. That critics have read in the film allusions to anything from John Ford's western *The Searchers* to screwball comedy certainly points to an extraordinary degree of intertextual reference, and indeed to an openness that can only be underscored by the film's vagueness in certain areas: its rather odd time frame and geography, for example; and its 'sharp scanting of information about the protagonists' prior lives' (Greenberg *et al.*, 1991–2, p. 21). This openness produces points of entry and identification to virtually all spectators, men just as much as women.

When, in 1978, Julia Lesage suggested that ambiguities are 'structured into almost every film to come out about strong women' (*New German Critique*, 1978, p. 91), she was referring to ambiguities at the level of narrative theme and characterisation. In the 1990s, the ambiguities are intertextual as well: the spectator is addressed as versed in the conventions of film genres and film language, and thus as capable of distancing herself/himself from narrative enunciation and content. This is a highly seductive mode of address. As Roy Grundmann argues:

> Smart film that it is, *Thelma and Louise* takes those principles [of media literacy], vulgarizes them, and throws them right back at the audience. But instead of pushing a single meaning, it allows the image to be appropriated by everyone in a different way. Thus, it can pass off its marketplace morals as high-flown ethical debate (Dowell *et al.*, 1991, p. 36).

The Accused, *The Color Purple* and *Thelma and Louise* all in some degree draw for their themes on issues named and put on the cultural agenda by feminism: most notably in these cases rape and violence against women. These themes are activated in diverse fictional settings and generic contexts across the three films: in the investigative narrative/courtroom drama; in the coming-to-consciousness narrative/in the buddy/road movie. As such, they appeal to a range of cultural competences, both general and specific: from an understanding or experience of sexual violence, or of being black in a white-dominated society; through a knowledge of film genres; to a familiarity with news events and stories or with an acclaimed novel by a black woman writer. If feminist readings of these films are available, then, they figure among a range of other possible readings. Choice is the watchword.

If these three films address feminist issues within the framework of popular feminism, two of them – *The Color Purple* and *Thelma and Louise* – do this, in some measure at least, from the standpoint of their female protagonists. Nevertheless, their address is more inclusive than such a statement might imply. If these films are indeed open to feminist readings, such readings are by no means privileged: they may be overdetermined by, or simply function as alternatives to, other types of reading. It may even be suggested that, while they flirt with popular feminism, these films actually preclude certain feminist readings: which then become available only by means of 'reading against the grain' (Ellsworth, 1984).

The Crying Game; Orlando; A Question of Silence/De Stilte Rond Christine M

If Hollywood's quest is to appeal to the largest audience possible, art cinema addresses itself to a more circumscribed body of cinema-goers: an audience defining itself, and constructed by the films themselves, as adult, sophisticated, cineliterate, discerning, cultured. Although not a hard-and-fast genre or category, art cinema does have certain defining characteristics. In textual terms, it tends to eschew the transparency, narrative linearity and narrative motivation characteristic of more mainstream forms of fiction cinema; institutionally, it usually involves relatively small production budgets and limited releases in particular sorts of exhibition venue (art houses, Regional Film Theatres, and film societies), and is supported by a distinctive apparatus of criticism.

Art cinema also tends to privilege visual style over narrative action and to a pervasive deployment of enigma, in everything from characterisation to narrative codes to enunciation. Defining itself as a *cinéma d'auteurs*, art cinema relies much more than Hollywood on critical intertexts as aids to unravelling the frequently opaque meanings of the films themselves. Understanding is most characteristically promoted in terms of directors' intentions or authorial expressivity: historically, the vast majority of art cinema directors have been male. Art cinema, too, has been associated with relatively high degrees of explicitness in the treatment of culturally taboo subjects, most notably of sex. Thus in this form of cinema a certain eroticisation of the body – particularly of the female body – together with a construction of femininity as enigmatic is not merely sanctioned but is almost a *sine qua non*.

Thus representations of sexuality in general, and of female sexuality in particular, which would be regarded as unacceptable in mainstream cinema are not merely tolerated but constitute a key component of art cinema's distinctive and somewhat daring self-image. It is perhaps surprising given this that aside from discussions of isolated productions by a small group of female film makers whose work is sometimes bracketed in the art cinema category (Agnes Varda, Nelly Kaplan, Marta Meszaros, Chantal Akerman, for example), art cinema as such has attracted negligible critical attention from feminist film critics and theorists.

In the past few years, a number of films have been released onto art house circuits in which the characteristic art cinema features of ambiguity and openness in sexual matters are combined in narratives centred around ambiguities of gender identity. In *The Crying Game* (Jordan, 1992) and *Orlando* (Potter, 1992), central characters are constructed as neither female nor male, but as both or either: their gender is a matter of performance or, following Joan Riviere's understanding of the term (see Chapter 11), of masquerade.

In Neil Jordan's *The Crying Game*, gender performatives structure a narrative centred upon a quest for atonement and for love. Jody (Forest Whitaker), a black British soldier held hostage by the IRA, is befriended by one of his captors, Fergus (Stephen Rea), who promises to look after Jody's lover, Dil (Jaye Davidson). After Jody is killed, Fergus escapes to London, assumes a false identity, searches out Dil, and falls in love with her. He is soon shocked to discover that Dil is male. However, although the 'truth' of Dil's gender is revealed (simultaneously to Fergus and to the film's audience) in a single brief shot, from Fergus's point-of-view, of Dil's naked body, this visually guaranteed knowledge neither puts an end to Fergus's resolve to keep his promise to Jody, nor forces any transformation in sexual identity or orientation on his part.

Indeed, Dil's masquerade of feminity (see Still 12.5) is represented as of no greater significance than any of the other disguises in the film: Fergus's London alias; the dissimulations of his IRA girlfriend Jude (Miranda Richardson) in the service of the Republican cause; even Dil's own rather less convincing assumption of maleness when he dons Jody's cricket whites towards the end of the film. As Jody has told Fergus, the part of the anatomy that is supposed to serve as the final arbiter of sexual difference is, after all, not so much a transcendental signifier as 'a piece of meat'.

What Fergus learns in his translation from the certainties and fixed identities of the Irish situation – in which one is either Protestant or Catholic, loyalist or republican, British or Irish, male or female, black or white (Ireland, says Jody, is the last place on earth where they call you 'nigger' to your face) – to the merging categories and hybrid identities of the Great Wen (as well as being both male and female, Dil is of mixed race) is that in the quest for love one need not be constrained by a matter so trivial as whether or not one's object is of the 'right' gender.

Orlando is a film adaptation of Virginia Woolf's novel of that name. It was written and directed by Sally Potter, the maker of the short film *Thriller*, which is discussed in Chapter 8. *Orlando*'s action, spanning the

12.5 The Crying Game: Dil's masquerade

years between 1600 and the present day, traces the passage of the aristocratic Orlando (Tilda Swinton) from one Elizabethan age to another – first as a man, then as a woman. Along the way, Orlando becomes the favourite of Elizabeth I (Quentin Crisp), falls in love with a beautiful Russian princess (Charlotte Valandrey), is appointed British ambassador to Central Asia, attends – as Lady Orlando – the literary salons of eighteenth-century London, loses her estate under Victorian laws of property and inheritance, and in the twentieth century gives birth to a daughter.

The film's episodic narrative is governed by Orlando's various transformations – although, in characteristic art cinema style, narrative is subordinated to an image that offers a sumptuous, colourful pageant of costume and setting. In both form and content, *Orlando*'s emphasis on spectacle and masquerade (Orlando's ever-changing costume is a designation of her/his gender as much as a visible mark of historical period) points to the fluid, the performative, nature of gender identity. The film's conclusion, however – unlike *The Crying Game*'s – is that even if there is nothing essential or fixed about gender identity, the pressure to be defined, in social terms, as either male or female remains; and that the gender identity assumed brings its own, often momentous, consequences. This is most evident when, in the nineteenth century, Orlando, as a woman, is constrained, deprived and dispossessed by laws that prevent her from owning or inheriting property in her own right.

How, then, will the twentieth-century Orlando – androgynous, but still clearly female, and the mother of a daughter – fare? *Orlando*'s play with gender performatives offers no postmodern fluidity of identities and limitless options; rather it treads a careful path between a quasi-postfeminist anti-essentialism and the (momentary, at least) fixity of identity necessary to political action. To this extent, like the novel upon which it is based, the film *Orlando* is certainly open to a feminist reading.

An international co-production, *Orlando* – unlike Sally Potter's previous films – has been promoted and exhibited as art cinema. Less overtly feminist than Potter's earlier work, it has been widely critically acclaimed and set alongside that tendency in contemporary British cinema most prominently represented by the work of Peter Greenaway, director of *The Draughtsman's Contract* (1982). If *Orlando* – whilst by no means a mass-market film – has reached a much broader audience than Potter's previous work, this has partly to do with changes in feminist cultural politics that have taken place over the past decade (Potter's last feature-length cinema film before *Orlando* was a British Film Institute production, *The Gold Diggers* [1983]). During this time many ideas born and nurtured within second-wave feminism have entered general cultural currency, though usually divested of the scare label 'feminist'.

Although it emerges in non-feminist cultural contexts, this is also true of the play of sexual identities popularly termed 'gender-bending', an idea and a practice far less shocking in the 1990s than when Virginia Woolf's novel first appeared. To this extent, *Orlando* does take on board feminist concerns, most notably a commitment to anti-essentialism which combines with an awareness that, however performative and provisional gender identity might be, being socially defined as a woman still brings with it significant social consequences. But at the same time, gender-bending need not necessarily be regarded exclusively – or indeed at all – as a feminist practice. Sally Potter herself confesses that whilst feminist ideas continue to inform her work, she hesitates now to use the label 'feminist', 'because it's become debased.... [I]f I use it, it stops people thinking' (Florence, 1993a, p. 279).

Released ten years before *Orlando, A Question of Silence/De Stilte Rond Christine M* (1982), though not claiming to be a feminist film, has been widely received as such, certainly in Britain. How much does this have to do with its textual features and how much with its reception contexts? Marleen Gorris's film about the investigation (by a female psychiatrist) and trial of three women who have murdered a male boutique owner displays many of the formal characteristics of art cinema: above all, the women's motives for the killing are never revealed; and the ending, in which all the women in the courtroom burst into spontaneous laughter, proposes something enigmatically different from the closure characteristic of classic narrative cinema. The central question raised by the film – why three ordinary women, strangers to each other, should for no apparent reason commit a murder – is not resolved within the terms of classic narrative logic. This, together with the fact that the women are seemingly not punished for their crime, has divided audience responses to the film very decisively along gender lines.

This gender gap has partly to do with the film's textual address. It has been suggested, for example, that *A Question of Silence* poses, at the levels of both theme and formal organisation, a women's culture which male, or patriarchal, culture overlaps but does not entirely contain. This 'wild zone' cannot be spoken and is not always conscious, but finds cultural expression in a number of ways: 'the violence of the crime and the negative disruption of laughter in the courtroom are [the women's] only forms of speech' (Williams, 1988, p. 112; see also Gentile, 1985; Montgomery, 1984). In its capacity to disturb, this unarticulable but recognizable wild zone refuses any causal logic, moral responsibility or balance, making for uncomfortable viewing for those who have investments in such things and who fail to recognise the separateness, the otherness of the wild zone.

Does this provide adequate explanation for male responses to *A Question of Silence*, which appear to have ranged from mild discomfort to enraged denunciation (one critic referred to the film's 'shockingly uncontrolled feminism')? Is it not equally likely that responses will be informed by the manner in which the film was exhibited (and received)? As a film embodying many of the textual features of art cinema, *A Question of Silence* could readily have been released, promoted, exhibited and received accordingly. For its British release, however, the film was taken up by the feminist distributor Cinema of Women, as their first venture into feature-film distribution, and as an attempt to draw upon an audience rather broader than that for the more self-consciously feminist films on their list.

COW recognised that art cinema might offer a space, if only a limited one, for radical cultural intervention: its elitist connotations, COW believed, would be modified by the exhibition strategy they chose. The film opened in a London cinema not normally associated with art house pictures, and was publicised as a 'Cinema of Women event' (Root, 1986). In the end, though, the success enjoyed by *A Question of Silence* derived from its enthusiastic reception by grassroots feminists rather than by broader audiences of women or by film buffs and critics, feminist or otherwise. And although *A Question of Silence* has received a certain amount of critical attention from feminists over the years, its flirtation with the notion of a separate women's culture, a 'wild zone' outside the sphere of language, has made it a problematic object for a feminist criticism committed to anti-essentialism and to the idea of the centrality of language in the production of both sexual difference and cultural meanings.

Desert Hearts; She Must Be Seeing Things; Born In Flames

Mandy Merck has suggested that 'if lesbianism hadn't already existed, art cinema might have invented it' (Merck, 1993, p. 162). This has to do partly with art cinema's quest to explore the 'mystery' of female sexuality, and partly with its self-proclaimed daring in the treatment of sexual matters. And indeed, in 'mainstream' art cinema, there is a long-established tradition of portrayals of love between women – see, for example, *Olivia* (Jacqueline Audry, France, 1951); *Les biches* (Chabrol, France, 1968); *Persona* (Bergman, Sweden, 1966); *The Conformist/Il conformista* (Bertolucci, Italy, 1970) (see Florence, 1993b). But so long as art cinema constructs femininity as enigmatic, its treatment of expressions of female sexuality – lesbianism included – will by definition be done, as it were, from the outside.

In recent years, however, a number of films have been made that, straddling the categories 'art cinema' and 'feminist independent cinema', offer representations of lesbianism from the inside: from a feminine, a feminist, or a lesbian standpoint. Donna Deitch's feature film *Desert Hearts* (1985), for example, is a straightforward romance set against the desert landscape of Nevada: the twist is that the lovers are women. By contrast with many portrayals of lesbians and lesbianism in mainstream if not in art cinema, both the lovers are attractive and their affair, while not without its ups and downs – in the absence of which there would of course be no story – is represented as liberating and joyful. For this reason, *Desert Hearts* has become a lesbian cult classic.

Also a lesbian love story, *She Must Be Seeing Things* (Sheila McLaughlin, 1987) goes beyond a romantic narrative involving overcoming the heterosexual world's resistance to a love affair between women. Taking such a relationship as given, it explores the dimensions of power involved in a particular lesbian relationship. Agatha (Sheila Dabney), discovering the intimate diary of her lover, Jo (Lois Weaver) – whom she believes is having affairs with men – is tormented by sexual jealousy. Meanwhile Jo, very much involved in directing a film, seems to have little time to reassure Agatha, who starts to follow her lover and spy on her. The parallels between Jo's film and her relationship with Agatha (in terms not only of content but also of the metaphors of vision and voyeurism in play in both) eventually become clear to the latter.

The episodic narrative of *She Must Be Seeing Things* is motivated largely by Agatha's fantasies about Jo, which are acted out in a succession of disconnected scenarios, in which the line between fantasy and 'reality' is blurred. How much is Agatha imagining? At the same time, it is clear that if the women's relationship incorporates a large component of fantasy, it also – and relatedly – involves engagements with power plays and sadomasochism. The film's treatment of the enactment of power in a love relation between women, controversial in a feminist or a lesbian-feminist context, has provoked heated debate, engaging opposing positions on the question of the politics and ethics of certain sexual practices (Alison Butler, 1987).

In *She Must Be Seeing Things*, the power/fantasy nexus is played out in a number of scenes involving games of butch-femme role reversal and gender masquerade. Agatha dresses as a man in order to pursue and spy on Jo (see Still 12.6); Jo offers an exhibition of femininity, performing a sexy routine in satin underwear for Agatha's voyeuristic gaze. But the film refuses any reading that would position Agatha straightforwardly as voyeur, bearer of the look, and thus as occupying a fixed 'masculine' position in the relationship. For if Agatha is the one who does the looking, Jo (who, as a film director, in any case occupies a powerful position in this respect) is by no means controlled by her look: on the contrary, in fact. If *She Must Be Seeing Things* flirts with sadomasochism as a component of a sexual relationship between women, this is constructed precisely as a flirtation, a game: neither of the characters remains either victim or oppressor for long. In this play of masquerade and fantasy, gender identifications – even in so apparently unlikely a setting as a same-sex relationship – are constructed as fluid and interchangeable.

A Question of Silence was – in Britain at least – a grassroots success with feminist audiences, whilst for various reasons, not all of them necessarily connected with the textual address of the film itself, appealing less to women cinema-goers more generally. This suggests that it would be a mistake to consider female cinema audiences as homogeneous. Audience responses to *The Color Purple* offer another case in point. While *A Question of Silence* divides feminist and non-feminist women, *The Color Purple* arguably separates black women from white women at the level of empirical response, if not also of textual address. Even a film like *She Must Be Seeing Things*, with its specific address to lesbian women, is capable of evoking varied empirical responses within this audience. Women's films, then, will not all necessarily speak to all women, nor address all women in the same way. This is as true, if in different ways, of avowedly feminist practices of cinema as it is of art cinema and of Hollywood.

In a discussion of 'women's cinema' (which she defines as a cinema

12.6 She Must Be Seeing Things: Agatha dresses as a man

by and for women), Teresa de Lauretis addresses the question of differences between women as these might ground a 'feminine aesthetic' of film reception – as against, that is, the aesthetic of textual organisation which, de Lauretis claims, informs feminist countercinemas (de Lauretis, 1985; de Lauretis, 1990; see also Florence 1993b). One of the films discussed in this context is Lizzie Borden's low-budget science-fiction fantasy *Born In Flames* (1983). The film's action is set in New York, ten years after a peaceful social-democratic revolution. Discontent simmers as women begin to realise how little they have gained from the revolution. The militant Women's Army is promoting street-level resistance to male harassment; Radio Regazza, an anarchist-style station run by young white women, is transmitting a mix of underground news and punk sounds; the black women of Radio Phoenix are broadcasting soul music; and a group of white intellectuals is attempting to carve a space for feminism within the male-dominated revolutionary party. After Women's Army leader Adelaide Norris (Jeanne Satterfield) is captured and dies in prison, these diverse groups of women band together for joint resistant action.

Any logic or coherence in the storyline of *Born in Flames* is of less significance than the sense of movement, activity and energy evoked by the film's organisation of sounds and images. Teresa de Lauretis argues that the film does indeed address the spectator as female:

> [B]ut it does not do so by portraying an experience which feels immediately one's own. On the contrary, its barely coherent narrative, its quick-paced shots and sound montage, the counter-point of image and word, the diversity of voices and languages, and the self-conscious science-fictional frame of the story hold the spectator across a distance, projecting toward her its fiction like a bridge of difference (de Lauretis, 1985, p. 165).

There is, in other words, no question here of that recognition of situations and identification with fictional characters proposed by cinematic realism. None the less, the spectator is caught up in the energy and pace of the film, and by the trajectory of differences it describes. But if the women in *Born In Flames* are diverse in terms of ethnicity, social class and sexual orientation, their eventual coming together for joint action entails no merging, no dilution or dissolution of differences; but rather a unity in diversity. Film maker Lizzie Borden proposes that all women viewers would have some point of identification with a position within the film, but that these points are varied (Friedberg, 1984): '[W]hat one takes away after seeing this film is the image of a *heterogeneity* in the female social subject' (de Lauretis, 1985, p. 168, my emphasis).

This reading of *Born In Flames* participates in the move in feminist debates on female spectatorship away from the view that the spectator inhabits an undifferentiated space, and towards awareness and celebration of the heterogeneity of the female spectator. At the same time, the film does perhaps demand of the spectator a certain degree of cultural competence around feminism (or feminisms). And to the extent that its four groups of women stand in for a range of political tendencies within the women's movement, *Born In Flames* speaks to differences within feminism as much as it speaks to differences between women.

Both *She Must Be Seeing Things* and *Born In Flames* engage issues of gender positioning and female spectatorship, insisting upon the fluidity and heterogeneity of both. The former, disrupting fixed notions of the relationship between looking and sexual difference, points to the elements of fantasy and power involved in every act of looking – a point which applies as much to those watching the film as to its fictional protagonists. *Born In Flames* engages more overtly with the spectator as a social subject, its fictional space insisting upon both differences between women and the potential of unity in diversity. As narrative features which, in textual and institutional terms, combine characteristics of both art cinema and feminist independent cinema, both these films have had theatrical releases in art house or other specialist venues.

Ties That Bind; The Body Beautiful

In the discussion of feminist independent cinema in Chapter 8, I point to the frequency with which film makers have either structured their work as autobiographical or quasi-autobiographical narratives, or have made use of autobiographical material for their films' content. Michelle Citron's *Daughter Rite*, for example, draws on an area of subject matter which, since the film was made in 1978, has become almost a defining theme or generic feature of feminist experimental and independent cinema: the mother–daughter relationship. *Daughter Rite* questions the reliability of its own source materials – home movie footage and a documentary that turns out to be fictional – as it simultaneously insists upon and relativises the daughter's account of the mother and of the relationship between mother and daughter. My argument is that this strategy draws the spectator into the painful and difficult emotions evoked by the film, while at the same time imposing a critical distance. In this move, the feelings and experiences described and worked through in the film are readable as personal and individual, and yet at the same time widely shared, if not universal.

The mother–daughter relationship continues to provide a rich seam of source material for women film makers (and increasingly, today, also for video makers [Baert, 1993]), who have deployed a range of cinematic languages and genres, from fictional narrative through dramatised documentary to experimental and avant-garde forms, to explore questions of identity. Above all, within experimental film making an established tradition of using 'personal' material sits well with a feminist concern to explore questions of identity through the mother–daughter relationship. In common with other types of experimental and avant-garde cinema, much of this work is produced on a modest scale, on low budgets – or no budgets – using artisanal, or craft-style, modes of production, and involving very limited theatrical distribution and exhibition (though in Britain, since the advent of Channel Four, limited broadcast television slots are now available for some work of this sort).

Ngozi Onwurah's episodic drama-documentary, *The Body Beautiful* (1991), a British Film Institute/Channel Four co-production, is an account of the film maker's relationship with her mother, and with her mother's body. Madge Onwurah, we are told in voice-over, was born in Newcastle upon Tyne in 1929; in 1957 she married a Nigerian medical student. The family moved to Nigeria, but with the civil war raging Ngozi and her mother were sent back to England: 'We would never live as a family again.' If Ngozi's father is revealingly absent, the presence of the mother is insistent: Madge Onwurah is played by herself, Ngozi by an actress (Sian Martin). The film proceeds as a series of vignettes, readable as image flashes from the daughter's memory: a little girl waits in a hospital corridor, watching as her mother is wheeled away on a trolley – she will give birth to a son, and have a cancerous breast removed; a walking stick hangs on a banister; Madge is helped into her bath. These memories chart the progressive mutilations – through childbirth, mastectomy, rheumatism – of Madge's body: 'pain had become an everyday occurrence'.

But Madge is heard as well as seen. Ngozi, now in her teens and a fashion model, displays her perfect body to the (male) photographer's

12.7 The Body Beautiful: Ngozi's body displayed for the fashion photographer's camera

camera (see Still 12.7). In voice-over, Madge speaks of 'the scale of beauty that stops at women like me'. Her image replaces Ngozi's as object of the camera's look, but this substitution is impossible: 'I had been muted' – changed, silenced. Later, seeing a beautiful young man who reminds her of her husband, Madge fantasises a tender and erotic sexual encounter with him. The image of the embracing bodies – old and young, mutilated and perfect, white and black – provokes the uncomfortable question, why is such an image so unsettling? It breaks so many taboos – around age, race, and sexuality – in visual representation. And indeed, even within the space of the film's fiction, the fantasy is unsustainable: the scene ends with Madge wincing in pain as the young man fondles her mutilated breast.

The adolescent Ngozi now begins to see her mother not simply as her mother, but as a woman. But as she kisses Madge's breast scar, Ngozi's voice-over acknowledges that had she not been her mother's daughter she could not have borne to do this. She speaks of the paradox of being 'the image' of her father (that is to say, as far as her mother's, and her own, culture is concerned, black), and yet in his absence formed by the mother whose body looks so different from her own. The visibility of the difference is underscored in the film's lingering closing image, which shows mother and daughter naked, entwined together: 'my mother is mirrored in my soul. . . . I am my mother's daughter for the rest of my life.' If the visible, the image, emphasises difference, the voices of mother, as well as of daughter, insist upon identification.

Ties That Bind (Friedrich, 1986) explores a mother–daughter relationship through rather different cinematic methods, and with a concomitant exploration of national identity. Shot in black and white, Su Friedrich's 'experimental documentary' is structured by an interplay of several sets of images: footage of the film maker's mother in various settings, and in what appears to be the film's 'present tense', frames actuality shots of marches, demonstrations and anti-militarist protests in the USA, also set in the film's present or recent past. These are punctuated by a series of images of a model house being constructed from a kit, and then destroyed. The film maker's voice emerges in words etched directly upon the film stock, conveying a sense of urgency and painful inarticulacy. The voice-over heard throughout the film is actually that of the film maker's mother, Lore Bucher. Lore was born in 1920 in Ulm, Germany, and in 1947 met and married an American serviceman whilst working in the postwar denazification programme. The couple later divorced.

Lore's voice-over recounts her own story: the rise of Nazism, the years of the Second World War and their aftermath, and the emigration to the USA with an American husband. The memories, some of them painful and shocking, are counterpointed by images that appear to guarantee the veracity of the 'oral history' account – the shots of Lore in the 'present' – while also commenting upon this account and drawing parallels, from the film maker's point of view, with current events in the USA and elsewhere: the rise of militarism, antisemitism, and so on. The sound and image tracks also interweave the mother's story with the daughter's quest for roots: for an identity which is to be her own, and yet which is sought in the mother's origins. In 1982, the daughter sets off on a pilgrimage to Germany, finds her way to Lore's home town, and looks for her mother's house. The significance of the repeated image of the house kit now becomes clear: the house is a fantasy object which stands in for what, psychically, constitutes the goal of the daughter's quest: an answer to the archetypal question, 'where do I come from?'

But, as Lore's account moves on to the war years, the concentration camps, the fierce bombings that ended the war and made her friends and relatives homeless, the house kit is smashed and burned and melts away. Tearfully, Lore says she is ashamed of being German: 'that people can live and be so brutal – it's really difficult to understand'. But if the mother's national identity is so painful and difficult, how is it possible for the daughter, for whom – as the images of protest on American soil suggest – being American is not unproblematic either, to seek roots in her mother's origins? *Ties That Bind* offers no resolution of the daughter's quest – unless it be in the very act of making a film – but slides to a conclusion in Lore's present: in 1980, she finally resumes the piano-playing she had enjoyed as a child but had abandoned when war came.

The Body Beautiful and *Ties That Bind* each chart a daughter's search for identity through a relationship with her mother (and, not incidentally, in the absence of a father), a relationship that inscribes desire at once for union/identification and separation/difference. Both daughters – Ngozi, British child of a Nigerian father; and Su, American daughter of a German mother – are hybrids. Ngozi's very visible hybridity becomes an issue for her precisely because of the gap between her outward appearance and her inner store of fantasies, memories and self-images. Su, born in a society in which second-generation immigrants – if they are white – can merge readily into the cultural mainstream, must perform a work of excavation in order to uncover the meaning of her own hybridity. The all-too-visible differences between Ngozi and Madge Onwurah belie the fact that within – in the soul – mother and daughter are mirrored. Complicated by the difficulties of a problematic history and national identity, Su Friedrich's quest for roots in her mother's past is in the end perhaps less capable of realisation than Ngozi's.

Neither of these short films has had a theatrical release, although *The Body Beautiful*, partly funded by Channel Four, has been broadcast on British television. In terms of its institutional conditions of production as well as in its textual organisation, the more obviously experimental *Ties That Bind*, funded by the New York State Council for the Arts, fits the more neatly of the two into the category 'avant-garde film'. At the same time, in Britain it was taken up by the feminist distributor Circles, and in consequence marketed as a feminist film, or at least as a film of feminist interest. If, for a variety of textual and institutional reasons, films like *The Body Beautiful* and *Ties That Bind* are less widely seen than, say, *Thelma and Louise*, they do offer a particularly focused addresss to women audiences, and constitute a highly productive strand within women's contemporary cultural production.

While the conditions of existence for a feminist countercinema as envisaged in the original *Women's Pictures* might no longer be in place in the 1990s, there is still a good deal of scope for productive exploration of the relationship between feminism and cinema, and between feminist film theory and different film practices. It is simply that the terms of the relationship, and thus of the debate, have shifted somewhat since 1982. Notwithstanding any changes in the cultural and political position of feminism, it is far less unusual today even than ten years ago for women to be making films. Moreover, a number of women and feminist film makers who were making experimental films in the 1970s have subsequently moved into feature production: Sally Potter, for example, has now directed two feature films. Female film directors, while still in a minority, are considerably less rare today, even in mainstream cinema. This does not mean that women are competing on equal terms with men; nor that every woman film maker will make feminist films, however defined. The point is rather that women who want to make films of any sort are less confined than hitherto to the low-budget, artisanal or oppositional end of the spectrum.

Born In Flames and *She Must Be Seeing Things* represent a type of 'women's cinema' that did not exist in 1982: the fiction feature which, straddling the categories 'art cinema' and 'feminist independent cinema', explicitly demands feminist cultural competences and addresses itself to particular subgroups within the female audience. It is in this area of film practice that there has been the most thoroughgoing and self-conscious engagement with feminist film theory. Although, for example, *She Must Be Seeing Things* is accessible in some degree without feminist cultural competences, it acquires considerably greater meaning in light of conceptualisations around vision, the look, and sexuality developed within feminist film theory; and overtly solicits readings grounded in such knowledge.

If other films engage less self-consciously with feminist critical–theoretical debates, many may still speak to feminist cultural competences: *Orlando* – and even *The Crying Game* – to a postmodern and potentially (though not necessarily) feminist sensitivity to the performative qualities of gender identity; the new Hollywood woman's picture to popular feminism; currents in the feminist avant-garde to feminist appropriations, across media, of autobiographical writing practices. But if the relationship between feminism on the one hand and these varied practices of cinema on the other is less close in the 1990s than it seemed feasible to anticipate in 1982, where does this leave feminist film theory? What, in this new order, is feminist film theory for?

Epilogue

In Chapter 1 it was argued that feminism has produced new knowledges, new ways of thinking; and that these can, indeed must, be deployed at the service of cultural politics: that is to say, of the critique and transformation of dominant ideologies and representations. Behind such a contention lie two assumptions: first of all, that knowledge is not neutral, but socially situated; and, second, that knowledge 'from below', in its capacity to transform ways of looking at and understanding the world, may be instrumental in changing the world we see and live in. This implicit advocacy of 'standpoint epistemology' presupposes a feminist position that places itself over against a dominant patriarchal culture.

Since the early 1980s, however, it has become increasingly difficult to hold to any assumption of a single feminist standpoint (or even, for that matter, of a unitary patriarchal culture). Some of the developments in feminist film theory charted in Chapter 10, and most especially those of the mid to late 1980s, may be regarded as in some sense symptomatic of this broader shift in feminist thinking, which may be summed up in the terms: difference, multiplicity, heterogeneity. In light of this, it is perhaps appropriate now to talk of feminisms, in the plural: 'Many different feminisms are generated from different conditions of women's lives,' contends the philosopher Sandra Harding, herself an advocate of feminist standpoint epistemology (Harding, 1994). One consequence of this shift is that feminist knowledges, their subjects as well as their objects, are increasingly now seen as multiple, and thus as potentially contradictory. Harding argues that 'difference must be centered within feminist analyses, and not just between them and the dominant culture' (p. 8). Another grounding premiss of standpoint epistemology is that knowledge – or knowledges – should be useful to those who produce it. To what extent has feminist film theory measured up to these benchmarks over the past ten years?

If in the early 1980s feminist film theory was already a body of knowledge of sufficient substance to be explicated as such in a book like *Women's Pictures*, it barely even existed as a discipline in the traditional sense. Few people were teaching feminist film theory, and in Britain certainly – and in varying degrees elsewhere – work on 'women and film' took place largely in academically marginal contexts such as adult education classes, or informally and collaboratively in women's movement venues or feminist reading groups. And because the subject was new and the literature limited, teachers and students were often in the position of inventing the subject as they went along.

In the 1990s, this is no longer the case. Feminist film theory has become academically institutionalised as part of the discipline of film studies (though film studies itself remains marginalised in relation to the more traditional disciplines). It is possible today to make a career by teaching feminist film studies in higher education, and by researching and writing in the field – although, again, few are in a position actually to make a living solely from these activities. A number of commentators have pointed to the dangers of this situation, arguing that, confined to the ghetto of academe, feminist film theory stands in danger of losing contact with its roots in feminist politics. It is perhaps significant in this regard that where feminist film theory has in fact gained a foothold in the academy, it has done so mainly in departments of and on courses in film studies rather than in the area of women's studies or feminist studies.

For the knowledge claims, and indeed the political investments, of the former are rather different, and certainly less obviously situated, than those of the latter. In short, there is a sense that a loss of political urgency and a decline in activism have accompanied the academic institutionalisation of feminist film theory. There is some accuracy in this proposition. In demanding attention to differences of class, ethnicity, and sexual orientation, feminist film theory has clearly embraced difference and multiplicity in the *objects* of its knowledge. But this welcome has yet to be fully extended to the *subjects* of feminist film theory's knowledge; and it is perhaps no coincidence that if any sense of political urgency is discernible in feminist film theory today, it lies largely in work produced by the subjects of 'other' feminist knowledges about cinematic representation, most notably by black women and by lesbians.

In a survey of courses in feminist film criticism in higher education in the USA, Janice Welsch points to the challenges posed by this state of affairs. She claims that feminist film theorists who draw upon semiotics (and also, it might be added, on psychoanalysis) have produced extremely radical ideas whilst, paradoxically, couching these ideas within traditional, patriarchal modes of scholarly discourse. On the other hand, she suggests, feminists whose thinking on representation has been less challenging to dominant styles of thought have often been more radical in the way they teach and organise their courses, and in their advocacy of forms of feminist oppositional cinema – most notably of the feminist documentary – that have been sidelined by the other tendency:

> Thus, feminist semioticians question the value of images studies and of realist documentaries ... on the grounds that both reflect dominant ideology; and feminist critics associated with realism challenge psychoanalytic and semiotic theorists on the grounds that they are complying with establishment criteria for academic respectability and acceptance in lieu of feminist political engagement (Welsch, 1987, p. 69).

The academic institutionalisation of a particular tendency within feminist film theory has consequences which connect with, but which also go beyond, the issue of political responsibility. Most immediately, perhaps, it shapes the formation of canons, that process of inclusion and exclusion which governs the films and the critical/theoretical texts taught in courses on feminist film criticism and theory. As Welsch's critique suggests, it is difficult within the terms of what she characterises as the academically respectable version of feminist film theory to deal with 'feminist-realist' films and criticism. This, as I have indicated, is true also of 'non-realist' fiction films (like *A Question of Silence*), which prove difficult to accommodate within the terms of semiotic–psychoanalytic criticism. On the other hand, the sociological tendency within feminist film theory lacks a critical vocabulary to deal with the modernist, and indeed with the postmodernist, aesthetics that have informed so many significant interventions in feminist film practice. Debates about difference and multiplicity in feminist knowledge suggest, however, that the issue is rather bigger and more complex than the realism-versus-antirealism debate.

Moreover, so long as a standpoint is inscribed in the very name of the discipline – *feminist* film studies – it can certainly not be assumed that those versions of feminist film studies that seem to conform with traditional academic modes of conceptualisation and debate will necessarily find a comfortable niche in the academy. As Charlotte Brunsdon has pointed out, courses in this area can generate expectations among students (and teachers) that often prove difficult to negotiate in a classroom situation (Brunsdon, 1991; see also Schwichtenberg, 1983). A body of knowledge that so frankly admits its situated nature will not necessarily find a comfortable home in an institution whose *raison-d'être* has little to do with the promotion of oppositional knowledge, nor of 'really useful knowledge'. In this contradictory situation, teachers and students share a special, and a difficult, responsibility. At its best, feminist pedagogy should draw upon, whilst refusing to stop at, students' lived experience. It should also open up a space for the sort of challenging thought that is all too often stifled in the more traditional disciplines and academic institutions. Maintaining a balance between intellectual rigour and avoidance of orthodoxy will never be easy: but it must surely be facilitated by a political commitment constantly to call to mind what the knowledges negotiated and generated in the classroom are being produced *for*.

Appendix: Film Details

What follows is an alphabetical listing of the films discussed in this book, together with details of year of release, director, production company, and running time. Video and 16 mm. film hire availability may be checked in the current *Films On Offer*, published by the British Film Institute. In Britain, Cinenova (113 Roman Road, London E2 0HU) distributes non-feature-length films and videos by women. In the USA, Women Make Movies (19 West 21 Street, 2nd Floor, New York, NY 10011) distributes feature-length and shorter films and videos by women. At the time of writing, some of the Hollywood and art cinema releases are available for purchase and/or for domestic video rental.

Following the list of films is a schedule of selected published listings of films and videos by, for and about women.

THE ACCUSED 110min/colour
1988/Jonathan Kaplan/Paramount/USA

L'AMOUR VIOLÉ/RAPE OF LOVE colour
1977/Yannick Bellon/Films de l'Equinoxe/France

ANNE OF THE INDIES 87min/colour
1951/Jacques Tourneur/Fox/USA

THE BIG SLEEP 114min/black and white
1946/Howard Hawks/Warner Bros/USA

THE BODY BEAUTIFUL 23min/colour
1991/Ngozi Onwurah/BFI Productions–Channel Four/UK

BORN IN FLAMES 90min/colour
1983/Lizzie Borden/USA

CHRISTOPHER STRONG 77min/black and white
1933/Dorothy Arzner/RKO/USA

THE COLOR PURPLE 154min/colour
1985/Steven Spielberg/Amblin Entertainment/USA

THE CRYING GAME 113min/colour
1992/Neil Jordan/Palace Productions/UK

DAUGHTER RITE 48min/colour
1978/Michelle Citron/USA

DESERT HEARTS 91min/colour
1985/Donna Deitch/Desert Heart Productions/USA

DRESSED TO KILL 105min/colour
1980/Brian de Palma/Filmways/USA

GIRLFRIENDS 87min/colour
1977/Claudia Weill/Cyclops/USA

JANIE'S JANIE 30min/black and white
1971/Geri Ashur/New York Newsreel/USA

JEANNE DIELMAN, 23 QUAI DU COMMERCE, 1080 BRUXELLES
225min/colour
1975/Chantal Akerman/Paradise Films–Unité Trois/Belgium–France

JULIA 117min/colour
1977/Fred Zinneman/Twentieth Century-Fox/USA

KLUTE 114min/colour
1971/Alan Pakula/Warner Bros/USA

LIVES OF PERFORMERS 90min/black and white
1972/Yvonne Rainer/USA

MILDRED PIERCE 111min/black and white
1945/Michael Curtiz/Warner Bros/USA

NEA/A YOUNG EMMANUELLE 105min/colour
1976/Nelly Kaplan/Films la Boétie/France

NORMA RAE 113min/colour
1979/Martin Ritt/Fox/USA

ONE WAY OR ANOTHER/DE CIERTA MANERA 79min/black and white
1974/Sara Gomez/ICAIC/Cuba

ORLANDO 93min/colour
1992/Sally Potter/British Screen Finance/UK–Russia–France–Italy –
Netherlands

PSYCHO 108min/black and white
1960/Alfred Hitchcock/Shamley/USA

A QUESTION OF SILENCE/DE STILTE ROND CHRISTINE M 96min/colour
1982/Marleen Gorris/Sigma Films/Netherlands

THE REVOLT OF MAMIE STOVER 93min/colour
1956/Raoul Walsh/Fox/USA

SALT OF THE EARTH 94min/black and white
1953/Herbert Biberman/Independent Productions Corporation/USA

SHE MUST BE SEEING THINGS 90min/colour
1987/Sheila McLaughlin/USA

STELLA DALLAS 105min/black and white
1937/King Vidor/Goldwyn/USA

THELMA AND LOUISE 130min/colour
1991/Ridley Scott/MGM–Pathe Comunications/USA

THRILLER 33min/black and white
1979/Sally Potter/Arts Council of Great Britain/UK

TIES THAT BIND 55min/black and white
1986/Su Friedrich/USA

UNION MAIDS 55min/black and white
1976/Jim Klein, Julia Reichert, Miles Mogulescu/USA

WHOSE CHOICE? 40min/colour
1976/London Women's Film Group–BFI Production Board/UK

WOMEN OF THE RHONDDA 20min/black and white
1973/Mary Capps, Mary Kelly, Margaret Dickinson, Esther Ronay,
Brigid Segrave, Humphrey Trevelyan/UK

YOUNG MR LINCOLN 101min/black and white
1939/John Ford/Fox/USA

Published Lists of Women's and Feminist Films
and Videos

Betancourt, Jean, *Women in Focus*, Dayton, Ohio, Pflaum, 1974.

Cook, Samantha, *Women's Film List*, London, BFI Education, 1989.

Dawson, Bonnie, *Women's Films in Print*, San Francisco, Booklegger Press, 1975.

Isis International, *Powerful Images: a Women's Guide to Audiovisual Resources*, Rome and Santiago, Isis International, 1986.

Lukasz-Aden, Gudrun and Strobel, Christel, *Der Frauenfilm: Filme von und für Frauen*, Munich, Wilhelm Heyne Verlag, 1985.

Root, Jane, *Women's Film List*, London, BFI Education, 1985.

Sullivan, Kaye, *Films For, By and About Women*, Metuchen, Scarecrow Press, 1980.

Sullivan, Kaye, *Films For, By and About Women, Series II*, Metuchen, Scarecrow Press, 1985.

Women's History Research Center, *Films By and/or About Women*, Berkeley, WHRC, 1972.

Notes

1 Passionate Detachment

1 This book does not include any account of the history of women's film making, partly because women's cinema and feminist cinema are not necessarily the same thing, and partly because the documenting the contributions of women in this field is in itself an enormous task, and one in which a certain amount of progress has already been made. Readers are referred to Henshaw (1972) and Smith (1975) for further information.

3 Textual Gratification

1 I have kept these terms in their original French in order to avoid confusion with my usages elsewhere in this book of 'history', 'story' and 'discourse'.

2 It is easy to see how an argument like this can generate rage among feminists. Even accepting the notion that the form taken by the Oedipus complex may be historically variable rather than universal, what is to be made of the apparently arbitrary elevation of the phallus as transcendental signifier?

3 There is a distinction to be made between notions of the *audience* as a social group, and of the *spectator* as addressed by the operations of a film text. This point is taken up in Chapter 9 and Chapter 10.

4 Making Visible the Invisible

1 In this context, patriarchal ideology is defined very broadly as an operation through which woman is constructed as eternal, mythical and unchanging, an essence or a set of fixed meanings. I am aware that the concept of patriarchy is a contentious one (Adlam, 1979; Beechey, 1979). I would nevertheless maintain that certain forms of patriarchal domination operate relatively autonomously of other social formations conditioning the position of women at different moments in history. Given this, the notion of patriarchal ideology is, I believe, tenable.

2 *Screen* is a British journal of film theory which had at the time been instrumental in taking up structuralist, semiotic and psychoanalytic debates in French film theory and making them available to English-speaking readers.

6 The Body in the Machine

1 In sociological terms, men constitute overall the vast majority of consumers of pornography. Although this is a more complex issue, it may also be argued that the textual operations of pornographic representations of women also construct a masculine spectator (see Chapter 3).

2 There is a distinction to be made between pornography and obscenity. While pornographic representations may be defined in terms of their sexual content and 'function', this definition is not necessarily a legal one. In other words, not all pornography is necessarily illicit. The term 'obscenity' tends to refer more specifically to pornographic representations which at any particular conjuncture fall within the scope of legal discourses.

3 A proper treatment of this question calls for a textual analysis of the rape sequence of L'Amour violé, which I am unable to undertake here. Such an analysis would take into account the specificity of cinematic codes as they construct spectator–text relations of fetishistic looking.

7 Real Women

1 This conclusion is arrived at from a reading of reviews of Julia which appeared in the British press during 1978 and 1979. It might be added that Lillian's memories of Julia emerge whilst Lillian is writing The Children's Hour, a play which deals with lesbianism. This fact and its significance are lost in the film.

2 Progressive realism is usually distinguished from socialist realism on the grounds of whether or not the representation originates in a socialist society. Although the film discussed here, Salt of the Earth, was produced in a capitalist society, I have retained the term 'socialist realism' throughout for the sake of consistency.

3 The book from which this quotation is taken refers to cinéma vérité rather than direct cinema, and the two terms are often in fact used interchangeably. I use the term 'direct cinema' here, partly to avoid confusion, but more importantly because I consider certain European film practices which have also been called cinéma vérité (the films of Jean Rouch, for example) to be grounded in views about truth, observation and the visible rather different from those underpinning American direct cinema.

9 The Production of Meaning and the Meaning of Production

1 These quotations, together with general information included in this chapter on the practices of the Independent Film Makers' Association, are taken from IFA internal documents on file in the BFI Information Department.

2 Information on Cinema of Women included in the present chapter is drawn largely from an interview I conducted with two members of the COW collective in April 1981.

3 For example, in March 1981, a local group of women organised a feminist film and video weekend course at the Midland Group Cinema in Nottingham, which is associated with the BFI's Regional Film Theatre network.

4 Examples include the Nottingham event mentioned in note 3, and 'Women's Own', a three-week season of films by women organised at the Institute of Contemporary Arts in London in the autumn of 1980.

Glossary

For extended definitions of concepts in feminist film theory, readers are referred to Annette Kuhn (ed.), *The Women's Companion to International Film*, London, Virago Press, 1990.

Analogical representation   A visual representation which reproduces the appearances of an external 'reality'.

Auteur theory   The notion that a single individual, usually the director, has the primary creative responsibility for – or 'authors' – a film.

Cinematic apparatus   The product of the interactions of the economic and ideological conditions of existence of cinema at any moment in history.

Cinematic specificity   Refers to elements of *signification* which operate only in cinematic language and in no other.

Classic realist text   A type of film organised according to a classic disruption–resolution narrative structure, and mobilising *analogical representation* as the means of telling the story.

Closure   Restriction of the range of meanings potentially available from a *text*.

Condensation   An unconscious process in which a single idea stands in for (condenses) several associations. Used originally in dream analysis, the concept has more recently been applied to the analysis of films as *texts*.

Continuity editing   A method of joining film shots which emphasises smooth transitions between shots, with ellipses of time and space made as unobtrusive to the spectator as possible.

Countercinema   Cinema which operates against, questions, and subverts *dominant cinema*, usually on the levels both of signification and of methods of production, distribution and exhibition.

Deconstructive cinema   Cinema based on breaking down, and possibly analysing, the modes of *signification* characteristic of *dominant cinema*.

Diegetic sound Sound which appears to emerge directly from the space of the film (for example, characters talking, sounds made by objects on screen).

Direct cinema A style of documentary film making developed in the USA in the early 1960s, dependent on lightweight mobile equipment, and attempting to minimise manipulation of the *profilmic event*.

Discours A register of *enunciation* in which utterances inscribe both a source and a recipient within the address itself (for example, '*I* saw *you* yesterday'). The term is also used in relation to cinematic address.

Discursive A form of address largely or exclusively employing *discours*.

Displacement The process through which an idea's emphasis, interest or intensity is detached from it and passed on (displaced) to other ideas. The concept, which was introduced by Freud for dream analysis, has been adopted in the analysis of films as *texts*.

Dissolve A punctuation device joining film shots, involving the superimposition of a *fade out* over a *fade in*.

Distanciation A relation between spectator and text in which the spectator is 'estranged' from the representation and is thus in a position to take a critical, questioning stance towards it.

Dominant cinema The combination of institutional conditions of production, distribution and exhibition of films for world-wide mass markets with a distinct set of textual characteristics associated with the *classic realist text*.

Enounced In a speech act, the purport of what is said.

Enunciation In a speech act, the way in which the recipient is addressed or situated (see *discours, histoire*).

Essentialism In feminist cultural theory, any notion of sexual difference, femininity or masculinity which reduces these to anatomical attributes.

Extradiegetic sound Sound emerging from outside the space of the film image (for example, 'background' music, voice-over commentary).

Fade A punctuation device marking the transition between shots in a film. *Fade in*: the image gradually appears on an initially black screen. *Fade out*: the opposite of fade in.

Fetishism The (unconscious) disavowal of the threat of castration by idealising the original source of the threat: in Freudian psychoanalysis, the absence of the mother's penis. The term is used in feminist analysis of cinematic representations of women.

Histoire A register of *enunciation* which inscribes distance and impersonality. It characterises the narration of past events in which the speaker was not personally involved. The term is also used in relation to cinematic enunciation.

Ideology A society's representation of itself in and for itself, and the ways in which people both live out and produce those representations.

Masquerade In psychoanalytic theory, the exaggeration by some women of 'feminine' behaviours. Used in feminist film theory to refer to performative aspects of gender positioning or identification; and in studies in the *metapsychology* of female spectatorship.

Melodrama Most common usage in feminist film theory refers to a Hollywood genre of the 1930s to 1950s, in which family conflicts are acted out. The genre is characterised by excessive *mise en scène*, performance and *extradiegetic sound*.

Metapsychology In film theory, a study of the relationship between spectatorial subjectivity and the *cinematic apparatus*.

Mirror phase In Lacanian psychoanalysis, the moment at which the infant apprehends and masters bodily unity, exemplified concretely by its perception of itself in a mirror. The mirror phase is a crucial moment in subject formation, because it is a prior condition of a sense of self as separate from 'outside'.

Mise en scène In cinema, that which is within the film frame: settings, costumes, props, composition of the image and movement within frame.

Mobile framing Changes in the framing of a film image which are the effect of zooming and/or camera movements of various kinds: for example, tracks, pans, tilts and crane shots.

Myth A form of address that can operate in various media, in which second-order meanings are constructed in such a way that they become universalised concepts. For example, certain representations of women may construct 'woman' as an eternal essence, unchanging, natural and outside history.

Narcissism Love directed towards the image of oneself or its likeness. The concept has been used in film theory to explain the fascination of the film image for the spectator.

Narrative closure The resolution of the disruptions or questions set up by a narrative, which usually takes place at the end of the *plot*.

Narrative voice/narrative point-of-view The point-of-view from which a story is told (for example, the subjective point-of-view of a character – 'I', an impersonal narration, etc.).

Patriarchal ideology An operation of *ideology* which represents and constructs relations of domination of women by men.

Plot In the Formalist sense, the order in which narrative events are given in the telling of the *story*.

Profilmic event The arrangement or ordering of what is filmed, or what is in the field of view of the camera.

Rhetoric Mode of address, or *enunciation*.

Scopophilia The instinct or drive to pleasurable looking, discussed by Freud in *Instincts and Their Vicissitudes* and used in film theory to describe the pleasure of looking in cinema.

Semiotics The study of the operation of *signs* in society – that is, of the cultural constitution of processes of meaning construction – and applied to a study of cinema by Christian Metz and others.

Sign   The smallest unit of meaning in a process of *signification*, made up of *signifier* and *signified*.

Signification   The process of construction of meanings.

Signifier/signified   The twin aspects of the *sign*. The signifier carries the meaning, and the signified is what is referred to by the signifier.

Specularity   Relations of looking and seeing, often unconscious.

Story   In the Formalist sense, the events of the narrative given chronologically in order of their 'actual' occurrence (see *plot*).

Suture   The process whereby the spectator is constantly being caught up in, or 'sewn in' to, a film's *enunciation*.

Synchronous sound   Sound whose source is visible within the film frame (for example, words spoken by a character on screen).

Tendency/tendentiousness   An attribute of a cultural product resulting from the producer's conscious intent to articulate a political position through the work.

Text   The internal structure and organisation of a cultural product or set of representations: a novel, painting, film, poem or advertisement may be analysed as a text.

Woman's picture   A subtype of *melodrama* which offers the *narrative point-of-view* of a female character and addresses a female spectator through concerns socially coded as 'feminine'.

Bibliography

I Works up to 1982

ADLAM, DIANA (1979), 'The case against capitalist patriarchy', *m/f*, no. 3, pp. 83–102.

ALLEN, JEANNE (1980), 'The film viewer as consumer', *Quarterly Review of Film Studies*, vol. 5, no. 4, pp. 481–501.

ASSOCIATION OF CINEMATOGRAPH, TELEVISION AND ALLIED TECHNICIANS (1975), *Patterns of Discrimination Against Women in the Film and Television Industries*, London, ACTT.

AUGST, BERTRAND (1979), 'The lure of psychoanalysis in film theory', *University Publishing*, no. 6, pp. 18–20.

BARRETT, MICHÈLE, *et al.* (1979), 'Representation and cultural production', in *Ideology and Cultural Production*, London, Croom Helm.

BARTHES, ROLAND (1972), 'The structuralist activity', in R. and F. DeGeorge, *The Structuralists: from Marx to Lévi-Strauss*, New York, Anchor Books.

BARTHES, ROLAND (1973), *Mythologies*, London, Paladin.

BARTHES, ROLAND (1974), *S/Z*, New York, Hill & Wang.

BARTHES, ROLAND (1975), *The Pleasure of the Text*, New York, Hill & Wang.

BARTHES, ROLAND (1977), 'Introduction to the structural analysis of narratives', in *Image-Music-Text*, London, Fontana.

BARTHES, ROLAND (1979), 'Upon leaving the movie theater', *University Publishing*, no. 6, p. 3.

BAUDRY, JEAN-LOUIS (1974–5), 'Ideological effects of the basic cinematographic apparatus', *Film Quarterly*, vol. 28, no. 2, pp. 39–47.

BAUDRY, JEAN-LOUIS (1976), 'The apparatus', *Camera Obscura*, no. 1, pp. 104–26.

BEECHEY, VERONICA (1979), 'On patriarchy', *Feminist Review*, no. 3, pp. 66–82.

BELLOUR, RAYMOND (1972), '*The Birds*: analysis of a sequence', unpublished seminar paper, British Film Institute.

BELLOUR, RAYMOND (1979), 'Psychosis, neurosis, perversion', *Camera Obscura*, nos 3/4, pp. 105–32.

BENJAMIN, WALTER (1973), *Understanding Brecht*, London, New Left Books.

BENVENISTE, EMILE (1971), *Problems in General Linguistics*, Coral Gables, University of Miami Press.

BERGER, JOHN (1972), *Ways of Seeing*, Harmondsworth, Penguin.

BERGSTROM, JANET (1977), '*Jeanne Dielman, 23 Quai du Commerce, 1080 Bruxelles* by Chantal Akerman', *Camera Obscura*, no. 2, pp. 115–21.

BERGSTROM, JANET (1979a), 'Enunciation and sexual difference (part 1)', *Camera Obscura*, nos 3/4, pp. 33–65.

BERGSTROM, JANET (1979b), 'Reading the work of Claire Johnston', *Camera Obscura* nos 3/4, pp. 21–31.

BORDWELL, DAVID and THOMPSON, KRISTIN (1979), *Film Art: an Introduction*, Reading, Mass., Addison-Wesley.

BORZELLO, FRANCES *et al.* (1979), 'Living dolls and "real women"', *Camerawork*, no. 12, pp. 10–11.

BOS, MARY and PACK, JILL (1980), 'Porn, law, politics', *Camerawork*, no. 18, pp. 4–5.

BOVENSCHEN, SILVIA (1977), 'Is there a feminine aesthetic?' *New German Critique*, no. 10, pp. 111–37.

BRANIGAN, EDWARD (1975), 'Formal permutations of the point-of-view shot', *Screen*, vol. 16, no. 3, pp. 54–64.

BROWN, BEVERLEY (1981), 'A feminist interest in pornography: some modest proposals', *m/f*, nos 5/6, pp. 5–18.

Cahiers du Cinéma (1972), 'John Ford's *Young Mr Lincoln*', *Screen*, vol. 13, no. 3, pp. 5–44.

Camera Obscura (1976a), 'Feminism and film: critical approaches', *Camera Obscura*, no. 1, pp. 3–10.

Camera Obscura (1976b), 'Yvonne Rainer: an introduction', *Camera Obscura*, no. 1, pp. 53–96.

CIXOUS, HÉLÈNE (1976), 'The laugh of the medusa', *Signs*, vol. 1, no. 4, pp. 875–93.

CIXOUS, HÉLÈNE (1980), 'Poetry is/and (the) political', *Bread and Roses*, vol. 2, no. 1, pp. 16–18.

COMOLLI, JEAN-LUC and NARBONI, PAUL (1971), 'Cinema/ideology/criticism', *Screen*, vol. 12, no. 1, pp. 27–35.

COOK, PAM (1975), 'Approaching the work of Dorothy Arzner', in C. Johnston (ed.) (1975b), pp. 9–18.

COOK, PAM (1976), '"Exploitation" films and feminism', *Screen*, vol. 17, no. 2, pp. 122–7.

COOK, PAM (1978a), 'Duplicity in *Mildred Pierce*', in E. Ann Kaplan (ed.) (1978), pp. 68–82.

COOK, PAM (1978b), 'The point of expression in avant-garde film', in *Catalogue of British Film Institute Productions 1977–1978*, London, British Film Institute.

COOK, PAM and JOHNSTON, CLAIRE (1974), 'The place of women in the cinema of Raoul Walsh', in P. Hardy (ed.), *Raoul Walsh*, Edinburgh, Edinburgh Film Festival.

CORNILLON, SUSAN KOPPELMAN (ed.) (1972), *Images of Women in Fiction: Feminist Perspectives*, Ohio, Bowling Green University Press.

COWARD, ROSALIND (1976), 'Lacan and signification', *Edinburgh Magazine*, no. 1, pp. 6–20.

COWARD, ROSALIND (1981), 'Underneath we're angry: an open letter to the Advertising Standards Authority', *Time Out*, no. 567, pp. 5–6.

COWARD, ROSALIND and ELLIS, JOHN (1977), *Language and Materialism*, London, Routledge & Kegan Paul.

COWARD, ROSALIND *et al.* (1976), 'Psychoanalysis and patriarchal structures', in *Papers on Patriarchy*, Lewes, Women's Publishing Collective.

CURLING, JONATHAN and McLEAN, FRAN (1977), 'The Independent Film-makers Association – Annual General Meeting and Conference', *Screen*, vol. 18, no. 1, pp. 107–17.

DALTON, ELIZABETH (1972), 'Women at work: Warners in the Thirties', *Velvet Light Trap*, no. 6, pp. 15–20.

DELEUZE, GILLES (1971), *Masochism: an Interpretation of Coldness and Cruelty*, New York, George Braziller.

DYER, RICHARD (1979), *Stars*, London, British Film Institute.

ECKERT, CHARLES (1974), 'Shirley Temple and the house of Rockefeller', *Jump Cut*, no. 2, pp. 1, 17–20.

ECKERT, CHARLES (1978), 'The Carole Lombard in Macy's window', *Quarterly Review of Film Studies*, vol. 3, no. 1, pp. 1–21.

ELLIS, JOHN (1980), 'On pornography', *Screen*, vol. 21, no. 1, pp. 81–108.

ELSAESSER, THOMAS (1972), 'Tales of sound and fury: observations on the family melodrama', *Monogram*, no. 4, pp. 2–15.

EMMENS, CAROL (1975), 'New Day Films: an alternative in distribution', *Women and Film*, no. 7, pp. 72–5.

FEUER, JANE (1980), '*Daughter Rite*: living with our pain and love', *Jump Cut*, no. 23, pp. 12–13.

FRENCH, PHILIP (1971), *The Movie Moguls*, Harmondsworth, Penguin.

FREUD, SIGMUND (1900), *The Interpretation of Dreams*, in S. Freud (1953–74), vols 4 and 5.

FREUD, SIGMUND (1915), *Instincts and Their Vicissitudes*, in S. Freud (1953–74), vol. 14, pp. 117–40.

FREUD, SIGMUND (1927), *Fetishism*, in S. Freud (1953–74), vol. 21, pp. 152–7.

FREUD, SIGMUND (1953–74), *The Standard Edition of the Complete Psychological Works of Sigmund Freud*, London, Hogarth Press.

GLEDHILL, CHRISTINE (1978), 'Recent developments in feminist criticism', *Quarterly Review of Film Studies*, vol. 3, no. 4, pp. 457–93.

GORKY, MAXIM *et al.* (1977), *Soviet Writers' Congress 1934: the Debate on Socialist Realism and Modernism in the Soviet Union*, London, Lawrence & Wishart.

HALBERSTADT, IRA (1976), 'Independent distribution: New Day Films', *Filmmakers Newsletter*, vol. 10, no. 1, pp. 18–22.

HANET, KARI (1976), 'Bellour on *North by Northwest*', *Edinburgh Magazine*, no. 1, pp. 43–9.

HARALOVICH, MARY BETH (1979), 'Woman's proper place: defining gender roles in film and history', unpublished paper for an independent study with Professor Jeanne Allen, University of Wisconsin-Madison.

HASKELL, MOLLY (1975), *From Reverence to Rape: the Treatment of Women in the Movies*, London, New English Library.

HEATH, STEPHEN (1973), 'The work of Christian Metz', *Screen*, vol. 14, no. 3, pp. 5–29.

HEATH, STEPHEN (1975a), 'Film and system: terms of analysis, part 1', *Screen*, vol. 16, no. 1, pp. 7–77.

HEATH, STEPHEN (1975b), 'Film and system: terms of analysis, part 2', *Screen*, vol. 16, no. 2, pp. 91–113.

HEATH, STEPHEN (1976), 'On screen, in frame: film and ideology', *Quarterly Review of Film Studies*, vol. 1, no. 3, pp. 251–65.

HEATH, STEPHEN (1978), 'Difference', *Screen*, vol. 19, no. 3, pp. 51–112.

HENSHAW, RICHARD (1972), 'A festival of one's own: review of women directors', *Velvet Light Trap*, no. 6, pp. 39–42 and 44.

HICKS, CHERRILL (1980), 'COW flicks', *The Leveller*, no. 34, pp. 22–3.

HOME OFFICE (1979), *Report of the Committee on Obscenity and Film Censorship*, Cmnd 7772, London, HMSO.

IRIGARAY, LUCE (1977), 'Women's exile', *Ideology and Consciousness*, no. 1, pp. 62–76.

JOHNSTON, CLAIRE (1973a), 'Introduction', in C. Johnston (ed.) (1973b), pp. 2–4.

JOHNSTON, CLAIRE (ed.) (1973b), *Notes on Women's Cinema*, London, Society for Education in Film and Television.

JOHNSTON, CLAIRE (1975a), 'Dorothy Arzner: critical strategies', in C. Johnston (ed.) (1975b), pp. 1–8.

JOHNSTON, CLAIRE (ed.) (1975b), *The Work of Dorothy Arzner: Towards a Feminist Cinema*, London, BFI.

JOHNSTON, CLAIRE (1975c), 'Feminist politics and film history', *Screen*, vol. 16, no. 3, pp. 115–24.

JOHNSTON, CLAIRE (1975d), 'Independent film making on 16 mm: some problems', unpublished discussion paper, Society for Education in Film and Television.

JOHNSTON, CLAIRE (1975e), 'Femininity and the masquerade: *Anne of the Indies*', in Claire Johnston and Paul Willemen (eds), *Jacques Tourneur*, Edinburgh, Edinburgh Film Festival.

JOHNSTON, CLAIRE (1976), 'Towards a feminist film practice: some theses', *Edinburgh Magazine*, no. 1, pp. 50–9.

Johnston, Claire (1980), 'The subject of feminist film theory/practice', *Screen*, vol. 21, no. 2, pp. 27–34.

Kaplan, Dora (1972), 'First International Festival of Women's Films, part 3: selected short subjects', *Women and Film*, no. 2, pp. 37–45.

Kaplan, E. Ann (1976), 'Aspects of British feminist film theory', *Jump Cut*, nos 12/13, pp. 52–5.

Kaplan, E. Ann (1977), 'Interview with British cine-feminists', in K. Kay and D. Peary (eds) (1977).

Kaplan, E. Ann (ed.) (1978), *Women in Film Noir*, London, BFI.

Kay, Karyn and Peary, Gerald (eds) (1977), *Women and the Cinema: a Critical Anthology*, New York, Dutton.

Kinder, Marsha (1977), 'Reflections on *Jeanne Dielman*', *Film Quarterly*, vol. 30, no. 4, pp. 2–8.

Kristeva, Julia (1975), 'The subject in signifying practice', *Semiotext(e)*, vol. 1, no. 3, pp. 19–34.

Kristeva, Julia (1976), 'Signifying practice and mode of production', *Edinburgh Magazine*, no. 1, pp. 64–76.

Kuhn, Annette (1975), 'Women's cinema and feminist film criticism', *Screen*, vol. 16, no. 3, pp. 107–12.

Kuhn, Annette (1978a), 'The camera I: observations on documentary', *Screen*, vol. 19, no. 2, pp. 71–84.

Kuhn, Annette (1978b), 'Structures of patriarchy and capital in the family', in A. Kuhn and A. Wolpe (eds) (1978b).

Kuhn, Annette (1979), 'Feminine writing', paper presented to the Psychoanalysis and Cinema Seminar, University of Wisconsin-Madison.

Kuhn, Annette (1981), '*The Big Sleep*: a disturbance in the sphere of sexuality', *Wide Angle*, vol. 4, no. 3, pp. 4–11.

Kuhn, Annette and Wolpe, Annmarie (1978a), 'Feminism and materialism', in A. Kuhn and A. Wolpe (eds) (1978b).

Kuhn, Annette and Wolpe, Annmarie (eds) (1978b), *Feminism and Materialism*, London, Routledge & Kegan Paul.

Lacan, Jacques (1970), 'The insistence of the letter in the Unconscious', in J. Ehrmann (ed.), *Structuralism*, New York, Anchor Books.

Lesage, Julia (1974), 'Feminist film criticism: theory and practice', *Women and Film*, nos 5/6, pp. 12–14.

Lesage, Julia (1978), 'The political aesthetics of the feminist documentary film', *Quarterly Review of Film Studies*, vol. 3, no. 4, pp. 507–23.

Lesage, Julia (1979), '*One Way Or Another*: dialectical, revolutionary, feminist', *Jump Cut*, no. 20, pp. 20–3.

Lesage, Julia *et al.* (1975), 'New Day's way', *Jump Cut*, no. 9, pp. 21–2.

Lippard, Lucy (1976), 'Yvonne Rainer on feminism and her film', in *From the Center: Feminist Essays on Women's Art*, New York, Dutton.

Loader, Jane (1977), '*Jeanne Dielman*: death in instalments', *Jump Cut*, no. 16, pp. 10–12.

LONDON WOMEN'S FILM GROUP (1976), 'Feminist and left independent film-making in England', *Jump Cut*, no. 10/11, pp. 59–60.

LURIE, SUSAN (1981–2), 'The construction of the "castrated woman" in psychoanalysis and cinema', *Discourse*, no. 4, pp. 52–74.

MACCABE, COLIN (1974), 'Realism and the cinema: notes on some Brechtian theses', *Screen*, vol. 15, no. 2, pp. 7–27.

MCGARRY, EILEEN (1975), 'Documentary, realism and women's cinema', *Women and Film*, no. 7, pp. 50–9.

MAMBER, STEPHEN (1974), *Cinéma Vérité in America: Studies in Uncontrolled Documentary*, Cambridge, Mass., MIT Press.

MARCUS, STEPHEN (1969), *The Other Victorians: a Study of Sexuality and Pornography in Nineteenth Century England*, London, Corgi.

MARTIN, ANGELA (1976), 'Notes on feminism and film', unpublished discussion paper, British Film Institute.

MELLEN, JOAN (1974), *Women and Their Sexuality in the New Film*, New York, Dell.

METZ, CHRISTIAN (1974), *Language and Cinema*, The Hague, Mouton.

METZ, CHRISTIAN (1975), 'The imaginary signifier', *Screen*, vol. 16, no. 2, pp. 14–76.

METZ, CHRISTIAN (1976), 'History/discourse: note on two voyeurisms', *Edinburgh Magazine*, no. 1, pp. 21–5.

MITCHELL, JULIET (1974), *Feminism and Psychoanalysis*, Harmondsworth, Penguin.

MULVEY, LAURA (1975), 'Visual pleasure and narrative cinema', *Screen*, vol. 16, no. 3, pp. 6–18.

MULVEY, LAURA (1979), 'Feminism, film and the avant-garde', *Framework*, no. 10, pp. 3–10.

NEALE, STEVE (1976), '"New Hollywood Cinema"', *Screen*, vol. 17, no. 2, pp. 117–22.

NEALE, STEVE (1980), 'Oppositional exhibition: notes and problems', *Screen*, vol. 21, no. 3, pp. 45–56.

NELSON, JOYCE (1977), '*Mildred Pierce* reconsidered', *Film Reader*, no. 2, pp. 65–70.

New German Critique (1978), 'Women and film: a discussion of feminist aesthetics', *New German Critique*, no. 13, pp. 83–107.

NOWELL-SMITH, GEOFFREY (1976), 'Introduction to "Signifying practice and mode of production"', *Edinburgh Magazine*, no. 1, pp. 60–3.

OUDART, JEAN-PIERRE (1977–8), 'Cinema and suture', *Screen*, vol. 18, no. 4, pp. 35–47.

PARRY, GARETH and JORDAN, PHILIP (1981a), 'Booming porn trade has the law taped', *Guardian*, 24 February, p. 3.

PARRY, GARETH and JORDAN, PHILIP (1981b), 'Crime and the middle-class voyeur', *Guardian*, 23 February, p. 11.

PERLMUTTER, RUTH (1979), 'Feminine absence: a political aesthetic in

Chantal Akerman's *Jeanne Dielman . . .*', *Quarterly Review of Film Studies*, vol. 4, no. 2, pp. 125–33.

PLACE, JANEY and BURTON, JULIANNE (1976), 'Feminist film criticism', *Movie*, no. 22, pp. 53–62.

PROPP, VLADIMIR (1968), *Morphology of the Folktale*, Austin, University of Texas Press.

REISZ, KAREL and MILLAR, GAVIN (1973), *The Technique of Film Editing*, New York, Hastings House.

RICH, B. RUBY (1977), 'The films of Yvonne Rainer', *Chrysalis*, no. 2, pp. 115–27.

RICH, B. RUBY (1978), 'The crisis of naming in feminist film criticism', *Jump Cut*, no. 19, pp. 9–12.

ROSEN, MARJORIE (1973), *Popcorn Venus: Women, Movies and the American Dream*, New York, Coward McCann & Geoghegan.

ROSENFELT, DEBBIE (1976), 'Ideology and structure in *Salt of the Earth*', *Jump Cut*, nos 12/13, pp. 19–22.

RUBIN, GAYLE (1975), 'The traffic in women: notes on the "political economy" of sex', in Rayna R. Reiter (ed.), *Toward an Anthropology of Women*, New York, Monthly Review Press.

RUSSELL, LEE (1965), 'John Ford', *New Left Review*, no. 29, pp. 69–73.

SARRIS, ANDREW (1968), *The American Cinema: Directors and Directions 1928–1968*, New York, Dutton.

SMITH, SHARON (1975), *Women Who Make Movies*, New York, Hopkinson & Blake.

SPENDER, DALE (1980), *Man Made Language*, London, Routledge & Kegan Paul.

STERN, LESLEY (1978), 'Independent feminist film-making in Australia', *Australian Journal of Screen Theory*, nos 5/6, pp. 105–21.

STERN, LESLEY (1979–80), 'Feminism and cinema: exchanges', *Screen*, vol. 20, nos 3/4, pp. 89–105.

SUTER, JACQUELYN (1979), 'Feminine discourse in *Christopher Strong*', *Camera Obscura*, nos 3/4, pp. 135–50.

TODOROV, TZVETAN (1977a), 'Categories of the literary narrative', *Film Reader*, no. 2, pp. 19–37.

TODOROV, TZVETAN (1977b), *The Poetics of Prose*, Ithaca, Cornell University Press.

TURIM, MAUREEN (1979), 'Gentlemen consume blondes', *Wide Angle*, vol. 1, no. 1 (reprint), pp. 52–9.

VAUGHAN-JAMES, C. (1973), *Soviet Socialist Realism: Origins and Theory*, London, Macmillan.

WILLEMEN, PAUL (1980), 'Letter to John', *Screen*, vol. 21, no. 2, pp. 53–65.

WILSON, MICHAEL and ROSENFELT, DEBORAH (1978), *Salt of the Earth*, New York, Feminist Press.

II Works from 1982

ANG, IEN (1985), *Watching Dallas: Soap Opera and the Melodramatic Imagination*, London, Methuen.

AUTY, MARTIN (1985), 'But is it cinema?', in Martin Auty and Nick Roddick (eds), *British Cinema Now*, London, BFI pp. 57–70.

BAD OBJECT-CHOICES (ed.) (1991), *How Do I Look?: Queer Film and Video*, Seattle, Bay Press.

BAERT, RENEE (1993), 'Desiring daughters', *Screen*, vol. 34, no. 2, pp. 109–23.

BERGSTROM, JANET and DOANE, MARY ANN (1989), 'The female spectator: contexts and directions', *Camera Obscura*, nos 20/21, pp. 5–27.

BOBO, JACQUELINE (1988), '*The Color Purple*: black women as cultural readers', in Pribram (ed.) (1988), pp. 90–109.

BRUNSDON, CHARLOTTE (1986), *Films for Women*, London, BFI.

BRUNSDON, CHARLOTTE (1991), 'Pedagogies of the feminine: feminist teaching and women's genres', *Screen*, vol. 32, no. 4, pp. 364–81.

BURGIN, VICTOR, *et al.* (eds) (1986), *Formations of Fantasy*, London, Methuen.

BUTLER, ALISON (1987), '*She Must Be Seeing Things*: an interview with Sheila McLaughlin', *Screen*, vol. 28, no. 4, pp. 20–8.

BUTLER, CHERYL B. (1991), 'The *Color Purple* controversy: black women spectatorship', *Wide Angle*, vol. 13, nos 3/4, pp. 62–9.

BUTLER, JUDITH (1988), 'Performative acts and gender constitution: an essay in phenomenology and feminist theory', *Theatre Journal*, vol. 20, no. 3, pp. 519–31.

BUTLER, JUDITH (1990), *Gender Trouble: Feminism and the Subversion of Identity*, New York, Routledge.

Camera Obscura (1989), nos 20/21, special issue: *The Spectatrix*.

Camera Obscura (1990), no. 22, special issue: *Feminism and Film History*.

COOK, PAM (1983), 'Melodrama and the women's [sic] picture'. in Sue Aspinall and Robert Murphy (eds), *Gainsborough Melodrama*, London, BFI pp. 14–28.

COWIE, ELIZABETH (1984), 'Fantasia', *m/f*, no. 9, pp. 71–104.

CREED, BARBARA (1993), *The Monstrous-Feminine: Film, Feminism, Psycho-analysis*, London, Routledge.

DE LAURETIS, TERESA (1985), 'Aesthetic and feminist theory: rethinking women's cinema', *New German Critique*, no. 34, pp. 154–75.

DE LAURETIS, TERESA (1990), 'Guerilla in the midst: women's cinema in the 80s', *Screen*, vol. 31, no. 1, pp. 6–25.

DELEUZE, GILLES (1986), *Cinema 1: the Movement-Image*, London, Athlone Press.

DELEUZE, GILLES (1989), *Cinema 2: the Time-Image*, London, Athlone Press.

Discourse (1986–7), no. 8, special issue: *She, the Inappropriate/d Other*.

DOANE, MARY ANN (1982), 'Film and the masquerade: theorising the female spectator', *Screen*, vol. 23, nos 3/4, pp. 74–87.

DOANE, MARY ANN (1987), *The Desire to Desire: the Woman's Film of the 1940s*, Bloomington and Indianapolis, Indiana University Press.

DOANE, MARY ANN (1988–9), 'Masquerade reconsidered: further thoughts on the female spectator', *Discourse*, vol. 11, no. 1, pp. 42–54.

DOANE, MARY ANN (1991a), *Femmes Fatales: Feminism, Film Theory, Psychoanalysis*, New York, Routledge.

DOANE, MARY ANN (1991b), 'Dark continents: epistemologies of racial and sexual difference in psychoanalysis and the cinema', in Doane (1991a).

DOANE, MARY ANN *et al.* (1984), *Re-Vision: Essays in Feminist Film Criticism*, Los Angeles, American Film Institute.

DOWELL, PAT *et al.* (1991), 'Should we go along for the ride? A critical symposium on *Thelma and Louise*', *Cineaste*, vol. 18, no. 4, pp. 28–36.

ELLSWORTH, ELIZABETH (1984), 'Incorporation of feminist meanings in media texts', *Humanities in Society*, vol. 7, nos 1/2, pp. 65–75.

ELLSWORTH, ELIZABETH (1986), 'Illicit pleasures: feminist spectators and *Personal Best*', *Wide Angle*, vol. 8, no. 2 (1986), pp. 45–56.

FISCHER, LUCY (1989), *Shot/Countershot: Film Tradition and Women's Cinema*, Princeton, Princeton University Press.

FLECK, PATRICE (1990), 'The silencing of women in the Hollywood "feminist" film: *The Accused*', *Post Script*, vol. 9, no. 3, pp. 49–55.

FLORENCE, PENNY (1993a), 'A conversation with Sally Potter', *Screen*, vol. 34, no. 3, pp. 275–84.

FLORENCE, PENNY (1993b), 'Lesbian cinema, women's cinema', in Gabriele Griffin (ed.), *Outwrite: Lesbianism and Popular Culture*, London, Pluto Press, pp. 126–47.

FRIEDBERG, ANNE (1984), 'An interview with filmmaker Lizzie Borden', *Women and Performance*, vol. 1, no. 2, pp. 37–45.

GAINES, JANE (1988), 'White privilege and looking relations: race and gender in feminist film theory', *Screen*, vol. 29, no. 4, pp. 12–27.

GAINES, JANE and HERZOG, CHARLOTTE (eds) (1990), *Fabrications: Costume and the Female Body*, New York, Routledge.

GENTILE, MARY C. (1985), *Film Feminisms: Theory and Practice*, Westport, Greenwood Press.

GLEDHILL, CHRISTINE (1986), '*Stella Dallas* and feminist film theory', *Cinema Journal*, vol. 25, no. 4, pp. 44–8.

GLEDHILL, CHRISTINE (ed.) (1987), *Home Is Where the Heart Is: Studies in Melodrama and the Woman's Film*, London, BFI.

GLEDHILL, CHRISTINE (1988), 'Pleasurable negotiations', in Pribram (ed.) (1988), pp. 64–89.

GLEDHILL, CHRISTINE (ed.) (1991), *Stardom: Industry of Desire*, London, Routledge.

GREENBERG, HARVEY R. *et al.* (1991–2), 'The many faces of Thelma and Louise', *Film Quarterly*, vol. 45, no. 2, pp. 20–31.

HARDING, SANDRA (1994), 'Subjectivity, experience and knowledge: an epistemology from/for rainbow coalition politics', in Judith Roof and Robyn Wiegand (eds), *Who Can Speak: Questions of Authority and Cultural Identity*, Urbana, University of Illinois Press.

HEATH, STEPHEN (1986), 'Joan Riviere and the masquerade', in Burgin *et al.* (eds) (1986), pp. 45–61.

HERZOG, CHARLOTTE and GAINES, JANE (1991), '"Puffed sleeves before teatime": Joan Crawford, Adrian and women audiences', in Gledhill (ed.) (1991), pp. 74–91.

HOLMLUND, CHRISTINE (1991), 'When is a lesbian not a lesbian?: the lesbian continuum and the mainstream femme film', *Camera Obscura*, nos 25/26, pp. 145–78.

HOOKS, BELL (1992), 'The oppositional gaze: black female spectators', in *Black Looks: Race and Representation*, London, Turnaround, pp. 115–31.

JACOBOWITZ, FLORENCE (1986), 'Feminist film theory and social reality', *CineAction!*, nos 3/4, pp. 21–31.

KAPLAN, E. ANN (1983), *Women and Film: Both Sides of the Camera*, New York, Methuen.

KAPLAN, E. ANN (1985), 'Dialogue', *Cinema Journal*, vol. 24, no. 2, pp. 40–3.

KAPLAN, E. ANN (1986), 'Feminist film criticism: current issues and problems', *Studies in the Literary Imagination*, vol. 19, no. 1, pp. 7–20.

KNIGHT, JULIA (1992), 'Cinenova: a sign of the times', *Screen*, vol. 33, no. 2 (1992), pp. 184–9.

KOCH, GERTRUD (1985), 'Ex-changing the gaze: re-visioning feminist film theory', *New German Critique*, no. 34, pp. 139–53.

KUHN, ANNETTE (1984), 'Women's genres', *Screen*, vol. 25, no. 1, pp. 18–28.

KUHN, ANNETTE (1985a), *The Power of the Image: Essays on Representation and Sexuality*, London, Routledge & Kegan Paul.

KUHN, ANNETTE (1985b), 'Sexual disguise and cinema', in Kuhn (1985a), pp. 48–73.

KUHN, ANNETTE (1988), 'The body and cinema: some problems for feminism', in Susan Sheridan (ed.), *Grafts: Feminist Cultural Criticism*, London, Verso, pp. 11–23.

LAPLACE, MARIA (1987), 'Producing and consuming the woman's film: discursive struggle in *Now, Voyager*', in Gledhill (ed.) (1987), pp. 138–66.

LOVELL, ALAN (1990), 'That was the Workshop that was', *Screen*, vol. 31, no. 1, pp. 102–8.

MAYNE, JUDITH (1985), 'Feminist film theory and criticism', *Signs: Journal of Women in Culture and Society*, vol. 11, no. 1, pp. 81–100.

MAYNE, JUDITH (1990), *The Woman at the Keyhole: Feminism and Women's Cinema*, Bloomington and Indianapolis, Indiana University Press.

MAYNE, JUDITH (1991), 'Lesbian looks: Dorothy Arzner and female authorship', in Bad Object-Choices (ed.) (1991), pp. 103–43.

MERCK, MANDY (1993), '*Lianna* and the lesbians of art cinema', in *Perversions: Deviant Readings*, London, Virago, pp. 162–76.

MERZ, CAROLINE and PARMAR, PRATIBHA (1987), 'Distribution matters: Circles', *Screen*, vol. 28, no. 4, pp. 66–9.

MODLESKI, TANIA (1982), 'The search for tomorrow in today's soap operas', in *Loving With a Vengeance*, Hamden, Conn., Shoe String Press, pp. 85–109.

MONTGOMERY, SARAH (1984), 'Women's women's films', *Feminist Review*, no. 18, pp. 38–48.

MULVEY, LAURA (1989a), 'British feminist film theory's female spectators: presence and absence', *Camera Obscura*, nos 20/21, pp. 68–81.

MULVEY, LAURA (1989b), *Visual and Other Pleasures*, London, Macmillan.

NEALE, STEVE (1986), 'Melodrama and tears', *Screen*, vol. 27, no. 6, pp. 6–22.

OHMER, SUSAN (1990), 'Female spectatorship and women's magazines: Hollywood, *Good Housekeeping* and World War II', *Velvet Light Trap*, no. 25, pp. 53–68.

PENLEY, CONSTANCE (1985), 'Feminism, film theory and the bachelor machines', *m/f*, no. 10, pp. 39–56.

PENLEY, CONSTANCE (ed.) (1988), *Feminism and Film Theory*, London, BFI.

PENLEY, CONSTANCE (1989), *The Future of an Illusion: Film, Feminism and Psychoanalysis*, London, Routledge, 1989.

PETRO, PATRICE and FLINN, CAROL (1985), 'Dialogue', *Cinema Journal*, vol. 25, no. 1, pp. 50–2.

PRIBRAM, E. DEIDRE (ed.) (1988), *Female Spectators: Looking at Film and Television*, London, Verso.

Quarterly Review of Film and Video (1989), vol. 11, no. 1, special issue: *Female Representation and Consumer Culture*.

RADWAY, JANICE (1984), *Reading the Romance: Women, Patriarchy and Popular Literature*, Chapel Hill, University of North Carolina Press.

RIVIERE, JOAN (1986), 'Womanliness as a masquerade', in Burgin *et al.* (eds) (1986), pp. 35–44.

ROOT, JANE (1986), 'Distributing *A Question of Silence*: a cautionary tale', in Brunsdon (ed.) (1986), pp. 213–23.

ROSE, JACQUELINE (1986), 'Woman as symptom', in *Sexuality in the Field of Vision*, London, Verso, pp. 215–23.

SCHLESINGER, PHILIP *et al.* (1992), *Women Viewing Violence*, London, BFI.

SCHWICHTENBERG, CATHY (1983), 'Critical dialogue: sexual politics', *Jump Cut*, no. 28, p. 58.

Screen (1988), vol. 29, no. 4, special issue: *The Last 'Special Issue' on Race?*

SILVERMAN, KAJA (1988a), *The Acoustic Mirror: the Female Voice in Psychoanalysis and Cinema*, Bloomington and Indianapolis, Indiana University Press.

SILVERMAN, KAJA (1988b), 'Masochism and male subjectivity', *Camera Obscura*, no. 17, pp. 31–66.

SOBCHACK, VIVIAN (1992), *The Address of the Eye: a Phenomenology of Film Experience*, Princeton, Princeton University Press.

STACEY, JACKIE (1993a), 'Hollywood memories', paper presented at the Screen Studies Conference.

STACEY, JACKIE (1993b), *Star Gazing: Hollywood Cinema and Female Spectatorship in 1940s and 1950s Britain*, London, Routledge.

STRAAYER, CHRIS (1984), '*Personal Best*: lesbian/feminist audience', *Jump Cut*, no. 29, pp. 40–4.

STUART, ANDREA (1990), 'Feminism: dead or alive?', in Jonathan Rutherford (ed.), *Identity, Community, Culture, Difference*, London, Lawrence & Wishart.

STUDLAR, GAYLYN (1984), 'Masochism and the perverse pleasures of cinema', *Quarterly Review of Film Studies*, vol. 9, no. 4, pp. 267–82.

STUDLAR, GAYLYN (1985), 'Visual pleasure and the masochistic aesthetic', *Journal of Film and Video*, vol. 37, no. 2, pp. 5–26.

STUDLAR, GAYLYN (1988), *In the Realm of Pleasure: Von Sternberg, Dietrich and the Masochistic Aesthetic*, Urbana and Chicago, University of Illinois Press.

STUDLAR, GAYLYN (1990a) 'Masochism, masquerade, and the erotic metamorphoses of Marlene Dietrich', in Gaines and Herzog (eds) (1990), pp. 229–49.

STUDLAR, GAYLYN (1990b), 'Reconciling feminism and phenomenology: notes on problems and possibilities, texts and contexts', *Quarterly Review of Film and Video*, vol. 12, no. 3, pp. 69–78.

TAYLOR, HELEN (1989), Scarlett's Women: 'Gone With the Wind' and its Female Fans, London, Virago.

TRINH MINH-HA (1992), *Framer Framed*, New York, Routledge.

WALDMAN, DIANE (1988), 'Film theory and the gendered spectator: the female or the feminist reader?', *Camera Obscura*, no. 18, pp. 80–94.

WALKER, JANET (1984), 'Psychoanalysis and feminist film theory: the problem of sexual difference and identity', *Wide Angle*, vol. 6, no. 3, pp. 16–23.

WELSCH, JANICE R. (1987), 'Feminist film theory/criticism in the United States', *Journal of Film and Video*, vol. 39, no. 2, pp. 66–82.

WILLIAMS, LINDA (1984), '"Something else besides a mother": *Stella Dallas* and the maternal melodrama', *Cinema Journal*, vol. 24, no. 1, pp. 2–27.

WILLIAMS, LINDA (1988), 'A jury of their peers: Marlene Gorris's *A Question of Silence*', in E. Ann Kaplan (ed.), *Postmodernism and Its Discontents*, London, Verso, pp. 105–15.

Index

Note: Italicised entries are names of films; emboldened page numbers are definitions in Glossary